"*Getting the Reformation Wrong* gets the Reformation right. All students of the Reformation, whether academic or just interested, must read this book. It rightly sets the record straight about the great people and ideas of the Protestant and Catholic Reformations of the sixteenth century in a refreshingly engaging style."

ROGER OLSON, author of *The Story of Christian Theology*

"Dr. Payton's new book, *Getting the Reformation Wrong,* is a refreshing and stimulating look at the events of the sixteenth century and their implications. He combines a solid understanding of the scholarship with a sensitivity to the faith issues involved, particularly for Christians of all types who may be reading these pages. Ending with reference to the worldwide Protestant missionary movement, he urges his readers to consider the tension between the triumph and the tragedy that are both the legacies of these long-ago events in a way that moves the discussion of the challenges of being a Protestant Christian right up to the present."

HELEN VREUGDENHIL, assistant professor of history, Redeemer University College

"The title is provocative, but what James R. Payton Jr. has in mind is not the overthrowing of generations of scholarship on the Reformation, but the use of the best scholarship to guide and correct misleading impressions often held by the common reader and Christian laypeople: for example, that the Reformation was a revolutionary bolt from the blue, that the principle of *sola scriptura* meant a wholesale rejection of Catholic theological tradition, that the Catholic Church was truculent over against the Protestant assault, refusing all efforts at reform, and the like. These notions are indeed false. On this basis of 'getting wrongs right,' the book proves to be a lively narrative that tells the story of the most important epoch in the history of the church in a clear, understandable, unfussy manner, yet one rich in detail. I appreciate especially Payton's sober conclusion on the tragic elements of what the sixteenth century wrought."

WALTER SUNDBERG, professor of church history, Luther Seminary, St. Paul, Minnesota

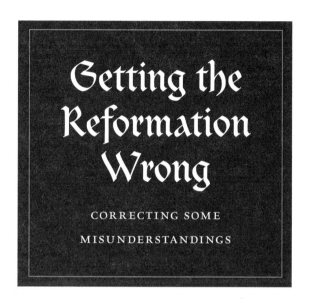

Getting the Reformation Wrong

CORRECTING SOME MISUNDERSTANDINGS

James R. Payton Jr.

IVP Academic

An imprint of InterVarsity Press
Downers Grove, Illinois

InterVarsity Press
P.O. Box 1400, Downers Grove, IL 60515-1426
World Wide Web: www.ivpress.com
E-mail: email@ivpress.com

InterVarsity Press® is the book-publishing division of InterVarsity Christian Fellowship/USA®, a movement of
students and faculty active on campus at hundreds of universities, colleges and schools of nursing in the United States
of America, and a member movement of the International Fellowship of Evangelical Students. For information
about local and regional activities, write Public Relations Dept., InterVarsity Christian Fellowship/USA, 6400
Schroeder Rd., P.O. Box 7895, Madison, WI 53707-7895, or visit the IVCF website at <www.intervarsity.org>.

Scripture quotations, unless otherwise noted, are from the New Revised Standard Version of the Bible, copyright
1989 by the Division of Christian Education of the National Council of the Churches of Christ in the USA. Used by
permission. All rights reserved.

Design: Cindy Kiple

Images: Martin Luther by Lucas Cranach the elder: The Granger Collection, NY

ISBN 978-0-8308-3880-6

Printed in the United States of America ∞

Library of Congress Cataloging-in-Publication Data

Payton, James R., 1947-
  Getting the Reformation wrong: correcting some misunderstandings/
James R. Payton, Jr.
    p. cm
  Includes bibliographical references and index.
  ISBN 978-0-8308-3880-6 (pbk.: alk. paper)
  1. Reformation. I. Title.
  BR305.3.P39 2010
  270.6—dc22

                                    2010008456

P	20	19	18	17	16	15	14	13	12	11	10	9	8	7	6	5	4	3	2	1
Y	27	26	25	24	23	22	21	20	19	18	17	16	15	14	13	12	11	10			

To Trevor

with whom I first learned

what it means to be a father

Contents

Acknowledgments

I AM INDEBTED TO NUMEROUS PEOPLE who have influenced and assisted me along the way in this project. First in order is Edward Panosian, under whose tutelage in a graduate program four decades ago I first encountered the fascinating field of the history of Christian thought and, more generally, church history. In my seminary training, Paul Woolley and Clair Davis offered further stimulus with their intriguing and challenging treatments of the field, and Norman Shepherd and Robert Godfrey both greatly advanced and enriched my understanding of the Reformation and its influence. Subsequent doctoral studies gave me the opportunity to explore the intellectual history of early modern Europe (a common academic designation for the Renaissance and Reformation eras) with Ken Davis and late medieval political and ecclesiastical history with Hugh MacKinnon. My doctoral program was enhanced by instruction from and interaction with Werner Packull and Walter Klaassen. All these, plus fellow graduate students in the field—Charles Nienkirchen (now professor of Christian history and spirituality at Ambrose University College), Dennis Martin (now professor of historical theology at Loyola University in Chicago) and Douglas Shantz (now holder of the Chair of Christian Thought at the University of Calgary)—helped hone my understanding and appreciation of the complex times, challenges and endeavors that shaped the sixteenth-century Reformation.

For the opportunity to teach upper-level courses on the late Middle Ages, the Renaissance and the Reformation, and church history, I am grateful to Redeemer University College. Among my colleagues there, Harry Van Dyke, Jacob Ellens and Darren Provost (now at Trinity Western University) encouraged and facilitated my further investigations into the Renaissance and Reformation eras, and discussions with Al Wolters especially helped clarify interpretative issues regarding the Renaissance. Among my other colleagues at Redeemer, Theodore Plantinga, Gene Haas, Mike Goheen (now Geneva Professor of Reformational Worldview Studies at Trinity Western University), Wayne Norman (now professor of psychology at Simpson University) and John Bolt (now professor of systematic theology at Calvin Theological Seminary) all showed interest and support, as well as offering good conversation partners for related fields of investigation. I am also thankful for stimulating discussions and shared interest with Clark Pinnock (professor of theology at McMaster Divinity College), and with Lyle Bierma (Jean and Kenneth Baker Professor of Systematic Theology), David Rylaarsdam (professor of historical theology) and Richard Muller (P. J. Zondervan Professor of Historical Theology), all of Calvin Theological Seminary. My current colleagues in the Redeemer history department—David Zietsma, Kevin Flatt and Helen Vreugdenhil—have graciously put up with a much-distracted department chair as I have devoted so much attention to this project during the past year.

Beyond these explicitly academic influences, I am further indebted to Joel Scandrett, formerly associate editor at InterVarsity Press, who enthusiastically represented this project and facilitated its acceptance by my publisher. To Drew Blankman, who stepped into Joel's shoes when the latter left InterVarsity for other pursuits and shepherded my manuscript through the stages leading to publication, I am grateful. As I have found before, the staff at InterVarsity Press are uniformly supportive and helpful; I am again indebted to them for their assistance along the way. Finally in this regard, I express appreciation to Judy Reveal, who has produced the name and subject indexes for this volume.

To all of these, I express my gratitude. For any infelicities and all errors remaining in this volume, I am solely responsible.

As always, I am grateful for the support and encouragement of my family. To my wife, Sharon, and to our children—Chris (and Liza), Trevor (and Erin), Jessica and Christopher—I freely express my thanks for the love we share as a family and the support we give each other in all our endeavors. Once again, I am indebted to you all.

This book is dedicated to my son Trevor. Over the years as he grew into maturity, we had many enjoyable, fascinating discussions about church history, Scripture and doctrine, and Christian living. He has stimulated me to be a better father, a more compassionate friend and a thoughtful scholar. In more ways than he can know, I am grateful to and for him.

Preface

This book is intended for readers from Christian backgrounds who recognize their roots in and look positively on the Reformation of the sixteenth century. I have written it especially for use in Christian university or college upper-level courses on the Reformation (whether in departments of history or religion and theology), as well as for more introductory courses on the history of Western civilization or religion courses that deal with the Reformation. The book is also for church pastors whose preaching or other teaching refers or appeals to the Reformation, as well as teachers in church settings who offer catechetical or other instruction in church history or the Reformation. This volume is thus particularly directed to people who look back on the Reformation as a significant movement that has shaped not only Western civilization but also the church world in which they find meaning in their lives. I trust that many in the larger Lutheran, Reformed/Calvinistic, Free Church and other Protestant communities, as well as interested Roman Catholics, will find this book of interest and help to them.

I am bold to hope that others whose personal religious commitments or academic interests are outside these areas will also use this book and find it beneficial. It purports to present a responsible, up-to-date, appreciative assessment of the sixteenth-century Reformation and should prove insightful for readers whether or not they are members of any of the religious bodies that arose out of that movement. But such readers should realize that this volume comes from and reflects a perspective in which a responsible historical treatment is itself only the penultimate goal, important as it is. The ultimate goal is to help those who are also committed, in one way or another, to the religious or theological value of the Reformation, that they might appreciate it and speak better and more responsibly of it.

I should make two qualifications about the title of this volume. For one thing, it speaks of "the Reformation" in the singular, not the plural. I am well aware of a recent trend in Reformation scholarship to use the plural;[1] indeed, in many ways, as the subsequent treatment will show, I am convinced that this seemingly slight modification offers a good window on what happened in the sixteenth century. However, for the most part, the intended readership of this volume will find itself in a Protestant tradition which either looks on the movement as "of a piece," or else thinks of its sixteenth-century roots as the "real" or "genuine" Reformation to which the other movements of the century did not quite shape up or from which they fell away. Using the plural in the title would not be well understood by much of this readership, so I have followed their instinctive predilections, which, it should be noted, accord with the way Reformation scholarship has referred to the movement until the last few years.

As a second qualification, the title of this book does not imply that learning what this volume offers will assure a right or final understanding of the Reformation. Claiming that kind of supposed objectivity or assertion of ultimate insight would be an arrogance for which no historian could ever expect absolution. Rather, what I intend with the title is to point out that there are some ways in which many people, despite better intentions and commitments to speak responsibly, have misunderstood and misrepresented the Reformation. This book builds on the wealth of careful Reformation scholarship of the last few generations which has done so much to flesh out and deepen our understanding of

---

[1]An excellent presentation of this perspective is found in the valuable work by Carter Lindberg, *The European Reformations* (Cambridge, Mass.: Blackwell, 1996).

the Reformation and its dynamics. Each of the chapters in this book draws on the wide-ranging and insightful investigations that have done so much to shape contemporary scholarly assessments of and perspectives on the Reformation. I would not deign to speak of a consensus, as if all Reformation-era specialists are in agreement; that is certainly not the case. But what this volume offers is a presentation of their assessments on a variety of basic questions and topics, which are so widely held that they seem unlikely to be challenged or changed through further research. That is to say, what is summarized and presented in this volume is "bedrock" Reformation scholarship as it has emerged from careful investigations over the past few generations, which offers a foundation on which to build in further study.

In the following treatment I have refrained from weighing down the text with the loads of references that could well be added. Notes are restricted to places where the perspective offered differs significantly from widely held notions and to references for quotations from or allusions to the written works of the Reformers themselves. In this regard, the translations from the Reformers and the church fathers which are not attributed to someone else are my own.

Will research into the Reformation continue? Undoubtedly. Will it generate further insights (and result in some disagreements)? Certainly. But will it undermine the foundation of Reformation scholarship so carefully laid by the past few generations? Not likely. In this book, I have tried to present this foundation in a way that reflects the strengths of Reformation scholarship and is accessible and helpful to interested readers. I hope it serves them well.

Introduction

Although I grew up in a Christian home, attended church regularly with my family, went to a Christian university and paid reasonably good attention through it all, I do not recall ever hearing about church history in all those years. Perhaps a pastor or teacher alluded to it in passing, but if so, it never caught my attention. Since I loved learning about history and had keen interest in biblical and doctrinal studies, but could not figure out how to bring those two together, I am fairly sure that if someone had referred to "church history" along the way, something would have clicked in my mind. When I finally discovered the field in early graduate studies, I was hooked. I took every course on church history or the history of Christian thought both in that program and in the seminary where I subsequently studied.

As a young, evangelical, would-be scholar, I was especially drawn to the history of the Reformation. After all, it had resulted in the various Protestant churches as over against the Roman Catholic Church. Since I was a committed evangelical Protestant, I desired to know as much as I could about the Reformation. Further, since I wanted to use whatever academic gifts God had given me in his service as directly as I could (whether in pastoral life or an academic setting), I plunged into studies of the history of the Reformation. This all led to obtaining a Th.M. (i.e.,

Master of Theology, a graduate program beyond the usual M.Div. seminary degree) in church history, with almost all my courses and my graduate thesis focused on the Reformation. Pursuing doctoral studies in early modern Europe was the next step in the academic portion of my spiritual journey. To make me a legitimate historian (and not just a religion expert), my graduate committee had me work in two minor fields outside church history, but the main focus of my doctoral studies was the intellectual history of early modern Europe—a field which included the Reformers' teaching. I received a Ph.D. in the field with a dissertation which explored the understanding of the significance of church history in the teaching of Philip Melanchthon and Martin Bucer, two leaders in the first generation of the Protestant Reformation.[1]

During all this I had become a pastor in the Reformed tradition, serving first a Presbyterian church in Pennsylvania and then a Christian Reformed one in Ontario. During the eight years I spent in the pastorate, my sermons and much of my other instruction drew significantly from what I had learned about church history and especially the Reformation. While the two congregations were dissimilar in background, in both of them members indicated appreciation for the instruction about and insights into the history of the church and the Reformation.

Eventually I was invited to join the faculty of Redeemer University College, where I became a history professor in 1985. In the years since then, I have taught the two-term, upper-level sequence in church history, as well as upper-level courses on the Reformation era. Throughout all this, I have kept current with the scholarly developments in Reformation studies and have produced both academic and popular articles dealing with various aspects of it. Along the way, though, I came to recognize some significant problems with the ways we who are committed Protestants speak about the Reformation—whether in churches or in classrooms.

To be sure, I am grateful that in the church circles in which I now move, people are aware of the history of the church to some degree, and

---

[1]James R. Payton Jr., "*Sola scriptura* and Church History: The Views of Bucer and Melanchthon on Religious Authority in 1539" (Ph.D. diss., University of Waterloo, 1982).

I resonate with the endeavors to point out our debt to the Protestant Reformers and their teaching. I think it important that Christian colleges offer instruction in church history and I am glad that they almost always deal with the Reformation, whether as a period in an introductory history course on Western civilization, as an upper-level history course, or in a course in a religion and theology department. I also recognize that it is more common now than it seemed to be in my youth to hear pastors or theologians refer to one of the main slogans of the Reformation in support of what they are teaching about faith or Scripture.

The challenge here is that a great deal of scholarly endeavor has gone into the study of the Reformation for the last century or so. During this period, critical editions of the Reformers' works have been painstakingly produced and published, and in the last three generations a plethora of secondary works has explored a bewildering diversity of topics on the Reformation. It is a daunting task to keep up with these developments, even for scholars whose main research and teaching responsibility is in early modern studies. However, few of those who teach about the Reformation in churches or Christian colleges have this kind of expertise. Pastors typically rely on what they were taught in seminary some years ago, plus whatever additional occasional reading they might undertake on the Reformation. Teachers in Christian colleges commonly need to teach an array of courses, some of them outside the areas of their scholarly preparation in graduate studies. Unless they are Reformation specialists, they usually end up relying on well-known older secondary literature.

Neither approach, though, will enable such people to keep abreast of Reformation scholarship. The result is that, however well intentioned, much of what is presented in churches and Christian colleges offers viewpoints and interpretations that have been weighed in the balances and found wanting by careful Reformation-era scholarship. However, since these scholarly contributions to the understanding and interpretation of the Reformation are generally unknown, what ends up being presented too often "gets the Reformation wrong" in several, sometimes serious, ways. This book attempts to address some of the common misunderstandings found in churches and college courses and offer viewpoints that reflect what Reformation scholarship has discovered through its more recent wide-ranging investigations.

The perspective in this does not look to scholarly Reformation specialists as gurus or high priests through whom alone initiation into sacred precincts is available. As in any field of scholarship, Reformation studies scholars are sometimes mistaken, and scholarly perspectives can be skewed by a variety of precommitments. Even so, the overriding concern of early modern European scholarship has been to come as close as possible to a careful understanding and interpretation of what transpired in that era. This has resulted in some remarkable, challenging discoveries and insights, which are incumbent on those teaching about the Reformation to reflect in the instruction they offer.

But, as I noted above, much of what I have encountered in churches and Christian college courses in these regards is flawed: "getting the Reformation wrong" is all too common a problem. I have identified several fundamental flaws in what is often presented about the Reformation. I have devoted a chapter each to a dozen of them in the work that follows. What we say about the Reformation too often presents—unintentionally, but nonetheless surely—perspectives that misrepresent what the Reformers actually taught or that have been thoroughly disproved by Reformation-era scholarship. Indeed, I have found that too much of what the contemporary evangelical and broader Protestant world thinks it knows about the Reformation is mistaken. Beyond that, I have often encountered perspectives on the Reformation which, however well intended as calls to live faithfully before God in our own day, make claims for the Reformation which the Reformers themselves did not accept or endorse.

This book arises from my ongoing fascination with and study of the Reformation. It was borne of a desire to expose, challenge and correct some misrepresentations of the Reformation which have become common. It comes as a call to appreciate, learn from and live out of the Reformation—not the Reformation of our fond imaginations, but the one which exploded on the European scene in the sixteenth century. Listening to it and learning from it may not only help us to more faithfully present the Reformation and what it taught, but also to see better how to live out the history of the church unfolding in our own day. On that, too, the Reformers have much to teach us, but what we learn from them may well take us in different directions than we might expect.

If we want to listen to and honor the Reformers, we need to know about the setting in which the Reformation arose: how and why the Reformation movement found support, how it unfolded, how it addressed the questions of its day and how it was challenged. We also need to explore how faithfully the Reformation was continued by the Reformers' successors, how to assess what resulted from it and how to view it in our day. Doing this is similar to what the Reformers themselves did as they surveyed the church in their day and tried to understand how it got that way. This is one way we can be faithful to the Reformers and the Reformation. I trust that this book will be a help to many in this worthy endeavor.

- 1 -

The Medieval
Call for Reform

ONE WAY IN WHICH SOME PEOPLE get the Reformation wrong is by overlooking or neglecting its historical rootedness. No matter how much significance we attribute to what the Reformation brought and the Reformers taught, the Reformation did not drop out of the sky from heaven. It arose "on the ground," in response to the oft-repeated call for reform which echoed down through the fourteenth and fifteenth centuries. In order to appreciate the sixteenth-century Reformation for what it was and did, it is necessary to see it against its historical background. Unless we do, we will certainly get the Reformation wrong: we will miss and misunderstand much of the significance of the Reformation, why it spread so quickly and what it meant to the peoples of Western Europe who encountered it.

To understand the Reformation's appeal to Western Europe, it is necessary to appreciate what the region had gone through in the two preceding centuries. To make sense of that, though, we need to recognize that the Reformation was not just an affair of doctrinal teaching, unaffected by and unrelated to the ebb and flow of society and culture. The Reformation did not take place only in churches or study groups. It broke loose in the hurly-burly of Western European life, not in a spiritually ethereal realm. As we will see in subsequent chapters, what had transpired in Western European society in the fourteenth and fifteenth centuries, and had continued into the sixteenth, shaped how people heard and understood the Reformation's message. Consequently, to avoid getting the Reformation wrong, we must know what had happened in the late Middle Ages in Western Europe.

To get into this, though, it is necessary to distance ourselves from a common notion in the present day—namely, that religion belongs in a personal, private sphere. No one held that attitude in the medieval or Reformation eras. The devastating problems we will consider below regarding weather, agricultural productivity and disease—all compounded by wars, peasant rebellions and the uncertainties involved in the emergence of national states in Western Europe—were not "secular" concerns, unrelated to the church. Since the church had long been the only unifying loyalty throughout Europe and its influence had significantly shaped the civilization that had developed in Western Europe earlier in the medieval period, people saw these "other" problems as issues in and for Western Christendom. The sort of overarching influence on all of society and culture for which many Christians yearn in the contemporary world was the norm in medieval and early modern Europe. Because of this, any problem—however "secular" it might be construed in the present day—had a significant religious component to it, and people expected that the teaching and practice of Christianity should provide solutions to it. The church's inability or failure to do this only exacerbated the frustration people felt toward the church and its leaders and prepared the way for other Christian leaders, in the sixteenth century, to receive a welcome hearing.

LATE MEDIEVAL CRISES IN WESTERN EUROPEAN SOCIETY

Historians hesitate to describe any era as a period of crisis, since crisis seems endemic to human existence in this world. No matter how peaceful, prosperous or pleasant a period may be, some crises will taint the era. Even so, few historians would hesitate to describe the late Middle Ages as a period of crisis.

The languid but basically steady development of Western Christendom in the aftermath of the destruction of the Roman Empire in the West—with the eventual Christianization and civilizing of the peoples of Western Europe—had led to a thirteenth-century zenith. Good government was expected and offered, as civil rulers followed ecclesiastical leadership. Western Europe was united in a single overarching loyalty to the church. Urban life had reestablished itself and was flourishing. Population was increasing. More and more land was under cultivation and regularly yielding good harvests. Schools and universities had been established and were producing leaders for church and society. Majestic Gothic cathedrals pierced the sky. All seemed to be going well (with minor problems, to be sure); there was no apparent reason to think that the path would change.

But that trajectory changed dramatically: from early in the fourteenth century through the end of the fifteenth, Western Europe reeled from one crisis to another, seemingly without a break. Harvest, health and hope all evaporated under what many viewed as heaven's wrath: how else could all the chaos be understood than as divine judgment? But with the undeniable corruption of the church from the absentee bishop of Rome down through the hierarchy to the lowly village priest, exasperated and desperate people recognized that the church itself needed to be renewed if it was to offer them any answers or solace. But not only had the administration of the church slid into a morass of corruption: the pattern of theological instruction adopted by the recently established universities seemed oblivious to human need while wrapped up in intellectual games. The determined cry *reformatio in capite et membris*—"reform in head and members"—echoed through the fourteenth and fifteenth centuries. It called for a drastic renewal of Western Christendom "from head to toe." When the Reformation came in the sixteenth century, it came to soil well prepared for the seed it would sow: Western Europe was looking for answers and direction, and the Reformers offered both.

We cannot extensively explore the problems Western Europe faced in the late Middle Ages here.[1] Even so, it will be helpful to consider

---

[1]Any good history of the late medieval period will deal with these problems *in extenso*. An excellent treatment is offered in Denys Hay, *Europe in the Fourteenth and Fifteenth Centuries* (London: Longman, 1966).

them in an overview fashion to enable readers to gauge the breadth and depth of what Western Europe had been struggling with for several generations by the time the Reformation arose. All these issues factored significantly into the sense of chaos loosed in Western Europe.

Agricultural failures. Although no one then recognized the situation, by the beginning of the fourteenth century virtually all of Western Europe's arable land had been brought under cultivation. With the agricultural practices of the time, further increase in harvests, which would have been necessary to meet the needs of an increasing population, was unlikely. This problem was exacerbated by a series of cold and wet growing seasons, which severely limited harvests, during most years in the first two decades of the fourteenth century. Decreased harvests resulted in less seed for the succeeding year's planting and less grain for food production. All this led to inadequate food supplies for Western Europe's population. Malnutrition ensued and a continent-wide famine arose. These problems were inextricably entwined. A virtually uninterrupted succession of such years devastated Western Europe: between 10 and 25 percent of the population died by 1320. However horrific this was, worse was coming.

The Black Death. The arrival of the Black Death (also known as the Bubonic Plague) a generation later compounded the horror.[2] It ravaged Western Europe from 1347 to 1351, killing between one-third and one-half of the continent's population. Periodic outbreaks occurred in various areas of Western Europe over the next 120 years. By 1450 the population of Western Europe had declined from what it had been in 1347 by between 60 and 75 percent. While other factors played a role in this precipitous decline, the main culprit was the Black Death.

The medicine of the time had no understanding of the etiology of this disease and no effective treatment for it. We now know that the

---

[2]For most of the following data on the Black Death, this treatment relies on the presentation by Robert S. Gottfried, *The Black Death: Natural and Human Disaster in Medieval Europe* (New York: The Free Press, 1983); see also the interesting collection of relevant material in Elizabeth A. Lehfeldt, ed., *The Black Death*, Problems in European Civilization (New York: Houghton Mifflin, 2005). For further consideration of the impact of the Black Death on Western Europe, see George Huppert, *After the Black Death: A Social History of Early Modern Europe* (Bloomington: Indiana University Press, 1986).

Bubonic Plague was passed via rats which served as hosts of infected fleas and that these rats had been brought to Western Europe on ships carrying on trade with the Far East. However, the presence of rats was nothing unusual throughout Western Europe and the awareness of epidemiology was rudimentary at best at the time. Fleabites were a common enough nuisance that no one particularly suspected how this form of the disease was contracted. The plague could also be spread by airborne means, through the coughing or labored respiration of infected individuals struggling with the disease. This pneumonic variant of the plague flourished in cold and wet climates—which, as noted above, had become increasingly common in Western Europe in preceding decades.

The disease struck, brought excruciating agony and killed quickly. In those infected by rat bites, incubation took about six days, then buboes developed (from which the disease gets its name) with the swelling of lymph nodes in armpit, neck and groin areas due to subcutaneous hemorrhaging. The blood in the buboes clotted, killing cells. This led to the poisoning of the neurological system. The mortality rate for this version of the plague was between 50 and 60 percent. The pneumonic variety incubated within two to three days, then body temperature fell quickly, lungs became congested, and severe coughing, which resulted in bloody sputum, ensued. Neurological disorders soon developed; the mortality rate for this form of the Black Death was above 95 percent.

As the trade centers from which the infection spread into Western Europe, the Italian cities were hit first. In 1348 Florence lost between 45 and 75 percent of its population to the plague within six months of the first infection.[3] In Venice, about 60 percent of the inhabitants died within eighteen months. From Italy it spread into the rest of the continent, wreaking havoc and spreading terror.

No medicinal practice, religious ceremony or incantation had any effect on the progress and spread of the disease. Apart from comforting those afflicted—which exposed those offering solace to the disease themselves—little could be done. Recognizing that those in close contact with infected persons most often developed the disease soon there-

---

[3]In his prologue to *The Decameron*, Giovanni Boccaccio described the course of the plague and some of the ways people reacted to it as it hit Florence in 1348.

after, many civic and medical leaders counseled quarantine: once anyone in a house manifested symptoms of the disease, everyone in that house was quarantined there. The result was that, with few exceptions, all the residents in that house eventually succumbed to the plague.

The Black Death spawned terror. There seemed to be no escape from this pestilence, and there was no understanding of it. The fact that it periodically reemerged in subsequent generations served to keep the plague's horrors close to the surface in people's minds. Life had always been uncertain. Death of mothers in childbirth, infant mortality, limited medical treatment for disease, ineffectual remedies for fever and infection, accidents at work and the dangers of warfare all were common concerns throughout the Middle Ages. Even so, Western Europe's mood during the thirteenth century was optimistic. But with the Black Death, life was not just short; it was too often forfeit. Large swaths of the population succumbed and the mood in Western Europe became pessimistic. A striking manifestation of that change was the emergence and widespread appropriation of the *danse macabre*—the artistic rendering of a person suffering from the Bubonic Plague as he or she succumbed, including what lay ahead in the afterlife.[4]

Wars and revolts. In addition, wars and revolts brought danger and destruction. While the on-again, off-again Hundred Years War (1337-1453) between England and France did not directly affect the rest of Western Europe, the uncertainties and devastation were sure enough for northwestern France where the predominance of the battles took place. Sporadic lesser wars elsewhere in the continent offered their own contribution to the unsettledness of the times.

Beyond these official bellicosities, most regions of Western Europe faced revolts of one kind or another during the last half of the fourteenth century and much of the fifteenth. With the widespread loss of population, the lords desperately needed the remaining peasants to work the fields and bring in the harvests. Some lords tried to increase the amount of time their peasants had to work for them, violating longstanding agreements. For their part, many peasants recognized

---

[4]On this, see the treatment by Johan Huizinga, *The Autumn of the Middle Ages*, trans. Rodney J. Payton and Ulrich Mammitzsch (Chicago: University of Chicago Press, 1996), pp. 156-72.

that their labor was more valuable than in the past, so they left their lords' manors and offered their services to those willing to pay them better. Some lords restricted access to what had been common lands for fishing or hunting, or charged fees for them; this was another novelty which chafed peasants. In various regions, further annoyances compounded these resentments, and peasant revolts broke out in France, England, Italy, northern Germany and Spain. Attacks on nobles and their estates led to brutal repressions. By the time the various revolts were suppressed, many lives had been lost and much devastation had occurred. The cessation of revolt did not commonly issue into agreement; force brought an end and imposed a settlement. Neither peasants nor lords were pleased with what resulted. To all alike, it seemed that the very fabric of existence had grown threadbare and nothing was sure for the future.

During the fourteenth and fifteenth centuries, Western Europe endured bad weather, poor harvests, famine and starvation, pestilence, and war. In a society which found its roots and supreme loyalty in Christianity, it is hardly surprising that these disasters received a Christian assessment. To many, it seemed that the fourth horseman of the Apocalypse had been turned loose (see Rev 6:7-8). Certainly this seemed to be divine punishment. What had humanity in Western Europe done to provoke God? What could be done to assuage his wrath? The church should have been the first line of defense in this regard, but it could not be. The church itself was stumbling through one crisis after another.

LATE MEDIEVAL CRISES IN CHURCH LEADERSHIP

In the early Middle Ages—the fifth through the tenth centuries—the church, headquartered in Rome, had led in the evangelization and civilizing of Western Europe. Along the way, this had resulted in Rome becoming the center of loyalty, aspiration and inquiry for the burgeoning churches among the various peoples of the continent. Rome's bishop came to be respected as the one who oversaw the evangelization efforts and who guided the various peoples and the whole continent in the pursuit of a Christian civilization. Western Europeans came to revere the pope as God's appointed representative on earth and as the disinterested arbiter of divine justice. In a real sense, they owed to him both their hope for the eternal future and their peace in the present.

By the end of the first millennium, all the peoples of Western Europe had embraced Christianity. With this the church became the only international body in the continent. Civil governments among the respective peoples were still developing, under ecclesiastical oversight, the various ministries and bureaucracies which would eventually attract respect and loyalty. But in the thirteenth century, loyalties to central governments and awareness of being a member of a distinct "nation" were only embryonic. Those loyalties would be greatly strengthened during the fourteenth and fifteenth centuries, as the governments of the various Western European peoples consolidated and managed to attract the respect and trust of the peoples they governed. The various peoples would become aware of being "English," "French," "Italian" or "German" and develop loyalty to their "nation."[5] Part of the reason this took place so readily in the late Middle Ages is the way the papacy specifically, and the church in general, frittered away the confidence which had formerly been placed in them.

Already in the thirteenth century, the highest point of the Middle Ages, the papacy began to come under some suspicion. Whereas earlier popes had been respected as dispensers of divine justice, the popes of the thirteenth century seemed to many to have become protagonists in the pursuit of justice, seeking to secure certain states of affairs which would serve the interests of church and papacy. This pattern began already with Pope Innocent III (1198-1216). His vigorous direction of European affairs pressured the monarchs of the three most powerful peoples (France, England, and the Holy Roman Empire) to yield to his directives. He was the first of a succession of seven "lawyer popes"—popes whose university training had been in canon (ecclesiastical) law, rather than in theology. Each of the seven lawyer popes of the thirteenth century followed the path of papal instigation of events, rather than the earlier one of papal assessment of events. Along the way, some civil and

---

[5]For an insightful treatment of the development of governments and of national loyalties in the fourteenth and fifteenth centuries, see Bernard Guenée, *States and Rulers in Later Medieval Europe*, trans. Juliet Vale (New York: Basil Blackwell, 1988).

ecclesiastical leaders became concerned with the shift in approach. Even so, during the thirteenth century the path of Western Christendom continued to be smooth. It became rocky early in the fourteenth century, however, with popes unintentionally but surely leading the way in this.

The Avignon Papacy (1309-1378). In 1309 a French prelate was elected pope, taking the name Clement V. In the Middle Ages, it was not uncommon for a non-Italian to be elected bishop of Rome,[6] so this initially provoked no consternation. However, while the newly elected bishop of Rome accepted the office, he resolutely refused to leave France to take up his charge and so conducted the office from his residence there. This pattern continued until 1378, with all seven of the popes elected in the period being French in nationality. Finally, in 1377 the last of them yielded to the many importunities which had been directed to him and his predecessors to return to Rome. Along the way, the papal court had settled in the town of Avignon; thus this period is known as the Avignon Papacy.

Little remained of the notion that the pope was a disinterested arbiter of divine justice. The reasons for this are not difficult to appreciate. For one thing, the Avignon popes regularly deferred to the wishes of the kings of France, who at the time ruled the wealthiest, most centrally organized and powerful kingdom of Western Europe. For another, of the 134 individuals "created" cardinal[7] during the period, 113 were Frenchmen. For rulers and peoples of the other emergent nations, the sheen of the papacy was tarnished. Favoritism stung, especially when it favored others.

Beyond the stain of clear national preference, the Avignon Papacy further besmirched the papal reputation by multiplying the ways it extracted funds from kings, peoples and clergy. Although "simony"[8] was

---

[6]However common this practice was then, it disappeared in 1523 with the death of Adrian VI (from the Netherlands), not to reappear until the election of John Paul II in 1978. For the intervening 455 years, all the popes were Italian in nationality.

[7]During the Middle Ages, a cardinal was a top-level power in the Roman Church, an advisor to the pope, and often lived at the papal court.

[8]The term refers to the practice of obtaining a religious office or practice in consideration of some monetary payment. The origin of the term is the story in Acts 8:18-21 in which Simon Magus attempted to purchase the ability to bestow the Holy Spirit—for which he was soundly denounced by the apostle Peter.

rigidly proscribed by canon law, skilled advisors found ways for popes to avoid the charge while pursuing the practice. In the estimation of much of Western Europe, any ecclesiastical office was for sale in Avignon. Among the slurs against "Roma" (Italian for "Rome," which the Avignon popes supposedly served as bishop) was a bit of graffiti often found in Western Europe during the period, an acrostic: *Radix Omnium Malorum Avaritia* ("the root of all evils is avarice")—a stinging indictment of the greed of the Avignon Papacy.

Beyond all this, though, the Avignon Papacy became known as a cesspool of moral depravity. Although the ecclesiastical demand for clergy of any hierarchical rank was celibacy, this requirement was often ignored. Even so, the peoples of Western Europe knew the requirement and expected that if any clerics should abide by it, the popes and cardinals should as the leaders of the church. Nevertheless, Avignon became known for cavalier indifference, not only to the rule of celibacy, but for any restriction on sexual appetites. The brilliant Italian author Francesco Petrarca denounced the Avignon Papacy for many violations of canon law, protocol and morality, the last of which played a pronounced role in his criticisms.[9]

At the beginning of the thirteenth century, the adulation in which the papacy was viewed was virtually boundless. Some suspicions arose during that century with the perceived machinations of the lawyer popes. But the Avignon Papacy brought scandal to the papal court rather than respect.[10] Many outspoken voices—theologians, monastic leaders and civil rulers—called on the Avignon popes to return to Rome and correct the grievous errors which had so badly damaged the papal reputation. Among these voices were two widely respected female monastics, St. Birgitta of Sweden and St. Catherine of Siena, who boldly denounced the papal court and summoned it to return to the path of rectitude. Finally, the last of the Avignon popes, Gregory VII, returned

---

[9]These can be found in Norman P. Zacour, trans., *Petrarch's Book Without a Name: A Translation of the "Liber sine Nomine"* (Toronto: Pontifical Institute of Medieval Studies, 1973).

[10]While this treatment is sharply critical of the Avignon Papacy, note that it is not some form of anti-Roman Catholic screed; even the most conservative of Roman Catholic historians recognize the problems with and acknowledge the corruption of the Avignon Papacy, and would hardly seek to defend it.

to Rome in 1377 in an attempt to begin reestablishing respect for the ecclesiastical leadership. After only a few months, though, he died. As hard as it would have been to imagine, something worse than the Avignon Papacy was about to befall Western Christendom.

The Great Schism (1378-1415). When the people of Rome discovered that after the death of Pope Gregory VII the cardinals intended to head back to Avignon, a crowd surrounded the papal palace and demanded the election of an Italian as bishop of Rome. The frightened cardinals elected the archbishop of Bari as pope in 1378; he took the name Urban VI. Little did they know just how different his lifestyle was from theirs.

Strictly ascetic in habits, he soon clashed with the cardinals. This became evident over the next few months after his election as he severely limited the various privileges to which they had become accustomed. Eventually several of them left Rome's summer heat for Anagni where they repudiated Urban's election because it had been decided under duress. To be sure, the provisions of canon law declared any such election invalid. However, the delay in rejecting it until the cardinals' perquisites came under fire served to raise serious questions in the minds of many theologians and canon lawyers. In any event these cardinals denounced Urban as a false pope and proceeded to elect someone else as pope—a Frenchman, who took the name Clement VII and promptly returned with his cardinals to Avignon.

However, Urban did not accept this deposition. He created several cardinals for his Roman court and claimed to be the true pope—as did the pope in Avignon. Each demanded the allegiance of all Christians and denounced both the other claimant and all his followers as servants of Satan. With all this, Western Christendom suddenly had two popes. The best minds among the theologians and canon lawyers could not come to agreement on which claim was the valid one and so the church found itself in schism. This debacle lasted from 1378-1415.

Rival papacies, with their courts, sought the allegiance of civil rulers, who were the ones who decided which of the popes they and their people would support. Western Europe was divided into two religious camps, each professing to be the true version of the church and de-

nouncing the other as false—but with no one able to decipher which
had the better claim. To continue to function in the manner that Western Christendom expected, both papal courts needed the full comple-
ment of financial support which Western Europe had previously
tendered to the church's center. But, of course, each had access to only
a part of what had been granted prior to 1378. Papal attempts to raise
contributions were often enough countered by a civil ruler wheeling
and dealing with the two papal courts to secure a reduction in payments, as the monarch bargained for the allegiance he and his nation
would bring to one papal court or the other. Periodically, a better deal
led to a transfer of that allegiance. Unsavory as this all seems, it made
sense to the monarchs: the more funds they could retain within their
domain, the more they had to use for the further consolidation of their
own governments. With the increased sensitivity to the well-being of
the residents the various monarchs governed, those residents ended up
developing loyalties to the monarch as a people and the idea of those
residents collectively comprising a nation emerged more fully into con-
sciousness. Loyalty to nation began to displace loyalty to the church as
the primary loyalty—not that people turned from Christianity, but that
they turned to the sure national center in their ruler, rather than the
uncertain international one in the pope (whoever he was).

The rise and collapse of conciliarism. Pressures from theologians,
canon lawyers, ecclesiastical hierarchs below the level of cardinal,
civil rulers, and a variety of male and female monastics to find a solu-
tion to this preposterous situation led to careful analysis of canon law.
In due course some canon lawyers came to see that certain provisions
in canon law could be interpreted in a way that spoke to the situation
and offered a way out.[11] This notion became known as "conciliarism"—
the idea that the papacy served the entire church as its administrative
head, but that ultimate ecclesiastical authority resided with a council
representing the whole church rather than in the papacy. Thus a pope
could not legitimately use his position to the detriment of the church—
as was obviously happening in the Great Schism. A council repre-

---

[11]For an outstanding treatment of the question, see Brian Tierney, *Foundations of the Conciliar Theory* (New York: Cambridge University Press, 1955).

senting the entire church should periodically be held to assess the state of the church and receive reports of the leadership rendered by the pope. If he proved derelict, then the church did not need to await his demise; it could remove him from office and replace him. The effect of this approach would have been to transform ecclesiastical government in a more democratic direction than had taken place even in any of the nations which had emerged. This was both conciliarism's strength and its weakness.

Conciliarism offered hope for bringing the Great Schism to an end. While not every canon lawyer, theologian and hierarch embraced the conciliarist approach, enough did to make it a viable option. Since it seemed the only possibility for resolving the impasse, it garnered much support in Western Christendom, whatever misgivings some had.

This was so evident that several cardinals in the two papal courts took up correspondence about adopting the approach themselves. In due course they summoned the Council of Pisa, which met in 1409. There the cardinals cast the votes, following a pattern which had become the norm in recent medieval councils. Most of the members of the two cardinalates met in Pisa, with a host of advisors and attendees from among the leadership of the theological schools, the monasteries, civil rulers and canon lawyers. At the Council of Pisa the cardinals declared both the incumbents in the papal sees of Avignon and Rome deposed and proceeded to elect another person as pope; he took the name Alexander V (1409-1410).

However, neither pope accepted the deposition; both continued to claim to be the true pope, entitled to the allegiance of all the church. Only now, thanks to the cardinals, Western Christendom had three popes. Given the new approach of conciliarism and the obvious ineffectuality of this first attempt to utilize it, much of Western Christendom remained uncertain who was the true pope. This was not the last gasp of conciliarism, for its basic approach continued to commend it to many as the only way out of the impasse. However, the Council of Pisa was the last time Western Europe trusted its future to the cardinals. Subsequent conciliarist endeavors adopted different understandings of who should vote, sidelining the cardinals, who had shown themselves so inept at handling the situation. Indeed, the cardinals had brought on the problem in the first place and their attempt to solve it had only exacerbated it.

Conciliarism continued to offer the only viable way out of the multipope mess. In due course, Emperor Sigismund prevailed on the papal successor in the Pisan line, John XXIII (1410-1415), to summon another council. It met as the Council of Constance, 1415-1418. With an attendance exceeding 3,500, the council showed how seriously Western Christendom saw the problem of the papal schism. At the council, voting was by nations. When the cardinals requested to vote as another group, equivalent to a nation, their request was denied. They could speak their mind within their national group, but the majority within that nation would make the decision. The first order of business for the Council of Constance was to declare its legitimacy and authority, and it did so in the decree *Haec sancta*. With that authority the council proceeded to depose all three popes—and, unlike the Council of Pisa, to "make it stick." Each was tried and convicted of crimes against the church and was stripped of any papal dignities.

Enforced and ensured by the authority of the emperor, this cleared the way for a response to the longstanding call for "reform in head and members." Soon enough, though, the council recognized that deliberating on and deciding how to effect reforms in so wide an arena was impossible in such a large gathering. So Martin V (1418-1431) was elected pope but sternly charged with pursuing and implementing reform in the several areas spelled out by the council. He would be required to call another council into session in five years (1423) at which he would report on his efforts in these regards. If he failed to impress the council, he could conceivably be stripped of papal dignity and the position given to another. According to the decree *Frequens* adopted by the council, that next council must be called five years after the Council of Constance concluded; that council would be followed by another seven years hence. From that point on, councils would be called every ten years—all to secure the well-being of the church.

The Council of Constance made a fateful decision as to how the pope could work to effect the reforms for which all of Western Christendom had been clamoring. Following up on its own approach to voting by nations and playing to the increasing identification the various peoples of Western Europe were making with their particular nations, the council allowed that the pope could make specific arrangements to secure reform with the distinct nations. To be sure, this would make for the requisite ecclesiastical flexibility to work with the particular patterns and needs found in the several nations. It would also allow the papacy to deal with the various nations in different manners. As it turned out, this had momentous consequences in the later fifteenth century and on into the sixteenth—but at the time of the conciliar decision, this approach seemed wise.

Martin V gave his promise to live up to these reform and reporting responsibilities. But once the Council of Constance came to an end, he directed scant attention to the issues of reform. As the fifth year came to an end, he dutifully summoned another council to meet in Siena, which at the time was enduring a renewed outbreak of the Bubonic Plague. When no one showed up for the council, he declared it suspended, ostensibly because of lack of interest. The civil rulers and the ecclesiastical leaders recognized that the pope had played the situation false, so when the next seven years had elapsed and the pope summoned a council to meet in Basel in 1431, they showed up in huge numbers—determined to seize control of the situation again, as their predecessors had in Constance.

In the meantime, Martin V had died and Eugenius IV (1431-1447) had been elected pope. He recognized the potential danger for his papacy in the determination evident at the council and declared the council prorogued to another venue, hoping to deflect interest and attendance through this subterfuge. However, the council declared that it had met in the name and by the authority of Christ, so that all the church—including the pope—was subject to its decisions. The council then rejected the papal attempt to move it and summoned the pope to the council to answer charges of contumacy toward the council. The pope had the good sense not to go to Basel, apologizing instead for his misguided attempt to move the council. But he was not going to let this situation stand.

The Council of Basel had adopted a different approach to voting than had been followed before. Rather than voting only by cardinals (as in Pisa) or by nations (as with Constance), the Council of Basel voted by committees. The attendees were divided into committees, without significant regard to rank or status; in the committee deliberations, every member had the privilege of speaking and voting, and the committee's decision rested with the simple majority. The council's decisions came via majority vote of the committees. This approach opened the door to influence from many more people, with some radicalism becoming evident in later decisions. Along the way, the pope wrote to a number of monarchs in Western Europe. They had supported conciliarism as a way of dealing with the church's problems and had offered support to the Council of Basel. The pope pointed out to them that what was taking place in the council could become the pattern in civil government as well. This was enough make some rulers mute somewhat their support for the Council of Basel.[12]

Basel plunged into the complicated issues of reform. It adopted a number of decisions designed to straighten out problems in a wide range of ecclesiastical and papal malfeasance. The Council of Basel was, indeed, dealing with issues of reform, but the vigorous, virtually democratic approach to restructuring government and practice made many civil rulers uneasy. Further, some experts in canon law began to question whether these more radical reforms could be implemented.

But Basel also managed to bring an end to the Hussite schism in Bohemia. The larger portion of the Hussites were reconciled to the rest of Western Christendom at the council, leading to great celebration and joy. The pope joined in this praise of the council and then called it to seize the opportunity just presented by missives from Constantinople to effect the larger reunion, the one with the estranged Eastern Orthodox. He made the most of this opportunity.

The Byzantine emperor and the patriarch of Constantinople had sent letters to both the pope and the council, seeking a meeting to work

---

[12]For an excellent and thorough consideration of this, see Joachim W. Stieber, *Pope Eugenius IV, the Council of Basel, and the Secular and Ecclesiastical Authorities in the Empire: The Conflict over Supreme Authority and Power in the Church* (Leiden: Brill, 1978).

toward reunion and, with that, to receive Western European aid against the threat posed by the Ottoman Turks. The pope suggested that out of concern for the Byzantines and the dire situation they faced from their Ottoman enemies, it would be better for the meeting to work toward reunion to be held in Italy rather than deep inland in Western Europe in Basel. This suggestion resonated with many theologians and civil rulers, who endorsed the idea, and in 1437 the pope declared the council transferred to Ferrara.

However, a large group remained suspicious of this endeavor as another attempt to derail the council. While a minority composed of the leading figures of church and state left for the Council of Ferrara (which ended up subsequently being shifted to Florence), a significant group refused to be prorogued. Building on the earlier response at Basel to the previous papal endeavor to shift locale, those who remained at Basel denounced the pope and summoned him to appear to answer charges. When he failed to do so within the allotted time, the council tried and deposed him. They then proceeded to elect another pope—thereby bringing on another schism, the very thing that conciliarism had been called into being to overcome.

With this, the Council of Basel clearly overreached itself and brought discredit to the whole conciliarist enterprise. Whatever noble sentiments it professed and whatever pronouncements it made regarding the state of the church and how to achieve reform, the council had drastically undermined itself. Finally, in 1449 the Council of Basel limped to an end. It prevailed on its "pope," who had received virtually no endorsements from within Western Christendom, to resign his "office" and went through the motions, to save face, of electing the current pope as pope—as though it still mattered what the council thought and did. To almost everyone else in Western Christendom, this was not the case.

Meanwhile the supposedly pressing need to deal swiftly with the Eastern Orthodox luminaries had come to naught. The Council of Ferrara/Florence met from 1438-1439 with the price of reunion set high: complete capitulation of Eastern Orthodox perspectives to Western Christian distinctives. The celebration held at the end of the council did not reflect the assessment of significant portions of the Byzantine contingent of representatives and the supposed reunion was rejected by the vast majority of Eastern Orthodox faithful in Byzantium. With that, Western Christendom did not send any appreciable aid to Constantinople, which fell to the Ottoman Turks on May 29, 1453.

The Renaissance papacy. Without moving toward the reform in head and members for which Western Christendom had been insisting for a century and a half, the church's leadership had consolidated again in a vigorous papacy. It was back in Rome, to be sure, and there was only one pope. Its greatest threat, conciliarism, had been discredited, and the hoped-for but moribund reunion with the Eastern Orthodox Church had nevertheless served to underline papal leadership.

Rather than pursue reform, however, papal leadership turned its interest toward the burgeoning Renaissance movement. Papal sponsorship of various artists, sculptors and authors served to beautify the Vatican and make Rome a center of the movement, but it did little to assuage the concerns of the rest of Western Christendom about the direction of the papacy. While the Renaissance papacy undoubtedly enriched Western art with its support of Raphael, Michelangelo, Bramante and others, it served to weaken yet further the confidence Western Christendom could muster in the papacy.

Along the way, the Renaissance papacy had made the most of the Council of Constance's decision that the pope could deal in distinct ways with the respective nations of Western Europe. Because papal authority had been badly tarnished since the early fourteenth century, the popes were hardly in a position to assert themselves vigorously against the more powerful nations of the continent. France, England and Spain (via the unification of the kingdoms of Aragon and Castile in the late fifteenth century) all became well-centralized, efficient kingdoms governed by strong monarchs. The Renaissance papacy had to deal with these nations with great discretion and caution. However, with nations that were less centralized, the pope did not face a united body governed by a monarch to whom all submitted without hesitation. With these nations the papacy was more high-handed and abrupt in demands. Preeminent among these nations was the huge but ramshackle conglomeration known as the Holy Roman Empire. Composed of more than three hundred states plus sixty-five free imperial cities,[13] "Germany" was anything but tightly centralized. Papal treatment of Germany in the fifteenth century rankled the German people greatly. The papacy would pay a high price for this in the sixteenth century.

The depths to which the Renaissance papacy plunged were evident in the case of Pope Alexander VI (1492-1503), a member of the Borgia family. He openly flaunted his violation of celibacy by promoting the children he had by different women to places of prominence. His daughter Lucrezia became a prominent figure in the papal court, and he created his nine-year-old son a cardinal—a papal mockery of the office if ever there was one! While his disreputable tenure did not become the norm, it was only an exaggerated version of the typically dissolute, spiritually destitute pattern offered by the Renaissance papacy. One of the last of the Renaissance popes was Leo X (1513-1521)—the pope in office when the "Luther affair" broke. On being elected pope, Leo declared, "God has given us the papacy! Let us enjoy it!" That utterance already speaks volumes about what the leadership of the church had become as the sixteenth century dawned.

Anticlericalism. During the late Middle Ages, a vigorous anticlericalism arose in Western Christendom. This does not necessarily mean that clergy were any more or less capable than they had been in earlier centuries. Part of the explanation could be that with increasing education available via the schools and universities, and with greater mobility possible because of urban life, more people became aware of what clergy should do or were doing in other regions. In this regard, they became dissatisfied with the lives their own clergy were living and with what those clergy were offering in their service.

This anticlerical sentiment was doubtlessly fed by the reports of clergy fleeing their parishes to avoid the Black Death. To be sure, many priests continued to meet with their parishioners, attended them in their sickness and presided at their funerals. But in a situation viewed

---

[13]These were cities not under the rule of one of the major states: they governed themselves under the general oversight of the emperor. Most often, these cities were major centers of trade. Their importance for the economy of the Holy Roman Empire, their periodic coalitions and confrontations, and their number all assured that centralizing imperial authority in Germany remained an elusive dream.

as a divine judgment, for a priest to default on his responsibilities toward his parishioners and flee only underlined the hopelessness experienced as the plague ravaged the region. This malfeasance would not be forgotten; it fed an anticlerical spirit.

Another reason for this spirit was the increasing awareness of how widespread the violations of celibacy were in Western Christendom. Greater levels of public knowledge about clerical requirements in this regard only served to highlight how much that requirement was flaunted by the clergy at all levels. One can get a sense of how widespread and pervasive this problem was by considering what happened in two dioceses when the respective bishops instituted a fine on priests who fathered children. In the diocese of Bamberg the bishop assessed a fine of five gulden for every child fathered by a priest; this resulted in one year in payments of 1,500 gulden. In the much larger diocese of Constance, the bishop instituted a fine of four gulden for any child spawned by a priest; from this, in one year the bishop collected 7,500 gulden.[14] That someone like Alexander VI, in the exalted position of the papacy itself, openly violated the rule of celibacy only emphasized the failure of the clergy at all levels to live by their stated responsibilities.

All this resulted in a virulent anticlericalism in the fourteenth and especially the fifteenth centuries. Even so, this must not be misunderstood as opposition to Christianity. Anticlericalism need not imply that people in Western Europe were dissatisfied with religion itself. Indeed, it would seem to imply the opposite: anticlericalism had little point if those criticizing did not care about religious practice. Given the crises Western Christendom had endured, the ministrations of clergy were more necessary and desired, not less. When clergy failed to provide them adequately, people denounced the failure.

Further, the anticlericalism of the late Middle Ages found a ready object in the papacy itself. With what was noted above about the disreputable steps the papacy had taken for several generations in sequence, it is hardly surprising that many people in Western Christendom were consummately dissatisfied with and openly critical of the papacy and the

---

[14]Information taken from Philip Schaff, *History of the Christian Church* (1910; reprint, Grand Rapids: Eerdmans, 1970), 6:668.

popes who filled that role. But this did not mean that the critics were ready to turn from the Christian faith or the church any more than Christians in twenty-first-century North America criticizing the way their denominational headquarters operates indicates that those critics are eager to turn to some other denomination or renounce the faith.

This rampant late-medieval anticlericalism indicates a longing for better Christianity, not less of it. It also indicates that long before Luther and the other Reformers came along, Western Christendom had become disenchanted with the way the church was being run and with its leaders. A faithful Christian—whether theologian, priest or monk—would be appreciated and receive a ready hearing, both as he criticized failed prelates and as he taught the faith. For this ready hearing to be possible, though, something also needed to change in the way the faith was presented, for that too had come to a critical pass.

LATE MEDIEVAL CRISES IN CHURCH TEACHING

The way the Christian faith was taught and proclaimed had undergone a significant transformation during the Middle Ages. During the fourteenth and fifteenth centuries, this development spun off into strange directions, resulting in at times bizarre but regularly confusing perspectives being presented as one group or another elaborated its distinctive viewpoints. Along the way most of the questions to which the sixteenth-century Reformers gave answers were broached. To get a sense of all this, we need to see how the teaching of the faith had developed in the Middle Ages.

Monastic schooling. With the collapse of the Roman Empire in the West under the Germanic onslaughts in the fourth and fifth centuries, schooling came to an abrupt end. The only place where learning survived was in the monasteries, where the learned treasures of antiquity—ancient works, some by pagan authors but most by the church fathers, plus the Scriptures themselves—continued to be studied and copied. This study was intended to serve monastic goals as it enabled monks to learn from the riches of the past in order to facilitate their ability to pray to God and learn his truth. But when Christian civilization arose and came to the point where it needed schools to train those who would lead in the civil sphere, the pattern and purpose of monastic schooling were not quite to the point.

The development of scholasticism. By that time, however, through increased trade with the Byzantine Empire and the Muslim states of the Near East and Spain and through the results of the Crusades, Western Europe had discovered a corpus of works that served its purposes—the works of Aristotle. Few of them had been treasured and copied in the monastic tradition, so Aristotle had not been well known. But his works, all focused on the world here below and all of which followed the same pattern of logical analysis and categorization, offered both a curriculum to be used and a way of thought to be followed. Monastic leaders decried learning about the world God had made through the works of a pagan, but philosopher-theologians enamored of the possibilities Aristotle proffered for better understanding the world argued that Aristotle could serve as a reliable guide. The defense offered in the thirteenth century by Albert the Great and his student Thomas Aquinas was that we should distinguish between the realms of nature and grace. In the former, all that was needed in order to learn appropriately was using human reason rightly and humbly. Since Aristotle laid out the patterns for using reason rightly, and followed them himself in his multifaceted exploration of the realm of nature, his works could be utilized to study the world of nature God had made. Where Aristotle had transgressed the limits of reason to propound notions which violated the teaching of Scripture—for example, the eternity of matter—Christian learning must humbly decline to follow the pagan philosopher and follow Christian teaching instead.

In due course this basic perspective carried the day. It was a significant development: for the first time, nature and grace were contrasted as realms or spheres. This also allowed for the articulation of the first Christian worldview, offering an explanation of how everything relates—all under the overarching direction of the creator God. This all helped to spawn the movement which came to be known as "scholasticism." This educational approach not only shaped the schooling offered in the schools and universities set up in the high Middle Ages, but also came to displace the prior monastic approach to instruction in the theological faculties which became part of the university set-up in medieval Western Europe.

Scholastic theology. To make a long and complicated story short, as scholasticism took over in the teaching of Christian doctrine, the logical patterns essential to Aristotelian thought also became dominant. While Scripture and Christian teaching still trumped whatever logical deductions might arise by simply following out Aristotelian logic, the ancient philosopher's stress on logic and rationality became the unquestioned norm. Given the rivalries between the Dominicans and Franciscans for the leadership in shaping the direction of the church in so many regards, it is hardly surprising that rival Dominican and Franciscan theological perspectives developed. A quick overview of this is necessary in order to understand the crisis in Christian teaching which was so painfully obvious by the end of the fifteenth century.

The pattern which developed, following Aristotelian perspectives, was that a distinctive assessment of the basic structure of all reality became the starting point for a scholastic theologian's articulation of how the realms of nature (the world here below) and of grace (divine revelation, salvation in Christ, the structures of the church—the whole of God's gracious provisions beyond what could be seen here below) functioned, how the two were related, and how they should consequently be understood. The scholastic pattern was to run everything through this grid with the result that the basic premise of the particular scholastic theologian dominated the whole package of his thought and teaching.

For Thomas Aquinas (writing in the mid-thirteenth century), and the Dominicans following him, the basic structure was reason itself. According to Aquinas, reason was the primary element in both God and humankind, made in God's image. So, in using reason to discover truth about nature, we are following God's pattern for us, a pattern we can discern because God also used reason to make the world. While the realm of grace was beyond the reach of mere reason itself, since God had revealed it to us in Word (the Scriptures) and deed, telling us about what he had done, faithful Christian exploration of the realm of grace required a careful use of reason again. Caution must be exercised to assure that the givens of grace as revealed set limits to what reason might otherwise conclude. Even so, a careful Christian thinker could understand the structures and, to some degree, the rationales of the realm of grace. For Aquinas and the Dominicans, the way to discern all this was to recognize and operate from the primacy of reason.

John Duns Scotus (writing in the last quarter of the thirteenth century), and the Franciscans after him, took a different approach. For them, the basic consideration was not reason, but will. Building on the ancient creeds' first affirmation that the creator God was the Father *Almighty*, Scotus argued that God can do anything he wills to do. His reason does not dictate to his will; among the possibilities he could have done he chose to do some in creation. For example, from Scotus's perspective, grass need not be green: it could be blue or purple. That it is green is because God willed it to be thus, not because of some requirement of divine reason. Thus will is the primary element in both God and humankind, made in God's image. From this approach, while one must use reason and logic to approach both the realms of nature and grace, one must remember that what one is examining is what God chose to do, among other possibilities, not what he necessarily did because directed by "reason."

For our purposes, the significance of this distinction between Aquinas and Scotus and their respective followers is the recognition that scholastic theology adopted a starting-point assumption about reality—the primacy of reason or of will—and from the insights (and limits) of that presupposition set forth the various elements of Christian teaching. This made for some disagreement between the two groups in their respective expositions of Christian doctrine. The arguments they brought against each other—and, indeed, within each group as one or another scholastic theologian sought to carry further the basic insights of his group—could be vehement as they propounded divergent views on various issues.

This came to a startling pass in the early fourteenth century with the teaching of William of Ockham. As a Franciscan, it is hardly surprising that he distanced himself from Aquinas's views; even so, he stepped away from much of Scotus's teaching, claiming to follow Scotus's lead into directions Scotus had not quite taken but which were worthy of pursuing. Ockham's teaching had the result of labeling both Aquinas and Scotus as *realists*, since both of them urged that the basic building blocks of their thought about nature had an ultimate reality in God's mind. In contrast, Ockham's approach said that all such building blocks were only names or terms useful to human beings for organizing our thoughts about the various patterns observable in nature without any ultimate reality in God's mind (at least as far as humankind could *know*). His perspective came to be known as *nominalism* (from the Latin term for *name*).

With this, Ockham seemed to be even more Aristotelian than either Aquinas or Scotus, since he rigidly followed out the question of what we can know by reason. As well, he seemed to stress the Christian emphasis on divine omnipotence more fully even than Scotus, since he argued that we should not claim to know what is in God's mind or will. As to the realm of grace, while we must use our minds to understand what God has said, according to Ockham we must not think that God is bound by what he has said in his revelation or done in the church in the past, since he is omnipotent. What we must do, then, is humbly believe what he has said and done, understand it as well as possible, and cast ourselves on his mercy, trusting him in all things.

Thus Ockham articulated another distinctive approach to the basic structure of all that is. For Ockham the realms of nature and grace were utterly distinct, because God had chosen (Franciscan approach) to make the realms operate in different fashions. We must use our reason to think through what we could learn about both, to be sure. Even so, while the realm of nature was accessible to reason, the realm of grace was not. Certainly much could be learned in the endeavor to think through what God had revealed and done in this realm, but however instructive this might be, the realm of grace does not ultimately bend to our reasoning; in this realm, we must simply believe. (This approach has often been labeled *fideism*.) Ockham repudiated the notion that, with whatever necessary humility, Christian thought could legitimately move from the realm of nature into that of grace, whether by reason (following Aquinas) or by will (following Scotus). In Ockham's distinctive scholastic grid, the two realms, while both structured by God, were profoundly distinct; indeed, what was true in one might well be untrue in the other. (For example, adding "1 + 1 + 1" led to different results in the realms of nature and of grace.) So, in regards to explicitly Christian teaching, humankind cannot rightly speak of "knowing" anything; we can only "believe" what is presented to us.

Ockham's teaching was startlingly different from his predecessors and caught on like wildfire in the more recently established universities,[15] with the preponderance of younger scholastic theologians following his perspectives. His teaching offered a different way of approaching issues than had been formulated previously and was consequently both stimulating and attractive. Moreover, it seemed to offer a way of articulating to some degree how the horrors that were befalling Western Europe could be assessed and appropriated as the way of God with Western Christendom and how people should respond to them.

While much more could be set forth on all this, at this point it is sufficient to note that from early in the fourteenth century, scholastic theology offered divergent paths to understanding the world here below and, even more, the ways of God with humankind. This eventually led to a proliferation of viewpoints on a host of doctrinal themes and questions with startlingly different conclusions—all claiming not only to be *a* way to view the issue but *the* way to do so. By the end of the fifteenth century, these issues included the question of how badly human nature was affected by original sin (completely depraved, partially depraved, somewhat wounded), how we are accounted righteous in God's sight (by faith alone, by faith plus works, by works alone), what religious authority we must follow (the Scriptures alone, the church hierarchy's teaching alone, the Scriptures as taught by the ecclesiastical hierarchy, conscience), how the sacraments worked (virtually automatically, only if accepted in faith, or basically as symbols to stimulate faith)

---

[15]In the older universities of Oxford and Paris, realism continued to prevail; however, nominalism came to dominate in the universities founded in the latter half of the fourteenth century—Vienna, Heidelberg, Erfurt, Cracow and Leipzig.

and the nature of divine predestination (foresight, divine decision, refusal on God's part to know). All these and many other questions became topics of intense discussion and argument among late medieval theologians.[16] The Reformers dealt with these issues in the sixteenth century, but in doing so they were not introducing questions but offering answers for questions which had long been contested within Western Christendom's teaching.

Mystics and preachers of repentance. During the fourteenth and fifteenth centuries, two other movements arose over against this scholastic argumentativeness. It takes little imagination to appreciate that priests and theologians schooled in the scholastic fashion would have difficulty speaking to the normal parishioner. The lofty flights of logic would be incomprehensible and the gamesmanship of scholastic wrangling could be baffling—even startling and unsettling.[17] Scholasticism of whatever variety seemed to have little to say to the common person about either doctrine or comfort.

One group of monastic leaders who had impact on the common folk in the time are known as the Rhineland mystics. Influenced by Meister Eckhardt, these men urged their hearers to open themselves to God's mercies by repentance and asceticism. John Tauler, Henry Suso, Jan van Ruysbroeck, Geert Groote and Thomas à Kempis all offered such counsel, each with his own distinctive emphases. Their message received a readier hearing than the preachments of scholastic theologians of the time.

Another group tackled the challenge of proclamation in a somewhat different fashion. In the face of a widespread sense that God was punishing Western Europe with all that it was enduring, Christian teaching found a different outlet in "the preachers of repentance." They preached to the common folk, calling them to repentance toward God

---

[16]For a challenging review of all this, see Heiko Augustinus Oberman, *The Harvest of Medieval Theology: Gabriel Biel and Late Medieval Nominalism*, rev. ed. (Grand Rapids: Eerdmans, 1967).

[17]One follower of Ockham's perspectives declared that for all we *know*, the Virgin Mary is in hell and Judas Iscariot at the left hand of God. However clever this might seem as a way to distinguish knowledge from faith, it would hardly be edifying or even accessible to the average parishioner.

as a way of alleviating his anger and finding mercy from him. However this pattern started, it soon caught on in large swaths of Western Europe, and a number of these preachers became well known—among them were Bernardino of Siena, Vincent Ferrer, John Capistrano and Geiler von Keysersberg.

These preachers would enter a region or town and hold open-air meetings, which began early in the day and sometimes carried on for several hours. Large crowds of peasants and some nobility flocked to them, and many sought to accommodate their lifestyles to the instructions offered. Their sermons were not doctrinal discourses; rather, they were calls to change one's life in ways that would please God. While there were minor variations among these preachers' directives, their advice boiled down largely to advising these folk to adapt and adopt the ascetic and penitential practices common among monks and nuns. Given the esteem in which faithful monks and nuns were held, and the sense that they were surely closer and more acceptable to God than many other clergy of the day seemed to be, the advice fit both the general notions the common folk already had and the predilections they shared in a time of apparent divine wrath. The problem, of course, was that such an ascetic and penitential lifestyle was exceedingly hard to sustain. So, whatever interest these preachers of repentance generated and whatever alleviation of fear and resuscitation of hope they engendered, their message proved difficult to follow.

Hunger for doctrine. As a final point, it is worth noting that the doctrinal diffusion brought much confusion in its wake as to what should be believed among both the scholastic theologians and those who could follow their arguments. For many of these latter, though, the whole scholastic enterprise had been discredited; a better way of doing theology seemed necessary as a way out of the argumentative morass. And the common people wanted and needed an approach to Christian truth that would make clear what the Christian faith taught and bring it to bear on the lives they lived. But the clamor was for better theology, not more of it. As the fifteenth century turned the corner into the sixteenth, Western Europe was not looking for more doctrine but for a clearer presentation of the Christian message.

CONCLUSION

During the late Middle Ages, Western Christendom stumbled through a series of crises without finding a way out of the labyrinth of problems. The fourteenth and fifteenth centuries were marked by intense, ongoing, multifaceted crises: the whole world seemed to be coming undone, with all supposed certainties in question and the previous century's optimism seeming laughably naive. Widespread consternation before the problems in agriculture, health, bloodshed and societal change found no alleviation from the mainstay of Western European civilization, the church. Indeed, that institution was lurching through its own series of crises, which would eventually lead to a profound disgust with and distrust of the leadership of the church. Anticlericalism took root and bore bitter fruit in a profoundly disappointed and frustrated Western Europe.

The hopeful beginnings of a new way of conceiving of and teaching about everything led to sharp conflict among the scholastic theologians. Eventually, this all issued into a delight in logical argument and dialectical artifice that discredited the whole enterprise and had people calling for another way to present the Christian message—one that did not speak above or beyond its hearers but to the depths of their being.

Throughout all this, Western Christendom forlornly kept calling for *reformatio in capite et membris*—"reform in head and members." For two centuries, this cry echoed throughout the continent. When it was finally answered in the sixteenth century with the Reformation, that movement was not initiating something new but was responding to a deep yearning, seeking to speak a relevant word into a desperate situation. Even so, it was not the first movement to respond with a significant answer: the Reformation was preceded and prepared for by the Renaissance.

– 2 –

The Renaissance

Friend or Foe?

ONE SURE WAY TO GET THE REFORMATION WRONG is to misunderstand its relationship to the Renaissance which preceded it. This is an important question which will ineluctably shape how the Reformation is understood—or misunderstood. Most treatments of the Reformation in conservative Christian circles include a sharp contrast between the Renaissance and the Reformation. This typically goes well beyond the unremarkable observation that they were distinguishable movements. The contrast is often much more pointed than that.

According to this common perspective, the Renaissance (1350-1550) and the Reformation both reacted against the corrupt medieval church, but they turned in dramatically different directions. The Renaissance was a human-centered movement, but the Reformation was a God-centered one. The Renaissance turned away from Christianity in favor of humanism, but the Reformation returned to biblical Christianity and called humanity to God. According to this schematic, the Renaissance was the forerunner of the Enlightenment, with its pride and confidence in human reason, but the Reformation called—and continues to call—humankind to humility before God.

This contrast is fundamental for much of what has been written and taught in these circles about the development of Western thought and civilization. Indeed, it would not be too much to say that this assessment has been accepted as almost canonical for understanding this portion of the history of Western civilization. This perspective is a foundational assumption in the widely used film series and book by the Christian apologist Francis Schaeffer *How Should We Then Live? The Rise and Decline of Western Thought and Culture.*[1] An influential treatment focused more on philosophical developments which draws on that basic perspective is found in Herman Dooyeweerd's *Roots of Western Culture: Pagan, Secular and Christian Options.*[2] Numerous other books purporting to deal with the Renaissance's influence on Western culture could be cited to the same effect—that the Renaissance was a human-centered movement which turned away from God and Christianity toward a vigorous humanism and prepared the path down which the Enlightenment would march.

However, this assessment of the Renaissance has not been limited to conservative Christian circles, even if it is now more commonly found there than elsewhere. It was commonly accepted through the first third of the twentieth century as the way of understanding how the Renaissance fit into the development of Western civilization. It helped spawn research into the Renaissance as well—with interesting and surprising results.

The question is not, though, how many have declared it or how often it has been asserted. The question is whether this contrast is valid. Does it offer a responsible, accurate representation of what is known about the Renaissance? The answer which scholarship universally gives to this question is clear.

---

[1]Francis A. Schaeffer, *How Should We Then Live? The Rise and Decline of Western Thought and Culture* (Old Tappan, N.J.: Revell, 1976). The film series was directed and produced by the author's son Frank Schaeffer, who points out that the film series is still considered a standard treatment in many conservative Christian high schools and post-secondary institutions (*Crazy for God: How I Grew Up as One of the Elect, Helped Found the Religious Right, and Lived to Take All [or Almost All] of It Back* [New York: Carroll & Graf, 2007], p. 260).
[2]Herman Dooyeweerd, *Roots of Western Culture: Pagan, Secular and Christian Options* (Toronto: Wedge, 1979), pp. 149-50; see also his *In the Twilight of Christian Thought: Studies in the Pretended Autonomy of Philosophical Thought* (Philadelphia: Presbyterian & Reformed, 1960), pp. 46-47.

Simply put, this contrast offers a great schematic but lousy history. Over the past three generations, careful scholarship has examined and thoroughly rejected this portrayal of the Renaissance. Undeniably, the Renaissance and the Reformation were different movements, with different emphases and foci. But the contrast as sketched out above has been thoroughly repudiated by scholars of the Renaissance. It is not too much to say that no scholar in the field accepts it today. While there are many differences of opinion among Renaissance scholars on a host of issues, the viewpoint presented above is rejected as a parody, not the pattern, of the movement.

But where did this view come from? How did it get so widespread? Why have scholars rejected it? And how might the relationship between the Renaissance and the Reformation be better construed? To answer these questions, we first need to consider something fundamental to the Renaissance itself—viewing history.

VIEWING HISTORY

For those who are not historians by training, it may be surprising to learn how young the academic discipline of history as we know it today actually is. Writing about history has been going on for many centuries, of course. But the scholarly discipline as we know it today—with its determination to adhere closely to data, interpret them elegantly but precisely, and offer as unbiased an interpretation as possible—is a young academic discipline. The view of the Renaissance which underlies the common perspective noted above arose along the way in that development; putting it in its context will help in assessing that view.

A history of history. People have been writing history for as far back as we know. From the earliest records of civilization, people have kept track of events that had taken place, listing and commenting on them. For a long time that record-keeping was oral, but eventually those records began to be written down and handed on from one generation to the next. These early accounts are often called *annals* (since they recorded what happened from year to year) or *chronicles* (if they took a broader scope). These could be bare lists of one thing after another, or they could be crafted to tell a story about a particular group, city-state, people or leader, often emphasizing the great things done by them.

Any such narrative was intended to drive home a point. The narrator was not particularly concerned to "get the facts straight," and he would have been nonplussed by a call to try to be unbiased in considering the data. Chronicles passed on what needed to be remembered and should be believed; their purpose was to entertain and instruct. Through them people could remember what they should remember, learn what they needed to know and see how to live.

The first to challenge this approach to the writing of history was Herodotus, an ancient Greek historian who lived in the fifth century B.C. His fascination with the past led him to seek out the chronicles of the various places where he lived or visited in his travels around the Mediterranean world. But as he heard these narratives, he ran up against jarring discordances among them. He urged that historical narratives could be more responsibly presented if their writers actually visited the places they wrote about, spoke with people who had witnessed the events and read the works of those involved in earlier ones.

Herodotus is sometimes called "the father of history," since his concerns anticipated the kind of careful approach which would eventually come to mark the study of history, once it emerged as an academic discipline many centuries later. To be sure, some ancient historians learned from Herodotus to be more careful to check the information they were using. But the old pattern of annals and chronicles persisted—right through the Roman and Byzantine Empires, down to the early modern world.

Throughout the Middle Ages the annal/chronicle approach to history continued. These narratives told about and commented on what had happened before, almost always from an unquestioned assumption of similarity with the writer's present. (That is the main reason why medieval paintings of the crucifixion of Christ clothe those around the cross in medieval garb and present the Roman soldiers wearing medieval armor.) Time had passed, but things had not changed. The idea of horizontal movement in time had not yet taken hold; there was only measuring up to or failing to attain a vertical standard. The actions and deeds of the past were seen and assessed on a scale of moral rectitude, an unchanging standard applicable in all times and places. Stories of the past could prove useful in this regard. Not only did they recount the glorious events of the past, but they served as "moral philosophy teaching by example," whether good or bad. Assessments were relatively easy. Since the standard of rectitude was unchanging (because given by God in the Decalogue or in some other fashion), the stories of the past served as lessons for right living in the present day.

In all this, there was no sense yet of historical distance. But in the later Middle Ages some reflective people began trying to sort out how things had gotten so badly off track in Italy and the rest of Western Europe. Among them were Francesco Petrarca and Giovanni Boccaccio, recognized as the first figures of the Renaissance. As Italians, they could still see the remains of the formerly great Roman Empire in the ruins scattered around Italy. Urban life had not entirely died out in Italy in the Middle Ages and a faint awareness of the glories of that empire persisted. In pondering the dislocation, Petrarca and Boccaccio came to question why human life and civilization in their own day were so far from what had once been in Roman antiquity, as they yearned for a resuscitation of that ancient past. This process of rumination opened a door onto a new way of conceiving reality, as it dawned on them that things do not remain the same throughout the ages, to be measured solely in a moralistic fashion by conformity to a vertical standard. Petrarca and Boccaccio intuited that as history passes, things can and do change. They sensed that history has a horizontal movement: things possible in one age were not possible in an earlier one, for example. Not only could the stories of the past be judged by a moral standard, as had so often been done, but they also needed to be assessed by asking what was possible or likely in a particular time, which was different from other times. The sense of anachronism had been born. It launched the Renaissance.

The sense of anachronism was a revolutionary notion. It offered a startlingly different way of viewing and appraising what had transpired in bygone days. It opened up new questions and spawned new perspectives about how to understand the past—and, consequently, how to assess the present. The idea caught on with a wide swath of the intellectuals of the day, who sought to help others imbibe this new outlook and live out of its rich possibilities in their day too. With this, another step in the Renaissance was taken.

This new openness to and appreciation of historical distance from the antiquity they yearned to see reborn in their day led Renaissance figures to speak of the intervening centuries as the period between— the "Middle Ages" or the "medieval" (from the Latin *medium aevum*) period. (Obviously, no one living during the medieval era would have spoken of that time as the "middle" ages: it was their present.) Historical distance allowed both critique and appreciation. It fed into yearning for change, a change amounting to a rebirth, a renewal of the ancient world—a "renaissance." The new sense of history's movement played a major role in initiating and carrying forward the Renaissance as a movement.

Not surprisingly, though, this new vantage point on the past did not immediately issue into a fully articulated and nuanced approach to studying and writing history. Renaissance figures eagerly worked their way through the questions and concerns of the day in what they took to be the brighter light of an ancient past, calling for a return to the sources *(ad fontes!)* of civilization for guidance, instead of drawing from the turgid wells of medieval civilization. Eager as they were to distance themselves from the intervening centuries, they did not recognize how much they still shared with that medieval period which had shaped them too. They continued, despite better intentions, often to treat history as a sort of moral philosophy teaching by example or as a way of arguing points against their opponents, rather than treating the past with some historical distance of their own. The older way of doing history continued but with new tools. It would take a while before history began to be written in a different fashion.

History "as it was." Among those who eventually led in this development was a brilliant and influential nineteenth-century historian, Leopold von Ranke. He urged that historians must attempt to view and present the earlier periods they studied "as they were" at the time in an (ostensibly) objective fashion. Careful attention to data would, he assumed, lead to disinterested presentation of the truth about the past.

Contemporary historical scholarship recognizes that such supposed objectivity is beyond anyone. Since at least the mid-twentieth century, historians have recognized that they all carry deep within themselves biases and predilections that keep them from seeing the past "whole and entire" and that shape the significance they see in the elements from the past which they end up focusing on (while leaving others to the side). But in the mid-nineteenth century, that self-criticism had not yet taken root and von Ranke's orientation inspired a generation of eager young historians who wanted to present the past for what it had been.

Along the way, in the generations after the Renaissance down to the mid-nineteenth century, no one had produced a history of the Renaissance as a movement. The designation had become well known and the significance of the movement had been appreciated, but no one had attempted a historical presentation and explanation of the Renaissance and what it was about until one of von Ranke's best students did in 1860.[3] His name was Jacob Burckhardt, by then a professor of history at the University of Basel.

BURCKHARDT ON THE RENAISSANCE

In 1860 Jacob Burckhardt published *The Civilization of the Renaissance in Italy*.[4] Coming as it did in the heyday of historical scholarship, the Swiss scholar's magisterial interpretation of the Renaissance as a movement found enthusiastic acceptance. It situated the Renaissance in the prior development of Italian cities and their republican ideals, discerning an Italian distinctiveness which led to the various developments in culture, society, art and outlook that came to be known as the Renaissance. As part of his wide-ranging and impressive presentation, Burckhardt pointed out the important role played by humanists in the Renaissance, on the one hand, and the emergence of individualism, on the other.

---

[3]In the preceding year, Georg Voigt had published a historical study of Renaissance literature in his *Die Wiederbelebung des classischen Altertums (The Revival of Classical Antiquity)*, but it did not treat the various other facets of Renaissance development and endeavor.

[4]Burckhardt subtitled the work *An Essay*. References below are to its second edition: Jacob Burckhardt, *The Civilization of the Renaissance in Italy: An Essay* (1878; reprint, London: Middlemore, 1954).

Burckhardt's elegantly written interpretation of the Renaissance heralded the movement as the harbinger of the modern world. He did not claim his was the only way the Renaissance might be understood. Indeed, in his introduction to the work he acknowledged that, given the breadth and depth of material to be examined, another scholar might well assess matters differently and come to a very different understanding.[5] Even so, Burckhardt's perspective was eagerly seized upon by many who discerned in it the historical roots of the philosophical humanism that by the 1860s had prevailed in much of Western culture. In so doing, though, they inferred a connection which Burckhardt himself did not make. This tendentious reading of Burckhardt was taken as his intent and was accepted for the next three generations as the way to understand the Renaissance. It ended up shaping how Western civilization was presented in textbooks used in schools and universities—leading, in due course, to the Renaissance/Reformation contrast under examination.

By the 1930s, though, this widely embraced view of the Renaissance began stimulating other scholars to delve more deeply into the Italian movement as a way of carrying further that interpretation with the results of their more specific investigations. This was when the commonly accepted interpretive scarf began to unravel. But before we turn to that development, we need to consider a bit more closely certain elements of the way the Swiss scholar's portrayal of the Renaissance had been taken.[6]

The appropriation of Burckhardt's perspective. As Burckhardt presented his understanding of the Renaissance, he pointed out the Renaissance figures' ready use of the Italian language self-designation *umanista*—"humanist." Many of Burckhardt's readers seized on this as the Western world's first encounter with this secularizing philosophy.

---

[5]"In the wide ocean upon which we venture, the possible ways and directions are many; and the same studies which have served for this work might easily, in other hands, not only receive a wholly different treatment and application, but lead also to essentially different conclusions" (Burckhardt, *Civilization of the Renaissance*, p. 3).
[6]Burckhardt's wide-ranging treatment offers a striking and in many ways compelling interpretation of the Renaissance. Our interaction with his views here will not offer an evaluation of the multifaceted treatment he offers; we restrict our consideration to the elements of it which ended up shaping the view of the Renaissance involved in the contrast vis-à-vis the Reformation.

Full blown in the nineteenth century of their day, it had supposedly first showed its bold physiognomy in Italy in the fourteenth and fifteenth centuries. According to the way the Basel professor's presentation was commonly interpreted, the widespread embrace of the designation by Renaissance figures indicated their focus on humanity as the center or measure of all things, excluding religious concerns in the process. Human reason could direct the way into the future in a fashion the sclerotic patterns of ecclesiastical dogmatism or religious faith that had dominated the Middle Ages would not have been able to negotiate. This reliance on human capacities opened the door to new vistas in art (such as distance perspective and nonreligious subjects) and new ways of conceiving of society (such as Machiavelli's *The Prince*) which owed little and did not defer to the previously dominant church culture. This all fit in with the widespread anticlericalism and the rejection of papal domination in Renaissance Italy.

Moreover, according to Burckhardt, individualism became a trademark of the Renaissance. In the common way of reading him, deference to either pope or tyrant sat ill with the republican sympathies of Renaissance leaders. With the rejection of such authority, and with the turning from Christian dogma to humanism, the various figures of the Renaissance were cast back on their own individuality for guidance. Necessity in this regard came to be celebrated as norm, and individualism became the nascent starting point for the various developments associated with and spawned by the Renaissance in its broad impact on Western Europe.

Thus the ecclesiastical and dogmatic dominance which marked the medieval centuries was forfeit. A relic from a bygone past, it had allegedly lost its grip on Renaissance figures, even if the common person continued deferential to the faith. The Renaissance vigorously turned away from the age of faith, toward a direction that would first become clear in the age of reason which arrived in the Enlightenment.

Burckhardt's presentation referred copiously to data from the Renaissance—events, writings, artworks—to substantiate his presentation. Artfully presented and elegantly written, his extended interpretive essay was engaging, compelling and convincing. As the only full-blown study of the Renaissance, it had no rivals; as a masterpiece of historical interpretation, it commanded respect. In the particular way Burckhardt's presentation was (mis)appropriated, it quickly became the way of understanding and interpreting the Renaissance that was heard in classrooms and assumed in scholarly circles.

Challenging the common view. The way Burckhardt's magnificent essay on the Renaissance had been taken commanded the field from the time of his book's publication in 1860 until the 1930s. During that time the academic discipline of history developed and became further refined. Artful and elegant presentations needed to be painstakingly rooted in the available data (primary sources, artifacts, non-anachronistic assessment, etc.). By the end of the first generation of the twentieth century, historical scholarship had become more exacting.

In the 1930s some scholars began to search more specifically through the data and primary sources from the Renaissance era, expecting to buttress and further elucidate what was taken as the Burckhardtian view, which had become de rigeur in scholarly circles. What those investigators found, though, ended up undermining the commonly received interpretation of the Renaissance in the matters noted above and, ultimately, driving it from the exalted position of canon to one of discredited misrepresentation. What did these scholars find that so undermined what had been so widely accepted?

Deficiencies in the common view. For one thing, as scholars in the twentieth century investigated the Italian Renaissance figures' self-designation "humanist" (Italian *umanista*), it became clear that the term had no philosophical import at the time. What Burckhardt's eager readers had done was to superimpose nineteenth-century philosophical humanism onto the usage of the term in the fourteenth and fifteenth centuries—a move Burckhardt himself did not make. But during the Renaissance *umanista* carried no philosophical implications. Rather, it had pedagogical ones: a "humanist" was someone who taught the "humanities"—the liberal arts. These Renaissance figures focused not on some perceived or alleged philosophical differences from their scholastic opponents, but on the pedagogical difference from them. Where scholastics concentrated on logic, dialectic and metaphysics, Renaissance humanists focused on grammar, poetry, rhetoric and history. Rather than ensconcing themselves in the "professional" schools at the universities (law, medicine and theology), the Renaissance figures emphasized the importance of preparatory or undergraduate education in its own right. Their purpose was to prepare their students to become capable and functioning members of society—not as specialists in law, medicine or theology, but as well-rounded individuals who could serve the needs of the burgeoning society in Italy. Burckhardt's readers had committed an egregious category mistake: they had misappropriated the understanding of "humanism" of their own day, with all its philosophical and humanity-centered implications, to interpret the "humanism" of the Renaissance, a movement that had no such philosophical emphasis or implications.

Further in that regard, careful Renaissance scholarship also discovered that the Italian Renaissance had no shared philosophical outlook at its core. Indeed, Renaissance figures offered a hodgepodge of philosophical loyalties. While Aristotelianism, Platonism, Stoicism and even scholasticism each found some devotees, most Renaissance figures were eclectic, showing special loyalty to no single philosophical tradition.[7] The reason for this is simple: they were not philosophers but pedagogues. Intent on preparing students for full lives spent in service of their communities, Renaissance humanist loyalties were to ancient patterns of education as better pedagogy than what had become the norm during the Middle Ages. They were not united or rooted in any philosophical orientation or construct.

In another regard, scholarship came to challenge the way Burckhardt's understanding of Renaissance individualism had been read. To be sure, the readiness to stand apart from and oppose the dominant form of education (scholasticism) that had prevailed in their day undeniably issued in a self-reliance or self-assertion which sat ill with the previously accepted patterns of medieval society dominated by the

---

[7]Paul Oskar Kristeller is especially noted for his contributions on this point: of his many publications in this area, see especially *Renaissance Thought: The Classic, Scholastic, and Humanist Strains* (New York: Harper Torchbooks, 1961), and *Renaissance Thought and Its Sources* (New York: Columbia University Press, 1979).

church. As we have seen, though, criticism of the church's failings and of ecclesiastical leadership was a general pattern throughout Western Europe during the fourteenth and fifteenth centuries. But it was heightened and edgier in Italy.

Scholars discovered that if seen in context, the greater intensity and boldness in this criticism as found in Italy betokened no distinctively Renaissance rejection of Christianity or faith in favor of individualism. Sharp criticism of the church and its leadership had been the pattern in medieval Italy already, prior to the onset of the Renaissance. Indeed, medieval Italy had always been the least obedient of the Roman obedience, with Italians individually and collectively going their own way.[8] Ecclesiastical law and papal pronouncement had often prohibited Christians trading with heretics and schismatics (intending the Byzantines) and with infidels (intending the Muslims), but that trade had continued to be the lifeblood of the Italian cities, which either skirted or simply ignored these pronouncements. Further, for the residents of Italy, Rome was not the ecclesiastical center from which missionaries had been sent or from which they had received guidance. The Italians owed their faith to earlier mission endeavors, prior to Rome's ascendancy as ecclesiastical center in the medieval West. Italian nostalgia for Rome turned to the ancient empire, rather than to the medieval church centered there. To criticize Rome vigorously indicated Italian resentment of papal leadership's opposition to greater Italian centralization, a pattern which had become unmistakable and deeply resented already in the medieval period and on into the Renaissance era. Finally, the cities and residents of Italy had experienced attempts at papal civil aggrandizement under the guise of seeking divine justice or, more crudely, via pronouncing crusade against Italian opponents.

By the time the Renaissance began, Italian anti-papal attitudes had been long standing. Vigorous criticism of Rome and rejection of papal

---

[8]See the treatment in Denys Hay, *The Italian Renaissance in Its Historical Background*, 2nd ed. (Cambridge: Cambridge University Press, 1977); see also Marvin B. Becker, *Medieval Italy: Constraints and Creativity* (Bloomington: Indiana University Press, 1981) for a discussion of this and many other facets of Italy's history in the period.

directives offered no indication of some new individualism rising against or repudiating ecclesiastical leadership. This had been a common Italian pattern, one which Renaissance figures imbibed with their mothers' milk. What those Renaissance figures offered was another way of approaching issues—that is, they found in the educational patterns of antiquity a way of better dealing with the pressing issues of their day. Twentieth-century Renaissance scholarship showed that this was no new Renaissance-era individualism; it was ancient education applied to contemporary questions.

Careful investigation also allowed Renaissance scholars to assess more straightforwardly a significant amount of data from the period dismissed by Burckhardt's epigones. He had recognized that many Renaissance leaders busied themselves with religious writings and practices, but—unlike those who appropriated his book to support their perspectives—he discerned no incongruity in their doing so.[9] Indeed, the evidence of ongoing concern with Christian teaching is abundant. Renaissance figures produced a great deal of devotional literature, careful textual studies of the New Testament and treatises on various doctrinal topics. Rather than dismiss these as holdovers from a superstitious upbringing, scholars have come to recognize them as evidence of the Renaissance figures' ongoing Christian commitment. To be sure, they were often opposed to Rome, anticlerical in attitude (as was common throughout Western Europe at the time and had long been so in Italy), and without the scholastic logomachies and the deference to canon law which had marked medieval writings about Christian teaching, but they were still undeniably and unreservedly Christian.

But what of Giovanni Pico della Mirandola's *Oration on the Dignity of Man?* This document has often been cited as evidence of a human-centered turn from Christian perspectives and a readiness to embrace philosophical humanism. In response, it should be noted that the title Pico gave to the address was only "Oration"; the rest of the title was

---

[9]Among the many examples Burckhardt offers in *Civilization of the Renaissance,* see his comments about Giovanni Boccaccio (p. 151), Alfonso of Aragon (pp. 164-65), Federigo of Urbino (p. 166), Giovanni Pico della Mirandola (pp. 263-64), Lorenzo the Magnificent (pp. 365, 416), Francesco Filelfo (p. 412), and Niccolo Niccoli, Giannozzo Manetti, Donato Acciaiuoli, Vittorino da Feltre and Maffeo Vegio (p. 377).

added subsequently to flesh out the intent of the speech. He hoped that the oration he had written would serve as the opening salvo of a public disputation of the "900 Theses" he had drafted, in which this young scholar, undeniably brilliant but audacious in his youthful exuberance, claimed to reconcile all the ancient philosophical schools (Aristotle, Plato, Stoics and Cynics) with each other and with both the Old and the New Testaments, the Jewish mystical writings and Christian doctrine. His challenge was never taken up, and a deadly disease brought an untimely end to this young scholar's contribution to the Renaissance.

But as Renaissance scholarship recognizes, the contents of the oration give no evidence of a turning away from Christianity—far from it, in fact! Rather, he exults that what he has learned has confirmed the Christian faith, which he insists is inviolable. Further, he urges his hearers to love God their Creator; extols the cardinal virtues of Christianity (faith, hope, and love); and comments that wisdom leads human beings to seek inner peace via theology. Moreover, he calls his hearers to recognize the great privilege God had granted humanity. Called to serve and honor him, humanity is exalted beyond the privilege of the angels themselves, since human beings have the freedom to choose to serve God and since God placed humanity, rather than angels, at the center of all reality.[10] However atypical this last segment may sound as a piece of medieval theologizing, it is a perspective that reflects the views of the Greek church fathers, faithful teachers from Christian antiquity. The comments earlier cited are standard fare in the writings of Christian piety. Is the total package he presents different from what would readily have been uttered by a medieval theologian? Indeed it is. Is it evidence of a philosophically inclined humanist turn away from God? Hardly. Rather, it betokens a deep, respectful, learned commitment to his Christian heritage and the deepest sources of the Christian faith. Giovanni Pico della Mirandola's *Oration on the Dignity of Man* offers clear evidence that the allegedly "human-centered" view of the Renaissance was way off the mark.

---

[10]See Pico della Mirandola, *Oration on the Dignity of Man*, in *An Italian Renaissance Reader*, ed. Paul F. Grendler (Toronto: Canadian Scholars' Press, 1987), pp. 383-411.

VIEWING THE RENAISSANCE

In the matters we have reviewed, the way Burckhardt's presentation on of the Renaissance had been appropriated became the dominant view until scholarly investigations demonstrated its flaws. Regrettably, it is still heard in many conservative Christian circles. However, in the consensus assessment of Renaissance scholars, it should be repudiated. One such scholar has sharply stated that this formerly dominant but still commonly encountered view "has only one major flaw: both in its general thrust and in virtually every detail, it is untrue."[11]

How then should the Renaissance be better understood in the present day? Specialist scholarship in the field now offers a different way of understanding the movement. While less edgy than the older assessment in the matters we have considered, it nonetheless has the undeniable advantage of accounting for all the relevant data. That consensus position is put well by Paul Oskar Kristeller: "Renaissance humanism was not as such a philosophical tendency or system, but rather a cultural and educational program which emphasized and developed an important but limited area of studies"[12]—namely, the *studia humanitatis*, the liberal arts.

For this, the Renaissance looked back beyond the medieval period to ancient Greece and Rome for guidance. Renaissance figures hoped to see a renewal of the strength of antiquity in their own day. They pursued that goal by learning and teaching ancient literature. To facilitate this, they also edited and published those works so that others could explore them as well.

The *studia humanitatis* of antiquity afforded these educators a wider vision of education than what had become the norm by their day— scholasticism. Renaissance leaders repudiated scholasticism's crabbed penchant for studies focused on the mind alone, leading only to abilities in argument and disputation. This would not offer Italian society what it needed to flourish. Society needed well-educated and articulate people who could present ideas in a winsome, convincing way that appealed to deeper springs than merely the intellect. Learning to speak

---

[11]Charles G. Nauert Jr., *Humanism and the Culture of Renaissance Europe* (Cambridge: Cambridge University Press, 1995), p. 2.

[12]Kristeller, *Renaissance Thought*, p. 10.

and write in a way that did not bludgeon others into intellectual submission but that persuasively wooed them to agreement offered the opportunity to contribute to the further development of Italian society. Well-crafted speech, elegance in language and winsome appeal to beauty and experience were needed, along with solid thought. The ancient educational emphasis on rhetoric offered that long ago, and Renaissance humanists sought to provide it in their own day.

Sometimes Renaissance figures were pilloried for turning to pagan sources. They could and did respond, though, that scholasticism was itself built on the foundation of Aristotelian logic. That was unquestionably a pagan product, but it had been accepted as viable for training in a Christian society. Learning from and appreciating the great works of pagan antiquity was thus not out of bounds for Christians. Beyond that, as Renaissance figures discovered, ancient Christians (such as Jerome, Basil of Caesarea and Gregory of Nyssa) had struggled with the legitimacy of their being so interested in the writings of the pagan authors of ancient Greece and Rome. As long before with these church fathers, so too in the Renaissance could scholars maintain Christian commitment while listening appreciatively to the winsome wisdom found in the literature of pagan antiquity.

But some Renaissance figures followed through with this predilection in another way, one that prepared the path the Renaissance would take north of the Alps. Vittorino da Feltre (1378-1446) enlarged the canon of ancient literature to be studied by including the works of the church fathers into the Renaissance humanist canon. For him, as for humanists in northern Europe soon after his time, the antiquity to be embraced and learned from included also the great literature of the ancient church. This datum serves as a fitting way to dismiss any further consideration of the discredited view of Renaissance humanism and to turn to the Renaissance as it developed north of the Alps—where it had direct contact with and influence on the Reformation.

THE NORTHERN RENAISSANCE

The Renaissance began influencing Europe north of the Italian Alps by the mid-fifteenth century. There the Renaissance took on even more

distinctly and obviously Christian overtones than it had in Italy. For the
northern nations, unlike the residents of Italy, classical antiquity had
little direct attraction, since their forebears had not participated in it—
indeed, they had been the "barbarians" who had brought an end to the
ancient world. The only element of antiquity that had direct resonance
with them was the ancient church. With the Christianization of Europe during the Middle Ages, the peoples there had been drawn into
the orbit of teaching spawned by the Greek and Latin church fathers.
So the call to go back to antiquity appealed, in the north of Europe, not
only to the classical world of ancient Greece and Rome, but also and
especially to ancient and undivided Christianity. The Renaissance in
the north quickly began to produce unquestionably Christian fruit.

Northern Christian humanism. This is not to say that the northern
Renaissance limited itself to specifically Christian concerns—it focused
also on ancient Roman law (especially in France) and the writings of
non-Christian authors of antiquity. But northern Renaissance humanism unquestionably devoted much of its attention to the ancient sources
of the Christian faith, the New Testament and the writings of the
church fathers, both Greek and Latin. Further, northern Renaissance
humanists' concerns focused especially (although not exclusively) on
the church, Christian doctrine and the reform for which so many had
long clamored. This was a more central concern in the Renaissance
north of the Italian Alps than it had been in Italy, important as it had
been there. Because of all this, it has become common among scholars
to speak of the Renaissance movement north of the Italian Alps as
"northern Christian humanism."

The northern Renaissance became a somewhat more diverse movement than its Italian predecessor. It first took root in the Holy Roman
Empire. Since northern Italy (Lombardy) was part of that empire, this
afforded the most ready pathway for dissemination of the movement
into the north. Thus Germany ended up leading the way in the northern Renaissance. The movement caught on also in France, England,
Spain, Hungary, Poland and Bohemia. The wide dispersion of northern Renaissance figures did not keep them isolated from each other,
since they wrote to each other in polished Latin to keep abreast of what

others were doing. Where a few enthusiasts for the Renaissance movement lived near each other, they often set up "sodalities"—groups which periodically met and discussed their endeavors. The northern Renaissance sometimes took on distinctive emphases in the various countries, as Renaissance figures wrestled with different questions. But it became a large, influential movement in Europe north of Italy.

The northern Renaissance diverged somewhat from its Italian counterpart by becoming a much more bookish movement. With the invention of the movable-type printing press in the fifteenth century, northern Renaissance humanists had much wider possibilities to publish the works of antiquity, pagan and Christian alike, than the Italian Renaissance humanists had known. They took advantage of this and offered critical editions of ancient works.

The leader in this was Desiderius Erasmus, who published a critical Greek edition of the New Testament in 1516 and editions of the works of several church fathers, thereby providing primary sources to use in educating, challenging scholastic theology and reforming the church. Indeed, Erasmus became known as the prince of the humanists, but also as the leader of a genuine movement for reform within the church.[13] He had many friends in the various royal courts of Europe and in the ecclesiastical hierarchy. In the first two decades of the sixteenth century, many young scholars rallied to him as a standard of excellence and as a leader of the most promising movement for reform of the church which had come along to that point. They styled themselves "Erasmians." Seeking to emulate his wit, scholarship and literary elegance, they followed him also in opposing scholastic theology and returning *ad fontes*, studying the New Testament and the works of the church fathers.

Relationship to the Reformation. All this had great effect on the Reformation as it unfolded under Luther's leadership after 1517. Luther had not been trained in northern Christian humanism; he was a product of a scholastic education. But many of those who rallied to Luther had been committed Erasmians. Most of these young scholars did not

---

[13]For a fine presentation of Erasmus which pays special attention to his role as a leader for reform in Christianity, see Cornelis Augustijn, *Erasmus: His Life, Works, and Influence*, trans. J. C. Grayson (Toronto: University of Toronto Press, 1991).

discern differences between Erasmus and Luther for quite a while. (Although it is clear that both Erasmus and Luther quickly recognized they had different emphases.) Many of these Erasmians became followers of Luther and, in due course, Protestant leaders. By the Diet of Augsburg in 1530, all but one of the more than thirty Protestant religious leaders in the Lutheran camp had been trained in northern Christian humanism. Similarly, all those who became leaders in the nascent Reformed movement (following Zwingli in Zurich, Bucer in Strasbourg, and Oecolampadius in Basel) had been devoted adherents of the northern Renaissance. It is no exaggeration to state that, aside from Luther himself, the leadership of the Reformation was in the hands of northern Christian humanists.

Eventually many of these Protestant leaders came to recognize differences between Erasmus and Luther. But significantly, none of them ever repudiated Erasmus; indeed, Bucer and Melanchthon courted Erasmus to the end of his life (in 1536), seeking to get him to declare for the Protestant movement. Further, in 1542, Bucer called Erasmus "the father of the Reformation." Gifted and insightful Protestant leaders as they were, these Erasmians-turned-Protestants did not recognize tension between the northern Renaissance of which they had been part and the Protestant movement to which they committed themselves.

Moreover, many of these Protestant leaders ended up establishing schools in the cities where they labored in order to present solid education from a Protestant perspective. Significantly, each of these schools offered the *studia humanitatis*—that is, they all had a northern Renaissance orientation. This is a striking indicator of how these Protestant leaders viewed the Renaissance and its relationship to the Reformation. They took the main focus and contribution of the former movement and used it for the latter one.

Further, they utilized the emphases of the Renaissance in the service of the Reformation. As scholars, these Protestants used the critical editions of the New Testament and the church fathers; some of them were involved in editing and publishing some of these works. Moreover, the Renaissance emphasis on rhetoric segued nicely into the Protestant emphasis on the proclamation of the Word of God. The Renaissance concern to persuade by winsome appeal to the deepest recesses of the human being served the emphases of the Reformation well.

Indeed, this whole line of argument can be sealed by pointing out that none of the "former" northern Renaissance humanists who became Protestant leaders ever denounced, repudiated or otherwise distanced themselves from the humanism in which they had been trained and to which they had been devoted. They might have disagreed with Erasmus on some doctrinal issue (especially on predestination and free will when that became a point of contention after 1525), but a difference in doctrinal perspective did not entail for them a distancing from northern Christian humanism. They never repudiated that Renaissance background—as surely they must have if they had seen it as a "human-centered Renaissance" as over against the "God-centered Reformation" which they pursued. Gifted and insightful as they were, they did not renounce it, because they did not accept the contrast that too many conservative Christians still accept. This contrast should be allowed to die the death it so richly deserves. To the Reformation, the Renaissance was friend, not foe.

- 3 -

Carried Along by Misunderstandings

Without Martin Luther, the Reformation as it took place in the sixteenth century cannot be understood. The movement as we know it began with him, and as it developed it swirled around him. Contemporaries understood this well enough. He was not the only figure involved, of course, and others played major roles, politically and theologically, from the beginning of the movement and in the following decades. Opinions have often differed as to the wisdom of the way Luther expressed his views and the correctness of those views. This difference of assessment began already during the Reformation and has continued to the present day.

There was nothing inevitable, though, about the role Luther would play in the movement, the particular impact it would have on Germany, or its beginnings in the first generation of the sixteenth century. With the advantage of hindsight, we can see how those elements all came together to shape and drive what came to be known as the Reformation, but no one could have had that advantage as the sixteenth century dawned. That something must surely take place sooner or later to meet the longstanding cry in Western Europe for *reformatio in capite et membris* was certain. What it would be, when it would happen, who would lead it, what role that person would play, where it would catch on and what effects it would have could not be known ahead of time. But that cry had been raised for two centuries already by the time Luther entered the Augustinian monastery in Erfurt in 1505, and in all that time no significant reform had yet begun.

A dozen years later, however, that Augustinian monk would post some theses on a church door, offering a public debate about various ideas and practices he wanted to challenge. This seemingly insignificant event in a small city in a swampy area of Saxony—an action by a young professor at one of the fledgling universities only recently founded in Germany—set in motion a movement beyond what that monk-professor intended or understood as he nailed those theses to the door. This movement would change the course of the church and Western civilization. Dr. Martin Luther had inaugurated a movement he had not foreseen or planned and which he would not ultimately be able to control. Even so, in one way or another, it swirled around him and his teachings. Acknowledging this is essential to getting the Reformation right, but it is possible to recognize this and yet get the Reformation wrong, even on this point.

A common way of doing this is the assumption that Luther came to his insights and almost immediately recognized and articulated their implications, and that people responded to his clear declarations. This is sometimes taken (especially among Lutherans) in the direction that Luther brought forward the truth, which some accepted but from which others turned away. Others (the Reformed) play it out a bit differently— that some who accepted Luther's teachings in due course saw further necessary implications and pushed them forward, while Luther and his devotees hesitated to go as far on the path as was warranted. Still others (Anabaptist in heritage, plus the various free churches) affirm that even those who had gone further than Luther still had not gone far enough.

No matter which version, this approach accepts that the initial proclamation of the Reformation's insights issued into precise understandings of what had been declared: the lines had been drawn and the choices were clear. This allowed for a straightforward decision between truth and error (however those two end up being distinguished among the adherents of these variations). Choices for or against Luther and his teaching arose from a clear confrontation with what he had communicated.

However, what actually transpired in the sixteenth century was not nearly as clean and neat as this myth, in all its variations, assumes; the reality was actually quite messy. Rather than initially advancing by sure understanding, the Reformation was carried along by misunderstandings. In its own way, this cluttered situation allowed the Reformation to develop and attract a wider audience. But in the early sixteenth century the challenges of communication—both speaking and listening—ensured that much that was said was not taken in the way intended by Luther (or other speakers). Part of this was due to the growth and development of Luther's own views, as he worked through and saw further implications of his own insights. Another contributing factor was that the people hearing him were not *tabulae rasae* waiting for ideas to be inscribed on their hearts and minds. They already had a host of issues and questions with which they were wrestling, and they ended up appropriating what they heard in ways that spoke to their issues and questions.

Undergirding all this, the unsettling socioeconomic changes and the religious tensions Germany had endured over the preceding two centuries had heightened frustrations and engendered an edgy readiness to find ways to restore things to right—whatever that might mean. Given the divergent, even contradictory, assessments of what "right" would be and how it would be achieved, it is not surprising that hearers discerned directives in the utterances of Luther and others, whether or not the speaker intended anything of the sort. Thus declarations were appropriated to ends far from what Luther had in mind. For the eager and enthused hearers of hope, though, the directives seemed both clear and obvious. All this made for a chaotic early Reformation movement, as German society jumped on the reforming horse and galloped off in all directions at once.

All this response and reaction to Luther was complicated by the intersection and entanglement of these misunderstandings. In what remains in this chapter, we will distinguish various streams in that turbulent river, as we consider several factors that contributed to these misunderstandings. However, this will result in a series of fairly distinct packages, much too neat and tidy in their separate presentations. "On the ground" in the sixteenth century, these all crashed together, making for a tangled clutter in the response to Luther. That some understood fairly well is clear, but that many embraced Luther early on without really understanding what he intended is undeniable. Even so, by endorsing him and invoking his insights for their purposes and projects, these helped turn the reform movement he had unintentionally kicked loose into a formidable juggernaut. This in turn made the task of those attempting to defend Rome and the church in that day much more difficult, since they had to wrestle with and respond to so much diverse material and so many contradictory assertions. This kept them from being able to fix on and respond to Luther as his thought was developing. Thus in its early stages the Reformation was carried along, in the main, by misunderstandings.

Luther's breakthrough. By all accounts, Martin Luther was an intense personality. During his years of study at the University of Erfurt prior to entering the Augustinian monastery there, he was known as a gregarious sort who loved friends, music and laughter. But the sudden death of a friend and a terrifying experience during a thunderstorm as he returned on horseback to Erfurt led to his promise to St. Anne to become a monk. It became clear from his earliest days in the monastery that he was consummately concerned with how to find peace with God.

This quest drove him in his days as a friar. It is unwarranted to dismiss this as evidence of some psychological imbalance or defect in Luther. Rather, because he was intense in all regards, the quest to find a gracious God could not be satisfied for him by some half-measure or cheap assurance that all would be well. Instead he took the teaching common in his day, plus the advice offered by more experienced monks, and lived it out punctiliously. That teaching urged people to do all they could, however much that might be,[1] to live righteously before God and love him, knowing that he demanded purity of deed and intention.

---

[1] This was commonly expressed in the directive *facere quod in se est*—a person should "do what is in his [or her] power."

God had demonstrated his love for humankind by sending his Son to become the Savior; Jesus Christ had suffered horrendously to achieve that salvation. Now people must respond by living to God. In all this, divine grace was less talked about than assumed. Laid up in the church by the exalted Savior and present in the sacraments, grace had to be won by purely living up to the demands of the confessional, so that worthy reception of the Eucharist could grant peace. Since God expected a life fully given to him, it had become common to urge that those most likely to attain peace with God were monks and nuns, who could be totally devoted to prayer and righteous living, given their vows and lifestyle. Indeed they came to be known as "the religious," with everyone else something less than that in the church's estimation.

Luther's decision to become a monk reflected all this teaching. His life as a monk showed how assiduously he took this to heart. His frustrations with it, though, demonstrated its inherent failure. No matter how vigorously he lived up to and even exceeded the rigors expected in a strict monastery like the Augustinian one in Erfurt, he could find no peace. He always discerned that in some way he never measured up to the divine standard, as urged by ecclesiastical teaching and monastic practice. He knew that deep within he was not fulfilling the expectations, whatever his father-confessors offered by way of assurances to him. Overwhelmed by his inability to live perfectly unto God, he found himself pushed in the other direction. As he acknowledged to a trusted older friend and counselor, Johann von Staupitz, rather than loving this God whose standards were so rigid and unattainable, he hated him. Bitterly, Luther asked what penance he should be assigned for that.

Staupitz advised Luther that he needed to learn to rely on God and get to know him better. Staupitz arranged for his protégé to undertake graduate studies in theology at the University of Erfurt. Ever the dutiful monk, Luther accepted this assignment. Not surprisingly, he threw himself into it with the same fervor that he had shown in all his previous monastic undertakings. He excelled in these studies, eventually receiving a doctorate in theology. All the while, he had continued to seek to find a way to peace with God in what he had learned, but that goal had continued to elude him. In due course, Staupitz arranged to have Luther succeed himself as professor of Bible at the recently founded University of Wittenberg. Luther undertook the charge in 1512 and dutifully performed his responsibilities.

In a few years, his teaching led him to St. Paul's Letter to the Romans. Ever the careful teacher, Luther struggled with the meaning and significance of Romans 1:16-17, and specifically how the apostle could be so excited by the Christian message. Paul called it "the gospel," which means "good news," for in it "the righteousness of God is revealed." Luther, though, had always experienced this as *bad* news. That divinely righteous standard was unattainable; being judged by it brought only terror. But as he wrestled with the passage, he came to the conclusion that the apostle could look on this revelation of divine righteousness as good news because it was a righteousness granted to faith, not a righteousness by which sinners are measured. Luther had previously understood "the righteousness of God" as the standard which God expected humans to attain and by which he would judge them. As Luther had found out by awful experience, meeting that standard was impossible. But if God acted to count those who believed in his Son as righteous in his sight, then the Christian message was indeed good news, as it brought peace to burdened consciences and offered a sure confidence to those who believed.

According to Luther's own testimony, this insight flooded him with light and peace. As he ransacked his fertile memory for other scriptural passages about God's righteousness and approached them with these contrasting understandings, he found confirmation of his discovery and encouragement that this was indeed the main thrust of all God's promises to humankind. This insight changed Luther's life, as well as the future of the church and Western civilization. Luther recognized that this hopeful message needed to be proclaimed more broadly and heard more widely. However, in ways that he did not recognize at that time, this insight still needed to work more fully through his own perspectives until it saturated them.

Luther's developing thought. Over the last century, careful scholarly investigation of critically edited versions of Luther's early works has led to much clearer insight into how his thought developed early in his career. As a professor of biblical studies in the theological faculty at the University of Wittenberg, he had lectured on the Psalms (1513-1515), Romans (1515-1516), Galatians (1516-1517) and Hebrews (1517) by the time he nailed his theses to the church door there. These lectures, plus some sermons he preached, give clear indications of what he had wrestled with and how his ideas had grown already before and subsequent to his breakthrough regarding the apostolic utterance in Romans 1:17, "the just shall live by faith." While that tremendously peace-inducing and assurance-granting insight lit up the Scriptures for him in striking ways, he still did not immediately recognize the breadth and depth of the implications of that perspective in the ways he subsequently would. As with others who hit on a life-changing insight, so it was with Luther: it took a while before he intuited the connections between his discovery and many other concerns.

Luther brought his insights regarding justification by faith to bear on the books of Scripture he had already exegeted in his teaching, leading to some revisions of what he had taught. The insight about justification also shaped the questions he asked of the rest of Scripture. Over the course of the next several years, Luther reexamined all he had thought and been taught, seeking to refurbish it and bring it into conformity with the implications he was increasingly recognizing as inherent in the doctrine of justification by faith. This was not the work of an hour or a holiday. Unquestionably brilliant a thinker as Luther was, the process nevertheless took him a handful of years, which he himself acknowledged at several points in his life.

But with the publication of his *Ninety-Five Theses* and the hubbub they shortly occasioned, plus the other writings he soon published, the monk-professor in the humble Saxon university quickly became one of Germany's most public figures. Neither his supporters nor his opponents were willing to wait until he had finished ruminating on implications and was ready to produce a final, definitive version of his thought. He was called, even forced, onto the public stage and summoned to give account of his views and attitudes. He did so as he discerned them and could articulate them at the time. But they were often enough not yet honed and polished in ways he might have preferred. As a result,

Luther sometimes urged views which he would later significantly modify. Similarly, he sometimes only later discerned implications which had eluded him in earlier comments. Along the way Luther's thought became more polished and refined as a package, rooted in justification by faith. Beyond these distinctively intellectual concerns, developments in his relationship to the papacy and his interaction with civil authorities led to modifications of his perspectives.

What all this means is that Luther's views were in process for several years after the Reformation got underway. During that time those views sometimes changed—not always dramatically, but in significant ways nonetheless. What his readers and hearers had to work with, though, was what he had discerned by the time he wrote whatever piece they were reading or heard the proclamation he made that day. This offered rich soil for misunderstanding to take root and eventually bring forth fruit Luther found not to his taste.

In this regard, it is striking that while his perspectives on justification by faith would come to dominate Luther's theology, doctrine itself played a relatively insignificant role in his writing and speaking until the early 1520s. It does not come up clearly in the *Ninety-Five Theses*, although Luther's breakthrough in understanding the Pauline utterance preceded those theses. Given the spiritual relief he experienced through this perception of Romans 1:17, though, the themes that resound in his teaching and writing in these early years are clearly related, even if explicit focus on justification by faith is lacking. Luther repeatedly emphasized the scriptural basis of Christian faith, the need to reject human tradition in favor of Scripture, the importance of faith and the fact that salvation is through faith rather than good works. In all this, Luther pushed simplicity—not simplification, but shedding the accumulated clutter that had overlain the simpler, basic Christian faith.[2] All this is basic to what Luther would more expansively urge in his teaching about justification by faith alone, but even so, the doctrine is notable—given the stress Luther later laid on it—mostly by its absence in his teaching and writing in the years leading up to the Diet of Worms in 1521.

---

[2]For a fine presentation of this, see Hans J. Hillerbrand, *The World of the Reformation* (1973; reprint, Grand Rapids: Baker, 1981), pp. 35-36.

And there was a veritable torrent of these publications, especially between 1519 and 1521, as treatises, commentaries, tracts and polemics poured from Luther's pen. The simplicity Luther proffered and emphasized attracted people to his views; it would also help to spawn variant readings of what the Reformation was about. But Luther did not sense that problem quickly. He sought to proclaim the vivifying, liberating power of this simplified version of the Christian message, and he brought all the rich powers of his remarkable abilities into full play as he did so. Luther was an electrifying writer who produced gripping works written in a way that the average literate German citizen could read and understand. His writings became instant bestsellers and publishers had a hard time keeping up with the demand. He communicated with memorable slogans, a populist writing style and a winsome call for change in the way things were done in the church.

In his enthusiasm for his insights he manifested an understandable naïveté. He genuinely believed that the ecclesiastical and civil authorities would be delighted to learn of and embrace this more accessible presentation of Christian teaching. Like many other purveyors of sharply different perspectives in history, though, Luther found out that bureaucracies do not really appreciate having their apple carts upset. But he found that the average German welcomed his teaching and that many of them passed it on—at least, as they understood it or interpreted it. Both responses endeared him to the German people.

Luther and the humanists. The first to flock to Luther's side were the Christian humanists of Germany. Followers of Erasmus in desiring to see Christian teaching and the church reformed, they latched quickly onto Luther, whose *Ninety-Five Theses* boldly strode in that direction. Within two weeks, the Saxon professor's theses were distributed throughout Germany, almost entirely due to humanist enthusiasm. They knew nothing directly about Luther, but it seemed to many of them that he was doing boldly what Erasmus had been seeking subtly.[3] In short order they began reading, discussing and passing on whatever the Saxon professor of theology published.

---

[3]In a May 1, 1518, letter to Beatus Rhenanus, Martin Bucer expressed himself in this fashion; it was a common refrain among humanists in the early period of the Reformation movement.

Luther appeared to be the fulfillment of something specific they had hoped for. While a few humanists had been appointed to chairs of poetry or other responsibilities at some German universities, all their positions were outside the mainstream of required studies. To have a genuine impact on the future of university education, they needed a man "on the inside," within one of the faculties, who would lead a movement to transform the universities by moving toward the *studia humanitatis*. These humanists were convinced, as Erasmus had urged, that such a change would eventually contribute significantly to transformation in church and society. Humanist preferences in this regard tended toward a professor in one of the theological faculties. And here was Dr. Martin Luther.

Opposed to the traditional methods of scholastic theological training, the humanists sought a simpler, more basic approach to the study of the Christian faith. Their call to return to the sources seemed to resound throughout Luther's call to hear and rely on Scripture and the church fathers. While the *Ninety-Five Theses* were proposed for a public disputation, a scholastic practice loathed by the humanists as an exercise in intellectual gamesmanship, the humanists saw Luther's theses as breathing a different spirit. In his works they espied a humbler and gentler approach, one directed deeper than the mind and its dialectical fastidiousness. In Luther's works they discerned a deep openness to ancient wisdom that reached for and gently wooed the human heart.

The humanists initially did not realize that Luther had been trained entirely in the scholastic mode. They knew that he could not have become a member of a theological faculty without such training, of course: that was the norm in the early sixteenth century. But they assumed that somehow the Saxon professor had embraced their humanist perspectives. After all, he had managed to break free from that scholastic theological pattern and had embraced a better one. It was natural for them to assume that it must be the one they themselves inchoately yearned for. By the time it became unquestionably clear—sometime in the early 1520s—that Luther's orientation was not entirely synchronized with that of Erasmus, many of the younger humanists had been captivated

by Luther's teachings and had become his followers.[4] This did not mean
that they had turned their backs on Erasmus, whom they still revered;
rather, it meant that they had come, as humanists, to embrace the Reformation movement led by Luther. They would utilize their humanist
concerns to further that Reformation movement, since they saw no ir-
reconcilable conflict between the two movements. Even so, they came
to Luther initially because they had misunderstood him and where he
was headed. It proved to be—for themselves, Luther and the Reformation movement—a fruitful misunderstanding.

Luther the German hero. When Germans of various backgrounds
learned that Luther had stood up to the church and challenged some of
its practices, they were astonished and delighted. For many generations,
Germans had viewed themselves as devoted adherents of Christianity,
the most faithful of the Roman obedience. This was not just their own
self-congratulatory assessment; it was held by many throughout Western Christendom, including several leading hierarchs. In 1510 the papal nuncio Aleander commented that no other nation was so devoted to
Rome. Even so, the hand of the papacy had often fallen heavily on
Germany and its leaders, and the Germans chafed under it. Resentment toward Rome was long standing throughout the Holy Roman
Empire. But no matter how much frustration the Germans had known,
and no matter how much they had hoped for improvement, their relationship to Rome had continued much the same as it always had been.

Consequently, when Luther boldly challenged the church about indulgences and a wide array of related issues, hosts of Germans were
enthralled by the sudden appearance of a German hero willing to stand
up to the nation's main oppressor. Luther's subsequent disputations (at
Heidelberg in 1518 and Leipzig in 1519) and his various writings all
showed a fearless and gifted opponent to the malfeasances and abuses
of Rome. His 1520 *Open Letter to the Christian Nobility of the German
Nation Concerning the Reform of the Christian Estate* manifested deep

---

[4]Lewis Spitz has pointed out in several publications the intriguing datum that as of 1530 almost all of Luther's fellow Reformers were humanists who had identified themselves with his
perspectives before they had turned thirty years old, and that humanists beyond that age had
almost all remained with Erasmus in the Roman obedience.

concern for Germans' well-being and called the civil leaders to champion them in all their needs, including the spiritual and religious ones, as over against an oppressive Rome. With all this, Luther became a hero to the Germans. When he traveled to the Diet of Worms in 1521 (on a safe conduct provided by Emperor Charles V), his wagon ride turned into a triumphal procession.

In the meantime the papal legate Aleander—along with John Eck, Luther's redoubtable opponent at the 1519 Leipzig Disputation—had returned to Germany from Rome with the June 15, 1520 papal bull *Exsurge Domine*, which condemned forty-one of Luther's propositions. They expected to find a deferential German populace; instead they encountered, as an astonished Aleander reported back to Rome, a Germany which had rallied to Luther's cause. The papal nuncio estimated that nine out of ten Germans supported Luther—a dramatic, drastic change from what he had observed only ten years previously. The German allegiance to Luther did not dissipate when Pope Leo X declared Luther's excommunication as a heretic in the January 3, 1521 papal bull *Decet romanum pontificem*.

At the diet, Luther received no hearing from the emperor; he was faced with a demand for a retraction. The emperor expected but did not receive the support of all the German princes in condemning Luther (and thus endorsing the papal judgment against him). Several of them refused to yield to the emperor, who consequently hesitated until after the diet had recessed to sign Luther's condemnation (on May 26, 1521). At that diet, though, the assembled lords of the empire found no difficulty and no imperial challenge in composing and sending a gravamen to Rome protesting 102 offenses of Rome against the German people. The German lords resented Roman oppression and spoke out boldly against it. For some of them, Luther had steeled their resolve, whatever they may have thought about or understood from what he had written in his works, and they had refused to assent to his condemnation.

Spirited away surreptitiously by the forces of Elector Frederick as he returned from Worms, Luther was taken to the Wartburg Castle for safekeeping, to forestall actions against him as an outlaw in the empire. By the time he emerged from this refuge a few months later his influence had only increased, and his sudden reappearance only enhanced his stature among many Germans as a hero of their long-suffering nation. The Germans who turned to him in this way did not necessarily understand all he taught nor agree with what they heard from him. They supported him without particular regard for what he said or wrote: what he had done and what he represented were more important to them. They did not need to understand him, and many did not try to do so. He was a flashpoint for their national frustrations and they stood with him because of what he offered Germany in that regard.

As time passed, Luther's stock as a hero declined in value, as it became evident that neither opposition to Rome per se nor German nationalism was his main concern. As this became clearer, this element of support for Luther waned. But by then, the Reformation movement was well underway and beyond the need for this kind of uncritical advocacy. In the early years of the Reformation, though, it constituted a significant support for Luther and the movement he had inaugurated.

Luther as champion of the old order. Along the way in these early years of the Reformation, the enthusiasm for Luther as German hero took on specific, even contradictory, emphases. His 1520 treatise to the German nobility expressed confidence in them as he urged them to set things right for and among the German people. This resonated deeply, especially with certain members of the lower nobility.

To some of them, the imperial knights, developments in recent generations had been extremely unsettling. They had seen their economic status eroded by advances of the merchant classes and the agrarian changes of recent generations. Further, these knights' civil importance had decreased because of changes in their relationship to the emperor. Not surprisingly, they were yearning for a return to "the good old days." With Luther's 1520 treatise relying on the nobility (rather than the emperor) to lead the German people to the right path in several regards, some imperial knights detected in Luther a call to straighten out what had gone amiss. They interpreted this call as a summons to restore the old order.

Among them, Franz von Sickingen was foremost. He discerned in what he had learned of Luther's exhortation an invitation to change the status quo back to what it had been in earlier generations. Bold enough to oppose the emperor at the Diet of Worms, von Sickingen subsequently tried to rally other imperial knights in a rebellion which they hoped would lead to a reestablishment of the old order. This abortive "Knights' Revolt" of 1522-1523 was soon enough quelled. Luther expressed no support for this quixotic venture, but it was his teaching—or rather, what was perceived to be his teaching—that had set the match to the imperial knights' powder keg of resentment. This was not the kind of support Luther welcomed then or later; it was, however, some of the support he received in the early years, as the Reformation movement got underway.

Luther as champion of a new order. From the opposite end of the spectrum, many peasants understood Luther's teaching as endorsing their demands. His 1520 treatise, *The Freedom of a Christian*, had urged that a Christian is no one's slave but everyone's servant. The former emphasis resonated with many peasants, who chafed under the increased dues and restricted privileges recently laid on them by various civil and ecclesiastical lords. Some clergy and peasant leaders inflamed the resentment, appealing to Luther's 1520 treatise and some of his other writings. This all led to the outbreak of the Peasants' War, which swept through Germany from 1524 through 1526. Almost a third of Germany endured the horrors of this conflict, which left in its wake hosts of slain on both sides of the socioeconomic equation.

In early 1525 a declaration of the peasants' reasons for embarking on this venture appeared in *The Twelve Articles: The Just and Fundamental Articles of All the Peasantry and Tenants of Spiritual and Temporal Powers by Whom They Think Themselves Oppressed*. Remarkably moderate, given its context in the bloody civil strife, the document justified the peasants' cause by appeal to the gospel and divine justice. Since Luther was especially noted in Germany for urging the gospel and speaking about divine justice in recent years, this clearly indicated that the peasants—or at least the more articulate and literate leaders among them—connected Luther's teaching and the peasants' rebellion.

Luther's response made it abundantly clear that he rejected this association and that he repudiated the use of force to achieve gospel purposes. Further provoked, he even called on the authorities to suppress the rebellion with brutality—an invitation they eagerly heeded. Even so, these peasants had understood Luther's teaching as addressing their concerns and legitimizing what they had done. While many peasants looked with hostile disfavor on Luther after the brutal repressions that brought the Peasants' War to an end, their prior misreading of what he intended served to offer another strand of that early support for him which actually rested on misunderstanding.

Luther as Hydra. Luther became the stimulus and the release point for much built-up tension and religious expectation in Germany. His *Ninety-Five Theses* turned attention to him and his writings which soon followed, together with reports of what he taught, set him at the head of a movement for the reform of the teaching and practice of Christianity, which encompassed and affected all areas of life in the sixteenth century. Many other would-be spokespersons jumped onboard and issued pronouncements, short writings and pamphlets which attracted much attention themselves. These people identified their concerns with Luther's, asserted their insights as implications of his, and called for changes in church, teaching and society.

What ensued was a free-for-all movement, excitedly propounding rather vague and generalized conceptions of a new gospel, using terms and slogans picked up from Luther, and demanding practical changes in the way things were—but with some serious differences about the strategies to follow and what to change. This all became an amorphous, heterogeneous movement in which people identified with Luther, whether or not they had actually read anything from him or heard him speak. Luther did not endorse and often did not know what others were doing in his name in these early years; as we have seen, he eventually distanced himself from much of it.

Those who sought to defend the Roman communion as it existed in that day blamed Luther for the whole of what they saw in this chaotic situation. What Luther had begun numerous others had carried on. All of it needed to be answered, and those who rose in defense saw the whole movement, in all its variations, as Luther's spawn. It was no easy task to defend the status quo anyway, since few wanted it to continue unchanged. But sorting out what to defend, whom to respond to and what to say in response were major challenges. The various ideas about what the new faith actually meant were befuddled by generalizations and mutually inconsistent claims; responding to it all was enormously taxing. Rome's defenders were scrambling, and they produced uneven responses to the welter of things flying at them.

It seemed to these early defenders of Rome and the existent church that they were fighting a multiheaded opponent which attacked them from all sides. This hydra was Luther, but none of Rome's defenders was Hercules. The attacks were so diverse and uncoordinated, the situation so confused, that the would-be defenders produced little of lasting significance, while Luther pressed on from strength to strength as his insights into what he had discovered progressively shaped and honed his thought. Distracted by numerous other attacks, though, the defenders of Rome were kept off-balance as to what they needed to communicate and whom they should answer. This confused situation allowed the Reformation movement inaugurated by Luther to consolidate behind all the smoke and chaos of the time and to emerge stronger as the air cleared. By the time it became evident that many of whom claimed to follow Luther had little in common with him, Luther's perspectives had sharpened and become clearer to him and many followers.

Luther as leader. While this chapter has focused on the misunderstandings that carried the Reformation movement along in the early years after Luther posted the ninety-five theses on the castle church door at Wittenberg, it is important not to neglect the understanding that arose during the time. As Luther published his writings and honed his thoughts, several important figures read and understood well what Luther was saying. Many of those who would become close associates of Luther or otherwise become leaders of the Reformation movement in their own right came to embrace the message Luther proclaimed and to accept the insights he discerned.

Among these was Philip Melanchthon, the brilliant young humanist who joined the faculty of the University of Wittenberg as professor of Greek in 1519. He quickly came under the influence of Luther and embraced his older colleague's teaching. Indeed, for a few

years Melanchthon's own distinctiveness seems to have been subli-
mated. While he would eventually reassert himself and his own perspectives, he continued to look to Luther as the stimulus for his own
reformatory perspectives.

Another who embraced Luther's teachings was Martin Bucer, the
Dominican friar who first encountered Luther at the Heidelberg Disputation in 1518. Bucer was captivated and won by Luther's mild responses and keen insights into Scripture. The Dominican friar took up
correspondence with Luther and came over to the Reformation movement. Bucer soon enough sought and received dispensation to leave the
Dominican order. Eventually, he became the leading pastor and Reformer in the major imperial city of Strasbourg. While his perspectives
would eventually diverge from Luther's in certain regards, he first came
to the Reformation movement because of personal contact with Luther
and a wholehearted embrace of Luther's teachings.

Others who could be numbered in this list of early followers of Luther include Johannes Bugenhagen and Justus Jonas, who both became
theological leaders, and Georg Spalatin and Philip of Hesse, who
served in the realm of civil government as faithful adherents of Luther's
teaching. This list could be expanded, but all this serves to indicate that
while the Reformation kicked off by Luther was carried along in its
early years by misunderstandings, he nevertheless found some readers
and hearers who understood well what he intended in his teaching and
preaching.

In the years after 1521, Luther produced more thoroughly integrated, intricately elaborated presentations of his thought. He came
into his own as a leader of the Reformation movement. He saw much
more clearly the implications of his insights, especially by bringing
the doctrine of justification by faith alone more sharply to the fore.
He shaped and molded the whole of his teaching to reflect and buttress that teaching. This led to much better understanding. Even so,
it also led, as we will see in the next chapter, to some significant conflict with other Reformers.

- 4 -

Conflict Among
the Reformers

Another way in which people sometimes get the Reformation wrong is by assuming that the Reformers all agreed with one another, at least for the most part. Obviously some differences arose along the way, since soon after the Reformers' time the Protestants were found in different churches. But did the Reformers stand alongside each other in their views? As we will see in the next two chapters, they together held the doctrines of justification *sola fide* and of *sola scriptura*. To come together on these key points was certainly a notable mark of the movement, given all the discord which had marked late medieval teaching on virtually every mooted doctrinal point.

But it is simply not the case that every time Luther (or Zwingli or Bucer or some other Reformation leader) ran up the flag that all the others stood at attention and saluted. There were differences among the Reformers that led to conflict, including contrasting ways of coordinating their respective teaching, the strategies they adopted for pursuing reform and the ways they dealt with each other. This manifested itself already early in the Reformation and continued throughout the Reformers' lifetimes.

AN EARLY INDICATION

Martin Luther had been spirited away by Elector Frederick's forces to the Wartburg Castle for safekeeping[1] as he returned from the Diet of Worms, but almost no one else knew what had happened to him. Back at the University of Wittenberg consternation and confusion reigned. Had Luther been killed? Had he been surreptitiously imprisoned? With no information, the worst was feared. One thing was sure: he was gone. What should his colleagues do now? They had committed themselves to this movement. Should it be allowed to fizzle out? If not, how should it be continued? What should they do? After a few months, the professors at Wittenberg learned that Luther was safe, but he was no longer directing the Reformation movement—that fell to them.

Among Luther's colleagues at the time, two stood out—Andreas Bodenstein von Karlstadt and Philip Melanchthon. Karlstadt, who remarkably held doctorates in both theology and canon law,[2] had been serving on the theology faculty longer than Luther; indeed, he was the one originally invited by John Eck to debate at Leipzig in 1519. By comparison, Philip Melanchthon was a mere youth—but a brilliant one. By 1518, Melanchthon had already published two major works[3] and had attained a remarkable reputation as a scholar—at the ripe old age of twenty-one! In that year, he was appointed professor of Greek at the University of Wittenberg. His inaugural address in the summer of that year stirred Luther, with its call to revamp university curricula in a northern Christian humanist direction. Melanchthon quickly fell under Luther's spell and turned his formidable talents to theology, which in 1521 resulted in the Reformation movement's first treatment of Christian doctrine, the *Loci communes theologici* (which went through many editions in subsequent years). It is clear from the first edition of this striking work that Melanchthon had thoroughly imbibed Luther's

---

[1]Luther stayed at the Wartburg Castle from early May 1521 to March 7, 1522. He used the time there to translate the New Testament from Greek into German.

[2]"Canon law" is the field of jurisprudence devoted to the mastery of ecclesiastical law. It encompasses the practices, precedents and pronouncements which the church (or its leaders) has adopted, enacted or promulgated over the centuries.

[3]These were a critical edition of the works of the Roman playwright Terence, published in 1516, and a grammar of the Greek language, published in 1518.

emphases. Indeed, it would not be too much to say that he had become "a little Luther" and not so much himself. He would subsequently recapture his own distinctiveness and step back from too close an emulation of Luther in coming years. He took the first steps in this direction in the months when Luther was ensconced in the Wartburg Castle.

These two worthy associates of Luther wanted to carry on the work begun by their colleague. Unsurprisingly, Karlstadt took the lead. It would unquestionably have been unseemly for Melanchthon to push himself forward as the director of whatever the Reformation would thenceforward become. As a professor he was by far the junior of Karlstadt, to whom the younger scholar readily deferred in these uncertain months. Further, as his subsequent life showed, Melanchthon was a cautious, pensive person, less well suited to serve as leader of a burgeoning movement. As a respected senior professor, Karlstadt enjoyed the respect of other professors and the academic credentials to continue the work begun by Luther.

Little is known about the deliberations that took place in Wittenberg; no consultations with Luther on these matters took place, though. What is known is that within a few months of Luther's disappearance Karlstadt was moving forward with reform initiatives. Desiring to simplify religious practice, bring it nearer the people and conform to biblical directives, Karlstadt introduced some changes in the worship practices at Wittenberg in early 1522. He denounced the use of special clerical vestments and opted instead for peasant garb. Further in this vein, he turned from the Latin liturgy to conduct key parts of the eucharistic celebration in German, the language of the people. In addition, as chief spokesman at the time for the Reformation movement, he denounced the religious imagery found in the churches in Wittenberg as a violation of the Decalogue's prescriptions. Soon afterward, excited crowds stormed through churches, knocking statuary from pedestals and smashing it. Melanchthon stood by uneasily during all of this, not at all sure that this was the direction the movement should take.

When Luther heard what taken place, he stormed back to Wittenberg. There he confronted Karlstadt and denounced what his senior colleague had done. So sternly did Luther distance himself from his colleague that Karlstadt soon left Wittenberg to pursue elsewhere his own vision of what reform should mean.

Did Luther oppose these changes Karlstadt had introduced? What had infuriated Luther was not the changes *per se*. Indeed, Luther would himself introduce a German version of the liturgy two years later in 1524, so that people could better understand what was happening (and what they were doing) in worship. Rather, Luther's overpowering concern was doctrinal: he feared that adopting these changes before the doctrine of justification *sola fide* was fully understood and grasped by the people would result in their thinking that by making these changes they were doing good works which would please God—and thus reintroduce the reliance on self and works which Luther had learned to loathe as a perversion of the Christian message. However desirable the changes foisted on the churches in Wittenberg by Karlstadt might have been, for Luther it was important to wait to introduce them until the people would recognize that adopting these changes would not commend them to God.

Luther resumed the leadership of the Reformation movement in Wittenberg. This incident in 1522, though, gives a précis of what would lead to conflict among the Reformers in coming years. Luther's views increasingly became explicitly rooted in his insights on justification *sola fide*. This would entail for him a specific strategy about introducing changes in church practices, and deviation would not be tolerated.

CONTRASTING DOCTRINAL STYLES

As we have already seen, almost all those who joined the movement launched by Luther had embraced northern Christian humanism. Given the educational patterns of the time, each of them had certainly received scholastic training, but they had all turned from it to humanism. A determination to return to the ancient sources, especially the Scriptures and the writings of the church fathers, a focus on winsome communication and a determination to train the whole person marked the perspectives of Ulrich Zwingli, Martin Bucer and Johannes Oecolampadius—three pastor-scholars who by the early 1520s were already playing leading roles in the Reformation movement.

In stark contrast, Luther had received no exposure to humanism in his education, which was entirely in the scholastic pattern. He had wrestled with the Scriptures and finally found an answer to his agonizing quest for peace with God, which had led to renewed study of Scripture and to the numerous publications which had spawned the Reformation movement. In the hurly-burly that ensued, Luther not only wrote at a furious rate, he also sought to reorient his own thought to comport with his new insights. As we have seen, though, this was a taxing and lengthy process for him.

Luther's scholastic background. Luther's mature theology did not leap full-grown from his forehead, like Athena from Zeus's in the Greek myth. He struggled with his views, evaluating what he had been taught in his extensive scholastic training—which had led, as it had with so few in his day, to a doctorate in theology. This is worth noting: although Luther had not been exposed to northern Christian humanism during his schooling, he had received as thorough a theological education as was then possible. He knew scholastic theology from the inside out; he had studied the Scriptures and theology in the medieval pattern for years. By the standards of his day, he was marvelously learned— beyond anyone else who joined the Reformation movement, none of whom had received the extensive and intensive theological training Luther had experienced. So, as he reconsidered and reevaluated what he had been taught, he had a lot of material to work with and a thorough training by which to reconsider it.

In thinking about this, it is important to remember that Luther was trained as a scholastic theologian. In his endeavor to reconsider and reevaluate everything he had been taught by relating it to his insight of justification by faith, he was engaging in a typically scholastic theological enterprise. As we have seen, scholastic philosopher-theologians fastened on a fundamental insight about God and humanity and that insight became the foundation of the whole of their thought. For Thomas Aquinas, that basic core was the primacy of the intellect; for John Duns Scotus, the fundamental axiom was the primacy of the will; and for William of Ockham, the grid was the absolute separation of the realms of nature and grace. So when Luther sought to review and revise all he had learned in order to bring it into conformity with justification by faith and its implications, he was following a traditional scholastic approach. To be sure, his grid was not just an intellectual construct for discerning metaphysical connections in the way reality cohered; with Luther, this reached deeper, into the recesses of heart and conscience. Even so, finding a basic postulate (for Luther, justification by faith alone) and rearticulating all teaching to comport with that postulate was the regular scholastic approach to thought. Luther's training had prepared him to engage in this endeavor, and his personal experience drove him to it. But it needs to be emphasized that Luther the Reformer pursued his liberating doctrinal insight in a typically scholastic doctrinal fashion, using it to shape the rest of his thought. Undeniably this led to profound depths in some of his perspectives. However, it also led to some genuine tensions in his interaction with other Reformers, who as Christian humanists recognized and rejected the scholastic approach to doing theology.

The core of Luther's thought. Justification *sola fide* became the bedrock of Luther's whole theology. The discovery of this understanding of divine righteousness and its relationship to faith as the good news of the Christian message had brought an end to Luther's personal spiritual struggle, but it proved to be far more than just a spiritual bromide. It reached into the depths of his being and from there rose to dominate all his thought, including his approaches to doctrine, to the reform of Christendom and toward other Reformers. This can be seen by considering anything in Luther's thought: the question of religious authority, his approach to hermeneutics, the question of the biblical canon, his views on predestination and free will, and even his understanding of the rationale for marriage![4] We will focus here on the way justification by faith alone shaped Luther's approach to reform, view of the state and guidelines for Christian living.

The 1522 confrontation with Karlstadt over the pace and pattern of reform set the mold for Luther's subsequent approach to reform initia-

---

[4]As Luther pondered his uncertain future, the former monk told his friend George Spalatin that he would marry "to spite the devil." Nothing in Luther's literary remains indicates whether his fiancée, Katharina von Bora (formerly a nun), found this endearing or romantic.

tives. Luther refused to adopt or endorse changes in church practice until he was sure that no one could possibly get the notion that by adopting these changes they were somehow securing a right standing with God. That would be a reversion to the very works-righteousness which Luther had denounced as a perversion of the Christian message.

So, out of concern for the weak among the congregation who only slowly grasped the basic Reformation message, changes could only gradually be introduced. Those changes must wait until the weakest members had so imbibed the doctrine of justification by faith alone that even they would not misunderstand the reasons for and result of whatever changes would be made. Luther's fundamental concern in all this was so to declare and teach the doctrine of justification *sola fide* directly and indirectly that all would be soaked with this sweet gospel rain. Only after that had transpired should anyone dare to introduce changes into church practices. By then, people would gladly accept the changes and not even consider them as somehow commending them to God or earning righteousness before him.

This assured a very slow pace of reform. Indeed, given the turnover in generations, it would assure that little could be changed in church practices. As previously noted, Luther did introduce a German version of the liturgy in 1524; this could be approved, since it would facilitate effective preaching and teaching. In due course, Luther also endorsed extending the chalice to the communicants in the Eucharist; this served to seal their commitment to the one in whom they found justification. In most other regards, though, changes were slow to be discussed and approved in the circles which closely followed Luther's teaching. As we will see, other Reformers saw this issue in quite a different fashion.

Luther's view of the state was also molded by his concern for the doctrine of justification. His teaching of the "two kingdoms" is well known but rarely understood. Luther distinguished between the kingdom of God's right hand (the church) and the kingdom of his left hand (the state). The church must live by the gospel. While the law would condemn sinners, the gospel offered the promise of righteousness from God. For Luther, law and gospel were found in every passage of Scripture; one might dominate, but either implied the other as its correlate.

Interpreting Scripture by this law-gospel dynamic enabled the church to serve God appropriately as the kingdom of his right hand.

By contrast, according to Luther, the state must not live out of the gospel, but from the law. Since Luther taught that not all the inhabitants of the state were or could be considered Christians, such people did not yet know and had not believed the liberating promise found in the gospel. Civil rulers, though, had to rule over all alike, no matter what their relationship to God might be. These rulers were obliged to enforce the natural law (which came from God apart from the Scriptures) and the civil law enacted by governmental decree. The former declared what people must not do in broad categories, and the latter specified those requirements for this undifferentiated community. Since gospel promise could not be enforced in this structure, the civil rulers of the state must not try to draw their enactments or judgments out of the Scriptures. Attempting to do so while being unable to propound the promise would present the Scriptures in a false light, one dominated by law. This would be a perverse misuse and misrepresentation of the Scriptures, according to Luther, since it would omit their main point and would suggest that they could be fulfilled by what one does. Justification *sola fide* has predetermined what Luther's views on the state must be. Again, some other Reformers would not agree.

It is not surprising that justification by faith alone shaped Luther's view of Christian life. It is worth noting, though, that it introduced a particular limitation in the way he allowed that believers should be directed as they sought to live before God. Luther considered it a corruption of the Christian message to teach that the law directs believers in this regard.

Luther allowed for two uses of the law but repudiated the third. The first use of the law was its general one to structure society and declare what must not be done if society is to continue and flourish; this was the law as it related human beings to each other. The second use of the law was to condemn sinners and bring them to an awareness of their sin before God; this was the law as it related human beings to God. Luther repudiated what came to be called the third use of the law, which some averred showed believers how God wants them to live to him. Luther bristled at this notion. He had learned by brutal experience that the law offered no comfort to human beings and only drove them to despair before God. To reintroduce the law as a guideline for Christian living must eventually lead, according to Luther, to a reversion to works-righteousness. Rather, Christians live by love—for God and for others. Again, justification by faith alone molded Luther's view of the guideline for Christian living. As with the other points noted above, though, some Reformers differed from him on this.

Many more such instances could be offered to show how justification by faith alone shaped and dominated Luther's perspectives, but these are enough to see that Luther's thought was thoroughly ruled by it. Indeed, it would not be too much to state that Luther detected a threat to justification by faith alone behind every blade of grass and under every rock in the landscape.

Luther's package of thought is undeniably vital and dynamic, arising from a lived, experienced relationship to God. But other Reformers had encountered other experiences which shaped their thought in ways that did not always coincide with Luther's predilections and preferences. This led to conflict.

The Christian humanist pattern. In considering the others who came to the Reformation movement, it is important to recall that they—and we are especially considering the early adherents Zwingli, Bucer and Oecolampadius—had all been exposed to scholastic theology to significant degrees, but that they had turned from it in disgust. Each had found northern Christian humanism a stimulating alternative, one that offered a vibrant way of reentering the theological contest—namely, by returning to the original sources, the Scriptures themselves and the works of the early church fathers. This orientation attracted them to Erasmus, the prince of the northern Christian humanists. Each of these three early Reformers corresponded with Erasmus. Bucer continued to do so into 1536, the last year of Erasmus's life. (Both Zwingli and Oecolampadius had died in 1531—Zwingli in a battle defending Zurich, and Oecolampadius succumbing to the plague.) All three of them welcomed and used Erasmus's critical edition of the Greek New Testament in 1516, and they all profited from the editions of the church fathers he published subsequently. Indeed, Oecolampadius worked with Erasmus on some of these in Basel. But all three of them identified themselves with the Reformation movement. As Reformers, though, their way of doing theology differed from Luther's, and their approach to reform diverged from his as well.

Northern Christian humanism in general found scholastic theology repugnant. Erasmus in particular denounced it. Exposed to it in his studies at the University of Paris, he declared that he rose from the study of scholastic theology not warmed to prayer but primed to argue. His investigations into the full texts of the writings of the church fathers manifested how widely they were misquoted, misused and misunderstood by the scholastic theologians. Beyond all this, Erasmus and his followers rejected the propensity scholasticism had for debate. From Erasmus's perspective, truth is not distilled at high temperature. Study of the ancient sources of the Christian faith should issue into the sort of interaction between discussants required by St. Paul when he wrote that Christians must "speak the truth to our neighbor" (Eph 4:25), and when he urged, "Above all, clothe yourselves with love, which binds everything together in perfect harmony" (Col 3:14). Little of either, it seemed to the humanists, could be found among the scholastics. Since this was so, scholasticism held no promise for presenting Christian truth effectively or winsomely. The sort of crude, vicious denunciation that too often accompanied the scholastic determination to show itself clever and shave distinctions closely led far afield from the kind of teaching found in Scripture and the church fathers. In the estimation of Erasmus and his adherents, theology must be done in a different way, by listening carefully to the teaching and doctrinal method of the apostles and the church fathers. It must be presented engagingly, humbly and invitingly, in open and genuine dialogue with all those ready to engage in the pursuit of truth. Name-calling and crude denunciation were vices to which no genuine Christian theologian dared stoop. Disputation raised only ire and produced only enemies; dialogue issued in discussion, respect and understanding.

With this approach that deemed scholasticism repugnant, the humanists also turned away from the deductionistic pattern of scholastic thought in which all truth was reduced to a single basic point from which everything was subsequently rethought and repackaged. For the humanists such dialectically belabored thought had little to do with what human beings faced in the complexities of life and less to offer as help in their struggles. The purpose of a genuine theologian was not to invite others to amazement at his dialectical finesse, but to set forth Christian teaching in an attractive, winsome fashion, with a life that squared with that teaching.

Zwingli, Bucer and Oecolampadius all turned to the Reformation movement as a genuine hope for the change long called for in Western Christendom. In so doing, they embraced the movement begun by Luther in 1517. However, none of them forsook their northern Christian humanist predilections as they did so. Specifically none of them traded in its approach to doing theology for a scholastic one, even the one adopted (in its distinctively Reformation dress) by Luther. The stage was thus set for conflict. It came in due course.

CONTRASTING FIELDS OF LABOR

The contrasting doctrinal styles of Luther on the one hand and his humanist followers on the other would have been enough to render at least some conflict between them likely. The fact that they labored in quite different circumstances, which made divergent claims on their attention and focus, was enough to assure the conflict.

Differing foci and emphases. Already by the mid-1520s, the reform endeavors of Zwingli, Bucer and Oecolampadius were developing a different focus than that of Luther. While Luther served as a professor of theology and worked for reform of the theological curriculum, these others were the leading pastors of significant cities: Zwingli in Zurich, Bucer in Strasbourg[5] and Oecolampadius in Basel. There were already significant differences in their respective intellectual backgrounds and predilections, as we have noted. Further differences arose from what

---

[5]During the sixteenth century the city was in German territory and its name was spelled *Strassburg* (German *Straßburg*); even so, in this book I will follow current scholarly convention in early modern European studies and give the city's name in its contemporary French spelling *Strasbourg*.

was necessary in their respective fields of labor.

Luther's struggle had been a personal one—that of an individual monk for assurance of his relationship with God. This eventually led Luther to a profound doctrinal breakthrough, which ended up permeating every aspect of his theology and all his perspectives. In contrast, Zwingli, Bucer and Oecolampadius had not gone through the sort of agonizing struggles Luther had endured. They had studied scholastic theology, but they had all turned from it as objectionable, becoming enamored instead of the perspectives of Christian humanism. Beyond this, though, all three of them were citizens of significant urban centers, and because of this, they were acquainted with the questions, anxieties and uncertainties that especially plagued the cities. But this experience and these concerns were unknown to and played no part in Luther's experience and his theological development. Luther came from a small town, situated within a large territory ruled by a sovereign prince, and he labored in a small town.

Luther's struggle and breakthrough led him to the reform of theology itself and to the academic reform of the University of Wittenberg's theological curriculum, but almost reluctantly also to reforms in the church and her practices. Zwingli, Bucer and Oecolampadius were turned off by the aridities of scholastic theology and turned on by the opportunity to go *ad fontes*, to Scripture and the church fathers. Learned already in those ancient sources, these three pastors embraced the emphases of Luther because those emphases presented the message of Scripture and the ancient church, and not just because Luther had said so. They had significant interest in the reform of theology too, but they lived in and labored for the Reformation within major cities of the time, as the leading pastors within those cities. This gave them a significantly different set of issues to face.[6]

The contrast is striking. Luther was a theology professor who regularly preached, but Zwingli, Bucer and Oecolampadius were pastors,

---

[6]To appreciate the import of this, it is necessary to keep in mind two basic assumptions which had prevailed for centuries in Western Christendom and still obtained as the Reformation began: (1) the membership of the city (or the state) and the church were the same, and (2) there was only one church (in many congregations) in a city (or state). Consequently, working for the reform of the city and the church were basically the same labor.

who ended up establishing schools. Luther worked to reform theology and the theological curriculum, but not so much parish life, while Zwingli, Bucer and Oecolampadius worked to reform preaching and liturgy—indeed, as well as theology—but especially parish life. Contrasting concerns inevitably led to differences in emphases and assessments as to what was important, what must be done and how the Reformation message could best take root.

It is worth noting that Luther's emphases were especially focused on the individual and his or her needs. The emphases of Zwingli, Bucer and Oecolampadius included individuals, of course, but reached beyond that to include the urban community. As Christian humanists, like their Italian Renaissance confreres, Zwingli, Bucer and Oecolampadius had special concern for the improvement of society, the development of responsible participation in government by its citizens and the improvement of social life and ethics.

The problem of the cities. Before proceeding further, it would be helpful to point out the special problems of the cities in the early sixteenth century. Cities had been growing again in northern Europe since the late eleventh century, so they were not a new phenomenon. But they had proven to be a special problem within Western Christendom, a problem which had not yet been resolved as the sixteenth century began.

The problem was that cities did not fit anywhere in the threefold structure of medieval feudal society. After the collapse of the Roman Empire in the West, as civilization slowly reemerged under the leadership of the church during the seventh to tenth centuries, Western European society had developed into three social classes: those who worked (the peasants), those who fought (the rulers and the knights) and those who prayed (the priests and the religious). This was simply the way society had been for as long as anyone knew. With no memory or evidence that society had ever known another structure, and without any sense of anachronism at the time, this threefold structure seemed self-evidently to be the way things had to be. Further, these three divisions seemed to cover the possibilities for legitimate Christian work: some tilled the ground, others defended those workers and yet others led in religious practice.

As trade reemerged in the north of Europe in the tenth and eleventh centuries,[7] merchants found it wise to set up permanent warehouses and trade centers. By the twelfth century, several of these had developed into cities, as more and more people moved to them to work in the new economic ventures or to provide goods for the traders to sell. This entailed leaving extended family and friends behind for an anonymous existence in an unknown, and often unfriendly, place. Many who headed with great hopes to the cities could find no viable employment in them. Crime increased as desperate people took what they needed to survive or found steady income from violence. Cities proved to be hotbeds for disease transmission, with the crowded conditions and the lack of sanitation.

And yet, the cities were unquestionably the engines that were driving the economic recovery of Western Europe: merchants bought and sold goods and offered markets for whatever extra merchandise enterprising individuals could produce beyond their immediate needs. The old barter economy gave way to an increasing reliance on money and credit. The cities were flourishing economically, as merchants became another class—a "middle" class between those who worked and those who fought—even while crowds within the cities suffered loneliness, disappointment, illness and danger.

In light of all this, it is scant surprise that clergy and hierarchs in these centuries frequently denounced cities as dens of iniquity. Violators of the sanctioned threefold structure of society, anonymous locales where neither family nor friend offered succor and love of neighbor seemed a forlorn impossibility, cities defied the standards of the church. The inhabitants of the cities (especially their successful leaders, the merchants and artisans) were engaging in commerce, an arena denounced by the ethical teaching of the church, which sternly declared that "the love of money is a root of all kinds of evil" (1 Tim 6:10).

---

[7]Trade had never completely died out in the Italian cities, even during the early Middle Ages. As Europe north of the Italian Alps became less dangerous for those who travelled with goods in the tenth and eleventh centuries, intrepid Italian merchants ventured into the region. Soon enough they either left representatives who worked for them there, or their successes stimulated residents of the region to turn to trade themselves. In this way, trade and merchandising developed in Western Europe beyond the Italian Alps.

Cursed with disease and danger, the cities already experienced evidence of divine wrath. Ecclesiastical jeremiads regularly declared cities and merchants condemned by God.

Like others in the late Middle Ages, citizens of the cities were already also caught up in the general religious frenzy, intensity and anxiety of late medieval religion. The further specific condemnation of their hopes and their lifestyle only added to the burden of the urban residents. And yet the cities continued to grow in numbers and economic influence. Few dared boldly declare what many sensed: that the cities, as the most vibrant element of whatever was happening throughout Western Europe, seemed in many ways to be experiencing divine blessing.

So as the sixteenth century dawned, the people in the cities labored under two problems in religious matters. First, as with everyone else in the late medieval period, the practice of religion was intense, anxious and demanding. The best it could do was to urge laypeople to take on semimonastic lifestyles, with all the arduous demands and ascetic requirements that entailed. Second, in the cities, virtually everyone suffered under the question of whether an urban lifestyle could be acceptable to God: it did not fit in the old, accepted three-tiered structure of medieval society, sanctioned by time and religious teaching.

Reformation and the cities. To these questions, the common Reformation message brought answers. The declaration that one was justified *sola fide*, and not by any kinds of good works one might try to do (including emulating the lifestyle of monks), answered the first question fairly straightforwardly. Further, the Reformation teaching that "all vocations are legitimate before God," who had made them all, spoke eloquently to the second. So the basic Reformation message addressed the main concerns of urban citizens in the early sixteenth century. It dealt with the fundamental anxieties of anyone seeking peace with God, but especially those caught in the hitherto religiously suspect realm of city living. With these answers coming from the ultimate source of religious authority, the Scriptures, the issue was rather clearly settled.

Thus the basic Reformation message greatly simplified religious life in the cities, allowing people in all good conscience to continue in their urban, middle-class lifestyle—and even to do it to God's glory. The Reformers' teaching thus recognized the sacredness of supposedly secular, middle-class life and the legitimacy of living in a city. The Reformation's perspectives thus undercut the sanctioned threefold structure of society by acknowledging other ways to live appropriately before God. It did not matter whether one fit into the three-tiered structure of feudal society, for God had already accepted the middle class and urban life itself in Christ.[8]

None of this yet implies any differences among the Reformers. However, the Reformers in the cities saw the necessity of responding to the particular problems of the cities—health questions, poverty, isolation from loved ones and so forth. To Zwingli, Bucer and Oecolampadius, Luther's "two-kingdom" approach fell short. Leaving urban life in the "secular" realm, unshaped by God's Word, seemed to them no way to deal with these problems. Relying on the wisdom of civil leaders alone—which is what Luther's approach to social life would require here, since he declared it wrong to use Scripture to provide answers or direction—had allowed these problems to develop in the first place. Perhaps Luther's division into "two kingdoms" might work in a large territorial state or a small town, where the old feudal structures were still largely intact and had not been as grievously undermined and brought into question as they had in the cities.

In the estimation of Zwingli, Bucer and Oecolampadius, the general uneasiness—intensified by its long standing—in the cities with the status and legitimacy of urban life called for something more incisive. Given the striking answers the Reformation had brought to the perennial questions of personal piety and peace with God, might not the

---

[8]In the last four decades, Reformation-era scholarship has carefully investigated the appeal of the Reformation to cities and how cities responded to and incorporated Reformation emphases: among others, see the groundbreaking work by Bernd Moeller, *Imperial Cities and the Reformation: Three Essays*, ed. and trans. H. C. Erik Midelfort and Mark U. Edwards Jr. (Philadelphia: Fortress, 1972), pp. 41-115; and Steven E. Ozment, *The Reformation in the Cities: The Appeal of Protestantism to Sixteenth-Century Germany and Switzerland* (New Haven, Conn.: Yale University Press, 1980). Specialized studies of significant cities and their relationship to the Reformation movement have also appeared: see, e.g., Thomas A. Brady Jr., *Ruling Class, Regime and Reformation at Strasbourg, 1520-1555* (Leiden: Brill, 1978).

further study of Scripture lead to appropriate answers that would also deal with urban life? Further, might this not show that not only should cities and the commercial activity that supported them be tolerated, but that they could even be celebrated as places and lifestyles which genuinely honored God? To find such answers, leaders would have to deal with the many concerns (health, welfare, the poor, etc.) for which the cities had often been castigated.

Among the leaders of the Reformation in the cities, all of whom were Christian humanists, the general answer was the same: although there were differences in emphasis as they sought to develop a Reformation response to these challenges, the general pattern was consistent. Zwingli in Zurich, Bucer in Strasbourg and Oecolampadius in Basel all turned to Scripture to discern what a society pleasing to God would look like. As we have seen, Luther rejected applying Scripture to civil life as a distortion of the Word of God, but the early city Reformers saw its promise for dealing with that corporate existence. Applying the Word of God meant applying the directives God had given long before to Israel, directives found in the law and in the proclamations of the Old Testament prophets. Thus Zwingli, Bucer and Oecolampadius tried to effect a *further* reform, beyond that of Luther—one that applied not only to the individual but to society as a whole. They ended up writing directives regarding schooling, care for the poor, begging, oversight of guilds, health matters, just prices and wages, and so forth. These were the kinds of questions that demanded to be dealt with in the cities. These specific applications of the Scriptures to such issues put them at odds with Luther's strong sense of what was right and wrong in using Scripture, but they were not driven by his concern to make sure the promise of Scripture came to the fore; they were concerned with the problems in the city.

This opens the door to another significant difference from Luther—namely, the pace of reform. As we have seen, Luther was cautious about this, concerned that the weakest member of the congregation must fully understand the implications of justification *sola fide* before proceeding to institute changes, no matter how desirable they seemed. In contrast, Zwingli, Bucer and Oecolampadius insisted on instituting such changes as soon as possible *for the sake of the weak*, so that they could be put in a better way to learn the fuller implications of Christian teaching. To be sure, the city Reformers usually preceded all such changes with public disputations about what was going to happen, so that people could see the differences and embrace the changes being made. Even so, the pace of reform in Zurich, Strasbourg and Basel was considerably faster than what Luther (and his strict followers) could approve. In their different approach, Zwingli, Bucer and Oecolampadius saw themselves as carrying further the implications of the Reformation movement—to enable God's grace to shape social, civil, corporate and congregational life in the ways Scripture indicated were pleasing to him. The Reformers in the cities were attempting to turn the cities from being the suspect rebels of medieval Christendom to the standard of God-glorifying life in the Reformation era.

For their efforts in these regards, they were criticized by their Lutheran compatriots as being "even more reformed" than Luther—a stance these Lutherans could hardly conceive of. But the name stuck, and the early stances of these city Reformers remained hallmarks of the subsequent *Reformed* movement.

Zwingli, Bucer and Oecolampadius laid heavy emphasis on the transformation of society; social ethics was a prime consideration for them. They looked to the Scriptures for guidance in this, especially to the law (with the prophets understood as particular applications of the law), as divine directives for living as a community before God. These early Reformed leaders agreed with Luther that the law restrained evil in society (the first use of the law) and that it served to convict sinners (the second use of the law), but they collectively also urged that the law of God tells Christians how God wants them to live (the third use of the law), both individually and communally. Indeed, in each of their respective cities, Zwingli, Bucer and Oecolampadius sought to achieve a "theocracy"—a society in which the will of God would set the norms and patterns for the community.

All three of them ran into trouble with the "city fathers," the councils which governed Zurich, Strasbourg and Basel. The pastors' determinations did not always mesh well with what the citizens were used to or the councilors desired. Even so, none of these early Reformed pastors gave up on the goal. Zwingli's and Oecolampadius' endeavors were cut short by their untimely deaths. Bucer achieved the most in this regard during his quarter-century of labors in Strasbourg (1523-1549). Significant in its own right, what he achieved was even more important because of its influence on John Calvin, who became a close friend and a neighbor to Bucer in the three years Calvin resided in Strasbourg (1538-1541), the years between the two periods of Calvin's own work in Geneva. But this Reformed emphasis on the third use of the law served to distance Zwingli, Bucer and Oecolampadius from Luther, who stringently opposed such a use of the law.

INTERACTION AMONG THE REFORMERS

Not only did justification *sola fide* shape Luther's views of doctrine and the approach to reform, but it also significantly shaped his views of himself and of the others who embraced the Reformation movement. This takes our considerations into a sticky area, which involves the way the Reformers interacted with each other as they confronted their differences.[9]

Luther's view of himself and others. As Luther surveyed what had transpired through the rediscovery and proclamation of the gospel, he declared time and again, "It was not I that did it, but the Word of God." With this he expressed genuine humility: Luther urged repeatedly that he himself was insignificant, but that the gospel was great, and that what he had accomplished was not his work but God's.

Even so, Luther was sure that God himself had entrusted him with this message. God had proclaimed the gospel anew through Luther; since that was the case, then all others should listen and heed. In due course, through struggles he had with others, Luther

---

[9]This has been examined in careful and painstaking fashion by the Lutheran scholar Mark U. Edwards Jr. in *Luther and the False Brethren* (Stanford, Calif.: Stanford University Press, 1975) and *Luther's Last Battles: Politics and Polemics 1531-1546* (Ithaca, N.Y.: Columbia University Press, 1983). My presentation in this section relies heavily on Edwards's studies.

came to view himself as a prophet like those of the Old Testament, a fifth evangelist after Matthew, Mark, Luke and John. Even with this self-conception, Luther did not suppose that any of his writings should be added to the canon of Scripture, but for him it did mean that he had been divinely authorized to give the proper understanding of the Scriptures. Further, since he was called by God to the awesome responsibility of this proclamation, he had the right to command.

Such an attitude was hardly likely to leave Luther open to discussion about his perspectives: that would imply uncertainty and would thus be unfaithful both to the truth he had discerned and to God's calling. It also would not leave him open to disagreement from others, even if they also claimed to stand with him on most issues. For Luther what was needed was bold proclamation. For any who would not learn to speak and teach properly, not dialogue but argument, disputation and debate were necessary. Luther often was extremely stubborn in the defense of truth as he had come to understand it; indeed, he showed himself time and again to be profoundly disputatious. The irony is that he thus ended up defending the Reformation message with a medieval scholastic mentality.

The question of how Luther might have dealt with others who also claimed to be teaching the truth but who did not exactly line up with his views is not just a theoretical one. Rather, the question is how he dealt with actual people like Zwingli, Bucer and Oecolampadius. These other Reformers had not gone through the searching and agonizing experience Luther had that led to his relief in discovering justification *sola fide*. They had been drawn to the study of the Scriptures and the church fathers through their northern Christian humanist inclinations. They were drawn by what Luther added to what they had already learned from Scripture; in this way they came to admit and confess gladly that sinners are received by God only through faith. For them, justification *sola fide* became essential to, though only part of, the whole package of God's teaching. This did not lead them to the fixation on justification *sola fide* as it had with Luther—which would have been the sort of scholastic approach to doctrine they repudiated as Christian humanists.

So others who joined the Reformation movement—including Zwingli, Bucer and Oecolampadius—sometimes placed the accents differently than Luther, and they made emphases which he found foreign. Luther could be very suspicious of the way they talked, especially if in their teaching he perceived threats to justification by faith alone, whether in the pace of reform or in the third use of the law. Indeed, it frequently happened that as Luther encountered the teachings of others he found different emphases than he would readily bring. He often upbraided such people and called them to a careful defense of and alertness to justification by faith alone. If they did not heed his advice, he could quite readily, if they continued to disagree with him, denounce them as servants of Satan, as those in league with the wicked one, seeking to divert people from the truth of the gospel. This is the tack he took with some fellow Reformers—including Zwingli, Bucer and Oecolampadius. While they, of course, protested that any such judgment was totally unwarranted and unfair, Luther nevertheless stuck to it.

The controversy over the Eucharist. We see this all most graphically in the very public controversy over the Lord's Supper which broke out among the Reformers in 1526 and dragged on until 1529. To begin to appreciate that conflict, it is necessary to step back from the view common among conservative Christians in the early twenty-first century that the Eucharist is nothing more than a memorial in which pious recipients humbly recall the death of the Son of God in their place long ago as they receive the elements of the Lord's Supper. This is not the place, and we do not here have the space, to treat the significance of the Eucharist in the history of the church and to discuss why that significance has diminished for so many conservative Christians in the present day. But a few points need to be made to enable such readers at least to see the background of the issue and what was at stake for the Reformers who ended up involved in the controversy.

While the memorial aspect of the Lord's Supper had never been in question in the history of Christianity, no one limited the Eucharist to that: from the New Testament[10] through the church fathers[11] down to the sixteenth century, all Christians taught and believed that through the Lord's Supper recipients somehow received the body and blood of the Savior. In the Lord's Supper, there is a real presence of Christ. In antiquity, the church fathers repeatedly warned against trying to understand or explain how this could be, acknowledging it as the merciful work of God, which cannot be fathomed.[12]

However, with Western Christendom's increasing reliance on Aristotle in the generations preceding the full embrace of scholastic thought, the Fourth Lateran Council in 1215 thought it could explain how one receives the body and blood of Christ when one receives what look and taste like bread and wine—namely, via "transubstantiation." According to this explanation, the "substances" of bread and wine "go across" (Latin *trans*) and become the substance of Christ's body and blood

---

[10]In building up to his exposition of the Lord's Supper in 1 Corinthians 11, Paul rhetorically asks, "The cup of blessing that we bless, is it not a sharing in the blood of Christ? The bread which we break, is it not a sharing in the body of Christ?" (1 Cor 10:16); his subsequent argument clearly indicates that he expects a positive response to both questions. In presenting the story of the disciples on the road to Emmaus, Luke points out that these disciples later told the other disciples "how he [the risen Christ] had been made known to them *in the breaking of the bread*" (Lk 24:35 [emphasis added]), using words which by the time he wrote (in the 60s) were used to refer to the Lord's Supper. As well, John recounted Jesus' striking words, "Very truly, I tell you, unless you eat the flesh of the Son of Man and drink his blood, you have no life in you. Those who eat my flesh and drink my blood have eternal life" (Jn 6:53-54); by the time John wrote (in the 90s), these words would unquestionably have been understood by his Christian readers to refer to the Lord's Supper.

[11]"We do not receive these as common bread and drink: as Jesus Christ our Savior, having been made flesh by the Word of God, had both flesh and blood for our salvation, we have been taught that the food blessed by praying his words, and from which our blood and flesh are duly nourished, is the flesh and blood of the same Jesus who was made flesh" (Justin Martyr *The First Apology* 66, my translation); see also Ignatius *Letter to the Ephesians* 20:2; Irenaeus *Against Heresies* 4:18, 5; Hippolytus *The Apostolic Tradition* 32:2; Cyril of Jerusalem *Mystagogical Lectures* 4:2-3; 5:20; Gregory of Nyssa *Catechetical Oration* 37; Cyril of Alexandria *Commentary on John* 6:54; Cyril of Alexandria *The Third Letter to Nestorius*; Ambrose *The Mysteries* 52, 58.

[12]"You ask how the bread becomes the body of Christ and the wine and water the blood of Christ. I tell you that the Holy Spirit descends and accomplishes these things which are beyond description and understanding. . . . The bread and wine are transformed into the body and blood of God. However, if you ask how this happens, let it be sufficient for you to hear that it takes place through the Holy Spirit—just as it was through the Holy Spirit that the Lord made flesh subsist for himself and in himself from the blessed mother of God. And more than this we do not know, except that the word of God is true and effective and omnipotent. But how this transpires is impossible to figure out" (John of Damascus *The Orthodox Faith* 4:13, my translation); see also Cyril of Jerusalem *Mystagogical Lectures* 4:6; Cyril of Alexandria *Commentary on John* 6:53; Ambrose *The Mysteries* 53.

when the ordained priest speaks the words of consecration, "This is my body" (Latin *hoc est corpus meum*). To be sure, the appearances remain the same: the elements still look and taste like bread and wine. This is miraculous, for it is the opposite of the way elements change in all other situations: they could look and even taste different, depending on what one might do with them, but their substances would remain the same as bread and wine. This miracle was possible because of the power of Christ's Word and the privilege granted the priest in his ordination to effect this transformation by the recitation of the words of institution. This viewpoint promulgated by the Fourth Lateran Council had been accepted and disseminated in the subsequent medieval period.

In the sixteenth century, though, Luther sternly criticized transubstantiation as the explanation of what transpires in the Eucharist as so much Aristotelian rationalistic foolishness. Even so, he affirmed the real presence of Christ. In the Lord's Supper, Luther found great comfort and assurance: he and all believers partook of the very body and blood of the Savior. In Zurich Zwingli—who had come to a Reformation stance independently of Luther by reading the Scriptures and the church fathers—also ended up attacking transubstantiation, but as the elaboration of an idea not required by the scriptural text. Turning away from the medieval doctrine, Zwingli spoke rather of the bread as a symbol of Christ's body, a symbol which helps recipients remember Christ's suffering and death until he returns.[13] Both these leaders had rejected transubstantiation, but they had nevertheless come to quite different assessments of what is received in the Lord's Supper. By 1526 each had heard of the other's views.

Luther denounced Zwingli's view as mere rationalism (i.e., evaluating Scripture and its comfort in terms of reason) and thus of a piece with the objectionable medieval theological approach. For his part, Zwingli responded that Luther's approach was itself an unpurged element of me-

---

[13]It is a misrepresentation, though, of Zwingli's view to describe it as a "real absence" of Christ from the Lord's Supper; he did not hold to a merely symbolic or memorial view, even though that is what he articulated most clearly. For him the "remembering" reflected the rich connotation of the Greek term *anamnēsis* in which the "remembered" thing becomes present again. However, he never found a way to articulate this clearly, to indicate how God extends grace to those who appropriately receive the Lord's Supper.

dieval sacramentalism, because it remained close to transubstantiation. (Luther had elaborated his position by urging that the body and blood of Christ were "in, with and under" the elements of bread and wine.)[14] Thus Zwingli argued that Luther was holding on to aspects of the very medieval system he had written so powerfully against.

Luther bristled. He asserted that Zwingli's approach was a return to "works-righteousness," since the recipient does the remembering, and thus whatever grace may come in the Lord's Supper comes because of that human remembering. This undermines justification *sola fide*—and so, of course, must be rejected. Zwingli countered that Luther's attitude was a hangover from tradition, without biblical warrant and thus ultimately against *sola scriptura*.

Luther declared that Zwingli's view attacked the Lord's Supper and emptied it of grace, making it of no benefit to the recipient because it was simply another good work. Zwingli responded that Luther's conception so filled the Eucharist with grace that everybody who partook, whether believer or not, received the body and blood of Christ. This, Zwingli averred, denied the very significance of faith itself. Luther did not back off from this challenge: even an unbeliever, he affirmed, indeed received and ate the body and blood of Christ!

Zwingli, Bucer and Oecolampadius were astounded. According to 1 Corinthians 11:27-28, some who are unworthy (i.e., believers who had not properly examined themselves and prepared for the Lord's Supper) might thus "eat and drink judgment" on themselves. But, from Luther's perspective, even a rank unbeliever receives Christ's body and blood? Luther responded, "Yes, because Christ is truly there!"

Personal vituperation. If this were all that took place in this controversy, it might be simply another regrettable example of theologians bickering—regrettable for the Reformation movement, and far too

---

[14]Luther's position has often, but erroneously, been identified as "consubstantiation." He did not use the term, and subsequent Lutheranism has repudiated it as rooted in a philosophical construction alien to its doctrinal stance. Even so, it is evident that, however erroneously, Zwingli understood something along this line as involved in Luther's view. (In this regard, it is interesting that "consubstantiation" could appropriately be used to identify the Eucharistic view of the late-medieval scholastic theologian John Duns Scotus. [I am indebted to Drew Blankman for this information.])

similar to the theological wrangling of late medieval scholasticism, but nevertheless born of a desire to appropriate the truth. But more was involved than just conflicting views. From the beginning of the controversy, Luther had excoriated Zwingli, Bucer and Oecolampadius as "false prophets," "minions of Satan" and "inspired by the wicked one." Luther loaded Zwingli and the others with invective—the very sort of hostile, coarse defamation for which monks and scholastics had long been known, and which Christian humanism (and especially its notable leader Erasmus) had denounced as unworthy of a Christian. So Zwingli, Bucer and Oecolampadius urged Luther to speak more temperately— which Luther interpreted as their satanically inspired attempt to have him go easy on truth. So he piled it on!

Zwingli and the others resolutely refused to engage in such name-calling and coarseness. They could resort to sarcasm, irony and other elegant weapons of verbal riposte, but they refused to stoop to the personal abuse which had so often besmirched scholastic theological debate. They acknowledged the great debt they and others owed to Luther for his endeavors to rescue the gospel and proclaim it clearly again in their day, but they declaimed against Luther's high-handedness and his seeing himself as an oracle.[15]

Eventually the Eucharistic controversy cooled down, and a measure of agreement was attained in 1536, some five years after the deaths of Zwingli and Oecolampadius. But Luther remained vigorous in his self-assessment and quick to denounce deviations from the path he discerned as the proper way to go. Even with his closest associates at Wittenberg, he could be abrupt and domineering. Philip Melanchthon especially experienced this. Beginning already in 1522, he distanced himself from too close an emulation of his colleague, seeking his own ways to articulate and advance the Reformation movement. Over the ensuing years, this led at times to emphases which Luther or his stringent followers at Wittenberg found questionable. While Luther usually defended Melanch-

---

[15]In a letter to Zwingli, Bucer sharply expressed his irritation, declaring that Luther's doctrinal tyranny was worse than what the church had suffered under the bishops of Rome; in a later letter to friends in Strasbourg, Bucer urged them to recognize that God had granted a great gift in Luther, but that they had to accept him as he was. Working for peace in the church would require them all, he noted, to put up with a lot from Luther.

thon against the criticisms of these others, occasionally Luther turned a sharp eye on Melanchthon. Especially in the 1540s, Melanchthon felt the heat from Luther on a variety of points. During these tense times, Melanchthon wrote to a friend that Wittenberg had become like a prison to him from which he would be only too happy to escape. To another he wrote that he had felt the wrath of Luther. The tensions eventually slackened, and Melanchthon did not end up leaving Wittenberg.

Respectful of their longstanding friendship, Luther still worked closely with Melanchthon. Indeed the younger colleague was chosen to give the oration at Luther's 1546 funeral. In that eulogy, he loyally stressed all that the church owed to Luther for the service he had offered her, expanding richly on this theme. Even so, it is striking that Melanchthon felt compelled to address the way Luther dealt with others. In so doing, he explicitly mentioned and endorsed the assessment of Erasmus that by the sixteenth century, Western Christendom was so desperately sick that God had sent it a violent physician.

SUMMARY

All this is not intended as an indictment of Luther; rather, it is a presentation of what transpired among the Reformers as they interacted with each other. As in other regards, so too in the question of conflict among them, Luther led the way. Given the ways his teaching and writing had been appropriated to endorse perspectives and justify actions which he had not intended,[16] it should occasion no astonishment that he became proprietary about his teaching. In the face of all this, it is also no wonder that he came to recognize, with genuine humility, the significant role he had been given to play in calling the church back to the gospel. It is hardly strange, furthermore, that he looked askance at what he perceived to be deviations from his main emphases. Moreover, it can hardly be a shock that he dealt with all this by utilizing his training as a scholastic theologian in the ways he integrated all his perspectives in a particular insight, conducted argument and dealt with his interlocutors.

---

[16]See the treatment of this topic in chapter three.

Given the quite different fields in which they labored and their common Christian humanist background, consciously chosen in contrast to the dominant scholastic approach to theology and argument, it is equally unsurprising that Zwingli, Bucer and Oecolampadius ended up serving the Reformation movement in a different way than Luther. They adopted and adapted the teaching and practice of the Reformation movement to address urban issues which faced them but were foreign to Luther's experience and concern. Their training and commitments as Christian humanists precluded them from responding in kind to the scholastic bombast and coarse personal abuse to which Luther resorted.

Neither Luther nor his Christian humanist associates desired conflict. All of them hoped that truth would prevail and all would agree. However, they differed in significant ways as to what that truth was, what it required, how to implement it and how to defend it. None of them wanted the conflict, but they disagreed on how to deal with and overcome it.

Even so, in the midst of all this, they agreed on how one finds peace with God and on the religious authority which directs us to this insight—the teachings of justification *sola fide* and *sola scriptura*, respectively. We turn to these doctrines in the next two chapters, to assess how adequately contemporary conservative Christian teaching comports with what the Reformers taught on these issues in the sixteenth-century Reformation movement.

- 5 -

What the Reformers
Meant by *Sola Fide*

Aₙyₒₙₑ who is at all familiar with sixteenth-century
Western Europe knows that the doctrine of justification *sola fide* played
a prominent role in the Protestant Reformation. This doctrine has often been styled the *material principle* of the Reformation.[1] All the Protestant Reformers insisted on it.

For Luther it became the grid through which all other facets of his
thought were passed: everything related to justification by faith alone.
While it did not serve as an integrating factor in the thought of the
other Reformers in the same way, they nonetheless vigorously emphasized it in all their endeavors. One the one hand, it served to distinguish what they declared from what late medieval theologizing and
pastoral instruction had urged; on the other, it amounted to a significant reclaiming of the ancient and apostolic understanding of what the
"gospel"—the good news—was all about.

The various traditions of Protestantism have continued to insist on
justification *sola fide*. It is a hallmark of Protestant teaching. Even so,

---

[1]This is correlated with what is then called the *formal principle* of the Protestant Reformation—
sola scriptura; see the treatment of this topic in chapter six.

some of what is proclaimed under the banner of "justification by faith alone" today is far from the teaching of the sixteenth-century Reformers; indeed it explicitly contradicts what they insisted on. This is one of the most glaring ways of getting the Reformation wrong.

In this chapter, we will consider what the Reformers taught on the subject, the clarifications they made regarding the doctrine and its too common contemporary misrepresentation. Our treatment will take a different form than in previous chapters, where we were considering historical backgrounds and influences. Here we are looking at what the Reformers taught and how they clarified it. It is important to establish this well, so that when we proceed to consider the way justification by faith alone is often presented in the present day, the Reformers' teaching will sit clearly before us and enable us to assess that contemporary presentation. So we will offer numerous citations from the respective Reformers' works to document their teachings and the ways they clarified what they meant by it. The contrast between their teaching and the contemporary misrepresentation will be abundantly clear.

We are justified by faith alone. The Protestant Reformers were united in emphasizing that justification is by faith alone. While there were minor differences among them as to how divine grace impacts us as we come to faith (as we will see), they nonetheless agreed on the main point of the doctrine. Human beings are sinners, unable to measure up to God's standard of righteousness. In the divine law court, sinners can have no hope in themselves or what they have done. But God has provided salvation through the life, suffering, death and resurrection of his incarnate Son. He took on human sin, so that all those who believe in him might take on his righteousness. United to him by faith worked by the Holy Spirit, humans are thus accepted by God as righteous. In his sovereign law court, he accounts them righteous: this is their justification, which is received by faith alone. On this all the Reformers agreed. To be sure, the articulation of this teaching was the fruit of the agonizing struggle of Martin Luther and his study of Scripture, a struggle which the others did not endure. But they recognized the doctrine as scriptural teaching.

The anxiety that dogged Martin Luther in the monastery arose from his diligent attention to the emphases in the teaching and pastoral counsel proffered in the late medieval church. Faith was taken for granted, since all acknowledged the Apostles' Creed. Exhortations focused on obedience to divine precepts. Any hope for a welcome before God at death and the final day depended on the number and quality of the good works thus produced. Those called "the religious"—the monks and the nuns—had the greatest chance of accumulating such good works, since their entire existence focused on worship and service. Seeking to find peace with God, Luther heeded these directives. He entered a strict Augustinian monastery and diligently set about living up to all the requirements it imposed, but without finding peace. He even exceeded the order's rigorous expectations, seeking to commend himself to God, but without coming to any sense that he could possibly measure up to the standard demanded by austere divine holiness. Nothing less than perfection would suffice, and he could not come near that. In all this, Luther fully inhabited the teaching commonly found throughout the church in his day, the teaching also familiar to the others who became Reformers with him.

Luther eventually found an answer to his quest through his discovery of justification *sola fide* in his encounter with Romans 1:16-17. Relief flooded his inner being; in short order, the doctrine of justification by faith alone began permeating and restructuring his understanding of Christian doctrine and life. By the early 1520s, his writings began evidencing how much his views had been reshaped from what he had previously heard in church and been taught in scholastic theology.

In *The Freedom of a Christian* (published in November 1520), Luther expanded on the doctrine. He brought forward passages in St. Paul's Letter to the Romans to show that the apostle summons people to believe the promises found in God's Word and to indicate how desperately such hope is needed, for sinners cannot possibly be righteous before God in themselves.[2] Against this background, Luther affirmed, "Therefore it is clear that, as the soul needs only the Word of God for its life and righteousness, so it is justified by faith alone, and not any works; for if it

---

[2]The passages are Romans 10:9; 10:4; 1:17; 3:23; 3:10-12, respectively.

could be justified by anything else, it would not need the Word, and consequently it would not need faith."[3] The Wittenberg professor went on to declare: "When you have learned this you will know that you need Christ, who suffered and rose again for you so that, if you believe in him, you may through this faith become a new man in so far as your sins are forgiven and you are justified by the merits of another, namely, of Christ alone."[4] As against what he and others had been taught, Luther explicitly stated: "He [who believes in Christ] needs no works to make him righteous and save him, since faith alone abundantly confers all these things."[5] Fifteen years later, Luther offered the same perspective in his 1535 commentary on St. Paul's Letter to the Galatians. As Luther expanded on the pregnant passage at Galatians 2:16-17,[6] he asserted: "But the work of Christ, properly speaking, is this: to embrace the one whom the Law has made a sinner and pronounced guilty, and to absolve him from his sins if he believes the Gospel. 'For Christ is the end of the Law, that everyone who has faith may be justified' (Rom 10:4)."[7] Many similar citations could be noted from Luther's writings throughout the rest of his career until his death in 1546.

Luther's close colleague in Wittenberg, Philip Melanchthon, produced the Reformation's first general treatment of Christian doctrine in his 1521 *Loci communes*. As he expounded on justification, Melanchthon urged, "Why is it that justification is attributed to faith alone? I answer that since we are justified by the mercy of God alone, and faith is clearly the recognition of that mercy by whatever promise you apprehend it, justification is attributed to faith alone." He goes on to explain, "Therefore, when justification is attributed to faith, it is attributed to the mercy of God; it is taken out of the realm of human efforts, works,

---

[3]Martin Luther, *The Freedom of a Christian*, trans. W. A. Lambert, in *Selected Writings of Martin Luther: 1520-1523*, ed. Theodore G. Tappert (Philadelphia: Fortress, 1967), p. 22.

[4]Ibid., p. 23.

[5]Ibid., p. 32.

[6]"Yet we know that a person is justified not by the works of the law but through faith in Jesus Christ. And we have come to believe in Christ, so that we might be justified by faith in Christ, and not by doing the works of the law, because no one will be justified by the works of the law. But if, in our effort to be justified in Christ, we ourselves have been found to be sinners, is Christ then a servant of sin? Certainly not!"

[7]Martin Luther, *Lectures on Galatians 1535, Chapters 1-4*, in *Luther's Works*, vol. 26, ed. Jaroslav Pelikan (St. Louis: Concordia, 1963), p. 143.

and merits."[8] Divine mercy provides what sinners could never hope to achieve; faith embraces that mercy in Christ and finds justification. This remained Melanchthon's teaching. In 1531 he wrote, "Faith alone justifies because we receive the forgiveness of sins and the Holy Spirit by faith alone. The reconciled are accounted righteous and children of God not on account of their own purity but by mercy on account of Christ, if they grasp this mercy by faith."[9]

Ulrich Zwingli also stressed the mercy of God for the justification of unworthy sinners. He wrote, "This is the gospel, that sins are remitted in the name of Christ; and no heart ever received tidings more glad."[10] Zwingli proceeded to expand on this teaching, eventually stating:

> For when man through repentance has come to the knowledge of himself, he finds nothing but utter despair. Hence, wholly distrusting himself, he is forced to take refuge in the mercy of God. But when he has begun to do that, justice makes him afraid. Then Christ appears, who has satisfied the divine justice for our trespasses. When once there is faith in Him, then salvation is found; for He is the infallible pledge of God's mercy.[11]

He wrapped up his treatment by asserting: "Through Christ alone we are given salvation, blessedness, grace, pardon, and all that makes us in any way worthy in the sight of a righteous God."[12]

In the preface to his 1536 *Commentary on Romans*, Martin Bucer elaborated on justification by faith alone and how it impacts those who believe. In his typically expansive fashion, Bucer urged,

> When Paul asserts that we are justified by faith, the faith whereby we assuredly believe that Christ is our Saviour and our sole peacemaker with the Father, he means that by this faith we are first of all delivered

---

[8]Philip Melanchthon, *Loci communes theologici*, in *Melanchthon and Bucer*, ed. Wilhelm Pauck, Library of Christian Classics (Philadelphia: Westminster Press, 1969), pp. 105, 106.

[9]Philip Melanchthon, *Apology of the Augsburg Confession*, in *The Book of Concord: The Confessions of the Evangelical Lutheran Church*, trans. and ed. Theodore G. Tappert (Philadelphia: Fortress, 1959), p. 119.

[10]Ulrich Zwingli, *Commentary on True and False Religion*, ed. Samuel Macauley Jackson and Clarence Nevin Heller (Durham, N.C.: Labyrinth, 1981), p. 119.

[11]Ibid., pp. 122-23.

[12]Ibid., p. 129.

from all doubt that God, on account of the death of Christ undergone on our behalf, forgives us all our sins, absolves us from all guilt, and passes judgment in our favour against Satan and all the ill we may have deserved.[13]

Bucer stressed strongly that this leads to a transformation of the one who receives such grace and mercy.

John Calvin stood with his fellow Reformers in strongly emphasizing the foundational significance of justification *sola fide*. In an early treatise written to guide the instruction of the citizens of Geneva, he declared: "For we are said to be justified through faith, not in the sense, however, that we receive within us any righteousness, but because the righteousness of Christ is credited to us, entirely as if it were really ours."[14] Later in his monumental *Institutes of the Christian Religion*, Calvin urged, "This [justification *sola fide*] is the main hinge on which religion turns."[15] His rich teaching can well serve to summarize the Protestant Reformers' shared perspective on justification: "He is said to be justified in God's sight who is both reckoned righteous in God's judgment and has been accepted on account of his righteousness. . . . Justified is he who, excluded from the righteousness of works, grasps the righteousness of Christ through faith, and clothed in it, appears in God's sight not as a sinner but as a righteous man."[16]

This commonality among the Protestant Reformers on the doctrine of justification by faith alone did not preclude some minor differences among them. Luther's words indicate why this could be so: "This is the great, inestimable treasure given us in Christ, *which no man can describe or grasp in words*."[17] The various Reformers reflected on how the great transaction promised in the gospel "worked," and they came to some-

---

[13]Cited in *Common Places of Martin Bucer*, trans. and ed. D. F. Wright, Courtenay Library of Reformation Classics (Appleford, U.K.: Sutton Courtenay, 1972), p. 162.

[14]John Calvin, *Instruction in Faith (1537)*, trans. and ed. Paul T. Fuhrmann (Louisville: Westminster John Knox Press, 1977), article 16 (p. 42).

[15]John Calvin, *Institutes of the Christian Religion*, ed. John T. McNeill, trans. Ford Lewis Battles, Library of Christian Classics (Philadelphia: Westminster, 1960), 3.11.1.

[16]Ibid., 3.11.2.

[17]Luther uttered this in a sermon he preached on March 14, 1522, which is reproduced in English translation in Tappert, *Selected Writings of Martin Luther*, pp. 256-59; this citation is at p. 257 (emphasis added).

what different insights. These sometimes reinforced each other, but at times they were in conflict. Luther emphasized the "sweet exchange" between the sinner and Christ and that sinners are united to Christ by that faith impelled in them by the Holy Spirit. Melanchthon's regular stress on divine mercy fits closely with this, although bringing a different accent. Zwingli tied justification to the divine decree of election, with faith the temporal manifestation of what God intended from eternity past for his chosen.[18] Bucer stressed that justification includes the reception of the Holy Spirit, who leads believers to live for God: "Hence he [St. Paul] never uses the word 'justify' in this way without appearing to speak no less of this imparting of true righteousness than of the fount and head of our entire salvation, the forgiveness of sins."[19] Calvin stepped back from Bucer's declaration when he asserted that justification by faith precludes "the sense . . . that we receive within any righteousness," but Calvin brought another emphasis when he asserted, "Christ, therefore, makes us thus participants in himself in order that we, who are in ourselves sinners, may be, through Christ's righteousness, considered just before the throne of God."[20] But these differences were variant modulations within the Reformers' concerto. The Protestant Reformers agreed in emphasizing justification *sola fide*.

But faith is never alone. From the perspective of those steeped in the medieval church's instruction, the Reformers' radical reduction of what was needed for justification was shocking. Urging that it came "by faith alone" seemed to undercut any call to holiness of life—the life spent doing good works. The defenders of the Roman church quickly pointed out that the Reformers' teaching would lead to indifference toward godliness.

In 1531 Melanchthon responded to this assertion as made in the *Roman Confutation* (a reaction to the Augsburg Confession). He observed, "Our opponents slanderously claim that we do not require good works, *whereas we not only require them but show how they can be done*."[21] Ac-

---

[18]"General Introduction," in *Zwingli and Bullinger*, ed. and trans. G. W. Bromiley, Library of Christian Classics (Philadelphia: Westminster Press, 1953), p. 34.

[19]Wright, *Common Places of Martin Bucer*, p. 162.

[20]Calvin *Instruction in Faith* 16.

[21]Melanchthon, *Apology of the Augsburg Confession*, p. 126 (emphasis added).

cording to Melanchthon, while justification is by faith alone, faith is never alone: the faith that justifies cannot be solitary. It cannot exist by itself, in supposedly blissful isolation. What Melanchthon here asserted was the common teaching of all the Protestant Reformers.

Luther was abundantly clear in this regard. He dealt with the charge that his teaching dispensed with a summons to holiness of life extensively and head-on in his *The Freedom of a Christian*. In expounding on that freedom, Luther urged, "This is that Christian liberty, our faith, which does not induce us to live in idleness or wickedness but makes the law and works unnecessary for any man's righteousness and salvation."[22] Freed from the impossible burden of trying to placate God by such works, the believer responds gladly to God: "Is not such a soul most obedient to God in all things by this faith?"[23] This determination to obey God is not just an option for one who believes and so receives justification: "Here the works begin; here a man cannot enjoy leisure; here he must indeed take care to discipline his body by fastings, watchings, labors, and other reasonable discipline and to subject it to the Spirit so that it will obey." Even so, as against what the medieval church had taught, "In doing these works, however, we must not think that a man is justified before God by them, for faith, which alone is righteousness before God, cannot endure that erroneous opinion."[24] But "a man cannot be idle. . . . The works themselves do not justify him before God, but he does the works out of spontaneous love in obedience to God and considers nothing except the approval of God, whom he would most scrupulously obey in all things."[25]

In Luther's teaching, there is no question that those justified do good works: "So the Christian who is consecrated by his faith does good works, but the works do not make him holier or more Christian."[26] Obeying God is not optional, merely a recommendation for believers so inclined: "But as faith makes a man a believer and righteous, so faith

---

[22]Luther, *Freedom of a Christian*, pp. 25-26
[23]Ibid., p. 26.
[24]Ibid., p. 34.
[25]Ibid., p. 35.
[26]Ibid., p. 36.

does good works."[27] As against the charges leveled by critics, Luther declared, "We do not, therefore, reject good works; on the contrary, we cherish and teach them as much as possible."[28] By faith, a believer lives for God: "This is a truly Christian life. Here faith is truly active through love [Gal 5:6], that is, it finds expression in works of the freest service, cheerfully and lovingly done."[29] Good works find their impetus in justifying faith: "Behold, from faith thus flow forth love and joy in the Lord, and from love a joyful, willing, and free mind that serves one's neighbor willingly."[30] Luther sums all this up clearly when he states, "Our faith in Christ does not free us from works but from false opinions concerning works, that is, from the foolish presumption that justification is acquired by works. . . . Righteousness does not consist in works, although works neither can nor ought to be wanting."[31] Good works issue from justifying faith, which seeks to obey God as fully as it can. Struggling against the sin that nonetheless still cleaves to them, believers realize that their obedience is not yet all it should, and someday will, be: "As long as we live in the flesh we only begin to make some progress in that which shall be perfected in the future life."[32] For Luther, faith was never alone.

Melanchthon stood forthrightly with his colleague in these regards. He urged, "Faith is nothing else than trust in the divine mercy promised in Christ. . . . This trust in the goodwill or mercy of God first calms our hearts and then inflames us to give thanks to God for his mercy so that we keep the law gladly and willingly."[33] At peace with God, believers yearn to serve him: "Faith cannot but pour forth from all creatures in most eager service to God as a dutiful son serves a godly father."[34] Such obedience is not dispensable: "You have here the sum and substance of the whole Christian life, faith with its fruits."[35] Faith

---

[27]Ibid., p. 37.
[28]Ibid., p. 39.
[29]Ibid., p. 41.
[30]Ibid., p. 43.
[31]Ibid., pp. 48-49.
[32]Ibid., p. 34.
[33]Melanchthon, *Loci communes*, p. 92.
[34]Ibid., p. 109.
[35]Ibid., p. 110.

cannot exist without producing this fruit: "For although faith alone justifies, love is also demanded. . . . A living faith is that efficacious, burning trust in the mercy of God which never fails to bring forth good fruits."[36]

Melanchthon sang the same song in his *Apology for the Augsburg Confession*. Defending the Reformers' teaching against their opponents, he noted, "We say, too, that love should follow faith, as Paul also says, 'In Christ Jesus neither circumcision nor uncircumcision is of any avail, but faith working through love' [Gal 5:6]."[37] He expanded on this by stating,

> Since faith brings the Holy Spirit and produces a new life in our hearts, it must also produce spiritual impulses in our hearts. What these impulses are, the prophet shows when he says [Jer 31:33], 'I will put my law upon their hearts.' After we have been justified and regenerated by faith, therefore, we begin to fear and love God, to pray and expect help from him, to thank and praise him, and to submit to him in our afflictions. Then we also begin to love our neighbor because our hearts have spiritual and holy impulses.[38]

He summed up his point succinctly: "So it is clear that we require good works."[39]

Ulrich Zwingli also insisted on the correlation between faith and good works. He wrote, "But we must add at once that the pious will not cease from good works simply because it is impossible to gain any merit by them. Rather, the greater our faith, the more and greater our works." Zwingli drew attention to the role of the Holy Spirit in this correlation by urging, "For since faith is inspired by the Holy Spirit, how can it be slothful or inactive when the Spirit himself is unceasing in his activity and operation? Where there is true faith, works necessarily result, just as fire necessarily brings with it heat."[40]

For his part, Martin Bucer was especially insistent on the good works that arise from justifying faith. Immediately after insisting that believ-

---

[36]Ibid., p. 112.
[37]Melanchthon, *Apology of the Augsburg Confession*, p. 123.
[38]Ibid., p. 124.
[39]Ibid., p. 127.
[40]Ulrich Zwingli, *An Exposition of the Faith*, in Bromiley, *Zwingli and Bullinger*, p. 272.

ers are justified by faith, Bucer went on to stress: "Furthermore, God breathes the power of his Spirit into those acquitted and declared righteous before him, to make immediate assault upon their corrupt ambitions and to urge on their suppression and extinction, and, on the other hand, to fashion upright attitudes to every aspect of life, to arouse and foster holy desires, conforming us speedily to the likeness of Christ." Bucer made the pastoral observation, "Unless we first believe that we have been accepted by him on the basis of mercy alone, we are unable to perform any good works." Using the same imagery as Zwingli, Bucer urged, "For anybody can see quite plainly that by such commendation of faith we are doing nothing more than arousing and stimulating genuine good works and sound righteousness, which of course can no more be absent where faith is present than heat can be lacking when the fire is burning." All this serves to mark the believer as the genuine article: "For that very righteousness and the good works wrought in us by the Spirit of Christ constitute the visible evidence of that unmerited acceptance of ours in the sight of God."[41]

John Calvin was no less firm in asserting that justifying faith is never solitary, as if it could exist by itself, without good works. In 1537 he made the point sharply: "Those who boast of having the faith of Christ and are completely destitute of sanctification by his spirit deceive themselves. For the Scripture teaches that Christ has been made for us not only righteousness but also sanctification [1 Cor 1:30]. Hence we cannot receive through faith his righteousness without embracing at the same time that sanctification."[42] He elaborated on this point by urging: "Now, as Christ is no minister of sin, so, after having purged us from the stains of sin, he does not clothe us with the participation of his righteousness in order that we may afterward profane with new stains so grand a grace, but in order that, being adopted as children of God, we may consecrate our life course and days to come to the glory of our Father."[43] What Calvin asserted later in the *Institutes* can serve not only as the summary of how he sees the conjunction of faith and good works,

---

[41]Cited in Wright, *Common Places of Martin Bucer*, pp. 162, 165, 166.
[42]Calvin *Instruction in the Christian Faith* 17.
[43]Ibid., 18.

but also as that of his fellow Protestant Reformers: "Let us sum these up. Christ was given to us by God's generosity, to be grasped and possessed by us in faith. By partaking of him, we principally receive a double grace: namely, that being reconciled to God through Christ's blamelessness, we may have in heaven instead of a Judge a gracious Father; and secondly, that sanctified by Christ's spirit we may cultivate blamelessness and purity of life."[44]

For Calvin and all the Protestant Reformers, we are justified by faith alone—but faith is never alone. Justifying faith leads to good works, performed in love toward God and our neighbors, in grateful obedience to God. Scholars have found minor differences in accent among the Reformers as they attempted to describe how God works within us by the Holy Spirit in justification. However, there is no disagreement among the Reformers on the certainty that justifying faith issues in good works. No Protestant Reformer ever allowed that a justifying faith could be solitary—no, not one.

Solitary faith? Given this unanimity among the Protestant Reformers, it is startling that within the larger Protestant world in the nineteenth to twenty-first centuries, the notion has developed and been widely disseminated that one can be justified by a faith that remains alone. Too often this is presented as what the Reformers taught and Protestants should believe. It is neither, but rather a misrepresentation and trivialization of the doctrine of justification *sola fide*.

This notion had its roots in the "revival" meetings and evangelistic campaigns that sprouted in the United States during the latter nineteenth century and continued well into the twentieth. Sometimes called "camp meetings," these events might last for several weeks, with services virtually every evening, often running several hours in length. Afterwards, the speakers and their "teams" would move on to other places to begin the process again. Criticized by many church leaders for "new measures," these meetings were marked by a variety of practices and endeavors which sought to bring someone to the point of "making a decision for Christ," of "walking the aisle," of "coming to the altar."

---

[44]Calvin *Institutes* 3.11.1.

These and other phrases were used to describe the speaker's vigorous challenge to individuals to come to a commitment right at that moment—whether rededicating oneself to Christ or coming to an initial conversion. Such converts would receive little follow-up from the meeting speaker, who would soon leave for another engagement. Depending on whether local churches welcomed or criticized such meetings, the speakers realized that their converts might not exactly fit within the molds of those churches. All this contributed to the speakers emphasizing the significance of the conversion experience as an unmistakable and undeniable turning point in which the convert stepped irretrievably from darkness into light.

Soon enough, the revivalist/evangelistic meeting style became a pattern for what transpired in many congregations. Preaching came to be focused on the simple gospel, issuing a call for people in attendance at the regular church services to "walk the aisle," "come to the altar" or "make a decision for Christ." Seeing this as Christianity's main responsibility, church members soon were taught to "share their testimony," to "witness for Christ," all with the intention of getting a person to make a decision for Christ—to believe in him. These would-be evangelists were taught to assist their converts to find a deep assurance of their new status with God. A simple syllogism, varied in its forms but similar in content, went like this: read from the Bible a promise of salvation for one who trusts in Christ; point out that the person has trusted in Christ; ask if God would lie; and get the person to conclude that he or she can thus have absolute assurance that God has granted him or her everlasting salvation.

Whatever one might say about the zeal for the message of salvation in Christ and for the spiritual well-being of others entailed in all this, it cannot be denied that this approach has some serious, debilitating limitations. The question is not whether God can use or has used it; as the Puritans used to say, God can strike a straight blow with a crooked stick. But this pattern has the unfortunate consequence of relegating Christian living—obedience to God, loving him and neighbor, good works—to the sidelines. The call to trust in Christ for salvation was allowed to stand alone, without the call to discipleship. Faith was left solitary, disconnected from faithful living. To be sure, such converts were often invited to attend church and become members, "get involved," read the Bible, pray and so forth. But these were nothing more than recommended and desirable options for those who chose them. For those who did not, though, their one-off faith was, they were too often assured, enough to get them into heaven.

Soon the religious landscape was littered with many who thought that this brief moment of religious intention was all they needed. "Carnal Christianity" came to be used as a designation for those who had professed faith in Christ at some time in the past but who were living the same kind of lifestyles as those who had never made any such profession. Even so, according to the common attitude—which soon enough was transmogrified into accepted teaching in many fundamentalist and some evangelical church circles—such "carnal Christians" were assured of being allowed into heaven, because they had once responded to an invitation to conversion and prayed for salvation in Christ.

The teaching that faith can be solitary—that it can stand alone, without any diligence to serve God and others and so do "good works"— has become commonplace in some evangelical and most fundamentalist Christian circles. This notion, which clearly falls far short of any idea of "discipling" others, is nonetheless presented as the gist of the Great Commission given by the resurrected Christ in Matthew 28:18-20. But that passage does not call his followers then or the church subsequently to make *converts*: it calls them to make *disciples*.[45] Further, this "solitary faith" is often presented in such circles as what the Protestant Reformation was all about, with its call to "justification *by faith alone*." Supposedly honoring both dominical commandment and Reformation heritage, solitary faith is presented as the quintessence of Christianity. Anything beyond that is optional.

This "solitary faith" idea is a distortion of the Reformers' common teaching, justification *sola fide*. It is more than slightly ironic that this

---

[45]Significantly, immediately after the call to "make disciples of all nations," Christ indicated what that would mean: "teaching them to obey everything that I have commanded you" (Mt 28:19-20). Even a generous interpretation of that directive will not allow the "solitary faith" notion to pass as a way of living up to this commission.

idea would actually legitimize the criticism brought by the Reformers' Roman opponents. This notion is flatly in contradiction to what all the Reformers taught. It is a trivialization of what they proclaimed: they called for a faith in divine promises of salvation in Christ, a faith that always led to sincere, grateful, determined endeavors to live whole-heartedly for God. That those who thus believed in God would not be able to live up to such a goal was a given, but no one thought that trying to do so was optional.

It is interesting to compare this contemporary teaching of "solitary faith" with the doggerel Tetzel used to peddle indulgences: "As soon as coin in coffer rings / the soul from purgatory springs." Luther was incensed by this trivializing of grace; the ninety-five theses were a reaction to the whole business. How would he and the other Reformers view the contemporary trivializing of justification by faith alone? They would undoubtedly excoriate it. They would be incensed anew by the contemporary Tetzels, who could well peddle such solitary faith with some updated doggerel: "A moment's fearful faith is given, / and God is stuck with you in heaven"; or "Walk the aisle! Pray the prayer! / One-time faith gets you there!"; or "Here's all you do: just one quick prayer. / So grace is cheap—what do you care?" or "Only a one-off faith you bring, / eternal passport to the King"; or "Cry out once and do not worry. / God accepts you in a hurry." Such "easy believism" (as this notion has sometimes been called) proffers a cheap grace with "eternal security," since "once saved, always safe" (another common phrase used with this notion).

It is troubling to see how far this falls short of the wise counsel of Ignatius of Antioch, one of the apostolic fathers. Trained as a young man by the apostle John in his old age, Ignatius offers a connection to the earliest days of the church just after the apostles had passed from the scene. In one of his letters, he wrote, "It is not a matter of promising now, but of persevering to the end in the power of faith."[46] This is certainly far removed—not only in time, but also in teaching—from the contemporary proclamation of "solitary faith." Ignatius seems better to

---

[46]Ignatius of Antioch *Letter to the Ephesians* 14:2, my translation.

understand what Jesus Christ meant when he said, "The one who en-
dures to the end will be saved" (Mt 10:22).

In this regard, the striking comment of another respected ancient
leader of the church is also worth pondering. Cyprian of Carthage was
addressing a somewhat different issue and problem, but *mutatis mutandis*
what he urged deserves careful consideration when he warned, "Through
the presumption of those who beguile with false promises of salvation,
the true hope of salvation is destroyed."[47] In this light, the contemporary notion is anything but innocuous.

This notion of solitary faith nonetheless has led many pastors and
evangelists to call their hearers (in the congregation or outside it) to be
sure they can recount the date and the hour when (or, the time and
place where) they "prayed the sinner's prayer" and thus were eternally
saved, no matter what they might do in the rest of their lives. This calls
people to rely on a spiritual birth certificate to know they are alive; the
Reformers called them to live.

This contemporary teaching seriously misconstrues what the Reformers unanimously taught. Justification *sola fide* has nothing to do
with a call to such solitary faith. This is one of the most glaring and
striking ways of getting the Reformation wrong. For the Reformers,
justification is by faith alone, but faith is never alone.

---

[47]Cyprian *The Lapsed* 34.

- 6 -

What the Reformers Meant by *Sola Scriptura*

WITH DOCTRINAL ISSUES PLAYING A SIGNIFICANT ROLE in the Protestant Reformation, the question of religious authority became a pressing concern. To deal responsibly with and choose among the competing arguments about what Christians should believe and practice, a religious authority was needed to show the way to go. But who or what would that be?

This was no new problem: theologians and canon lawyers had already been arguing about the question for almost two hundred years by the dawn of the sixteenth century.[1] Scripture, the writings of the church fathers, ancient creeds, conciliar decrees, papal declarations, liturgical traditions, canon law and the pronouncements of the theological faculties at the various universities all had some claim on the

---

[1]See the extended treatment of the question in Heiko Oberman, *The Harvest of Medieval Theology: Gabriel Biel and Late Medieval Nominalism*, rev. ed. (Grand Rapids: Eerdmans, 1967), pp. 361-422. Significantly, this is corroborated by Philip Melanchthon's observation in a treatise on religious authority which we will consider in this chapter: "It is a very frequent custom to contend as to just how much weight is to be attributed to the opinions of the church, the decrees of the synods, and the sayings of the Scriptures" (Philip Melanchthon, *The Church and the Authority of the Word, 1529*, in *Melanchthon: Selected Writings*, ed. Elmer Ellsworth Flack and Lowell J. Satre, trans. Charles Leander Hill [Minneapolis: Augsburg, 1962], p. 133).

mind of the church. In a vague and undefined way, it was generally recognized that Scripture played a leading role, but the questions regarding who could interpret it and how it should be interpreted were matters of dispute.

This may seem strange to many Protestants today, who acknowledge and perhaps readily appeal to the Bible as their sole religious authority—a view ostensibly learned from the Protestant Reformation. With this shared acknowledgment and the easy way that appeal is made, one might almost expect that all those concerned for Christian truth would end up in agreement. With more than twenty-six thousand Protestant denominations in existence as the third millennium began, though, it appears the problem is a bit more complicated.

What much of Protestantism thinks the Reformers taught about religious authority is a significant misrepresentation of what they actually taught. A simplistic "Scripture good, tradition bad" notion has become so common that it has even tainted a recent version of Scripture, translated for and widely used in the larger evangelical church community.[2] But such a notion gets the Reformation wrong: indeed, it trivializes the Reformers' views on religious authority. The question of religious authority was, undeniably, a major concern of the Reformers and a significant component of the Reformation movement. The Reformers came to greater clarity as the movement progressed, as they wrestled with the implications of what they believed and the ways what they said was misunderstood or misappropriated in their day.

Reformation scholarship has labored diligently on this question in the last generation or so. One of the major contributors to these investigations comments helpfully on what has been learned when she notes, "It is by now a well-known fact that the Reformers did not reject the tradition of the Early Church, which in their eyes was to be sharply distinguished from the corruptions of mediaeval ecclesiastical structures."[3] This stands in sharp contrast to what many think the Re-

---

[2]See my "The New International Version and the De-Catholicizing of Scripture," *Perspectives: A Journal of Reformed Thought* 8 (November 1993): 10-13.

[3]The comment is by Irena Backus in her *The Disputation of Baden, 1526 and Berne, 1528: Neutralizing the Early Church*, Studies in Reformed Theology and History (Princeton, N.J.: Princeton Theological Seminary, 1993), p. 81.

formers taught about religious authority. If we are not to get the Reformation wrong on this undeniably important topic, we will need to do what Reformation scholarship has done—namely, to consider carefully what the Reformers themselves actually taught about religious authority, to see what they meant by *sola scriptura*. So, as in the previous one, this chapter will look closely at what the Reformers themselves said, offering numerous citations from their written works to show what they intended as they asserted *sola scriptura* and how they clarified and qualified that assertion.

INTRODUCTION TO *SOLA SCRIPTURA*

As the Protestant Reformation unfolded, the question of religious authority came to the fore. To assert justification *sola fide* meant a dramatic turn from what had become commonplace teaching in Western Christendom. Legitimizing such a departure from what had been taught entailed appeal to a religious authority which could rule out other considerations. *Sola scriptura* became the Protestant Reformers' common answer to such a demand. While there were subtle but still important differences among them in their views of the complete contours of this answer,[4] these need not concern us here. Their overarching agreement on *sola scriptura*, given the uncertainties which bedeviled the question of religious authority as the sixteenth century dawned, is startling.

All the Protestant Reformers dealt with the question to some degree. Some, though, paid it particular attention. For this reason, Luther, Melanchthon and Bucer will require more attention than will Zwingli and Oecolampadius. Calvin, as a second-generation Reformer, pulled together and polished what had been urged by his predecessors in the movement.

LUTHER AND *SOLA SCRIPTURA*

As Luther struggled to his breakthrough in understanding Romans 1:16-17 and thereby found the peace with God for which he had so long

---

[4]I have dealt with some of these in my unpublished "*Sola scriptura* and Church History: The Views of Bucer and Melanchthon on Religious Authority in 1539" (Ph.D. diss., University of Waterloo, 1982).

fruitlessly searched, he soon turned a critical eye on the various claimants to religious authority in his day.

Coming to **sola scriptura.** As he did so, Luther quickly recognized a
number of human traditions which had developed in ecclesiastical practice that were in conflict with justification by faith alone and its implications. Luther repudiated them and undermined the authority supposedly claimed for them.[5] Frustrated that his extensive training in
scholastic theology had not opened up this understanding to him, he
quickly relegated scholastic theology and the pronouncements of its faculties at the universities to insignificance as religious authorities. As he
examined canon law and the various papal decisions, he found no help
in this regard, either; he quickly consigned them to the ash heap.[6] He
found even the writings of the church fathers a mixed bag in this regard,
since they did not address the question of justification by faith alone
straightforwardly. At the Leipzig Debate in 1519, John Eck forced Luther to assert that the Council of Constance had erred in its condemnation of Jan Hus. Luther had come to the conclusion that even a church
council (esteemed in Western Christendom as an ecumenical council)
could err. As against all else, Scripture had opened up to him the wonder of justification *sola fide*—indeed, only Scripture had done so.

Interpreting Scripture rightly: Law and gospel. As professor of Bible
at the University of Wittenberg, Luther had the opportunity to pursue
his instincts regarding Scripture's authority more intensely. Eventually
he came to a hermeneutical approach which enabled him to discern
justification everywhere in Scripture: he urged that both law and gospel are found in every scriptural passage. Where the passage brought
forward demands from God, it was law—which no one can fully live up
to. Since the same God is the God of grace and free forgiveness, the law

---

[5]See Luther's examination and repudiation of the alleged biblical warrant for several of these
in his *A Reply to the Texts Cited in Defense of the Doctrines of Men*, in *Selected Writings of Martin
Luther, 1520-1523*, ed. Theodore G. Tappert (Philadelphia: Fortress, 1967), pp. 223-29.
[6]The papal bull *Exsurge Domine* threatened Luther with excommunication and declared that his
books should be burned, and when the bull was promulgated in Rome in June 1520, a number
of Luther's books were consigned to the flames. In northern Europe, the proclamation of the
bull was accompanied by the burning of Luther's books in Louvain, Cologne, Mainz and Ingolstadt. On December 10, 1520, Luther countered by burning the papal bull and numerous
volumes of canon law.

emphasis demanded the gospel promise as its necessary correlate. If a passage offered promise, it came from a gracious God, whose grace humans need because they are sinners. So, conversely, the passage implied our need as sinners and the grace offered by God. With this approach, all of Scripture proclaims justification *sola fide*, since it always drives people to Christ. In this fashion, Scripture stands supreme, without any equal as religious authority.

Nothing else among the claimants to religious authority could match it. Scripture stood superior to all else, and these other claimants had to be judged by Scripture as norm. However helpful they might be, they were far below Scripture in the authority with which they spoke. Luther had discovered what would become known as the formal principle of the Reformation, *sola scriptura*. This did not quite settle the question, however.

The allegation of subjectivism. At the Diet of Worms in 1521 Luther was called to recant what he had written. He asked for time to consider his answer. When he answered skillfully the next day, pointing out that much of what he had written could not be denied (as Christian truth or as criticism of papal tyranny toward the German nation), the archbishop of Trier broke in and asked how Luther could possibly think he alone understood Scripture rightly. He went on that Luther thus set his own judgment above that of many hierarchs and famous theologians down through the centuries, whose teachings had been confirmed by church councils. The allegation of subjectivism was clear and forthright. Luther answered that unless he were convinced by appeal to Scripture and good reason, he could not recant. Even so, when he was spirited away from Worms for safekeeping to the Wartburg Castle, the question whether he alone could be right in his views tortured him. He eventually came to insights that allowed him to face and respond to this challenge.[7]

The allegation of subjectivism soon became an accusation regularly hurled at Luther by his opponents. His steadfast determination to stand by his views, in the face of much to the contrary in church teaching and practice, seemed willful and rebellious to them. Both

---

[7]Roland Bainton, *Here I Stand: A Life of Martin Luther* (Nashville: Abingdon, 1950), pp. 140-50.

then and in subsequent centuries, this accusation was leveled at Luther and, through him, at the whole Protestant Reformation. There is no denying that Luther stood his ground in the face of much opposition or that he refused to budge in his convictions, whatever others said about that. But there is an important consideration that needs to be kept in mind in this regard, one that is too rarely acknowledged as a significant factor.

Doctor of theology. It needs to be remembered that Martin Luther had earned a doctorate in theology. According to the academic regulations honored in his day, that accorded him special privileges. Those who had only earned lower degrees could teach, but they were restricted to the enunciation of the major text—in biblical instruction, Scripture itself; in theological studies, Peter Lombard's *Sentences*, the chief handbook of medieval theology in Western Christendom—and to the glosses which respected scholars of bygone days had added to the text. Such instructors were strictly prohibited from adding their own interpretations or glosses to the material presented to the students: that privilege was restricted to those who had earned a doctor's degree. Thus, when Luther set forth his perspectives, often enough in contrast to the words of earlier scholars, he was using the privilege he had earned by his extensive studies. Thus, while he engaged in such confrontation of earlier scholars much more frequently and with more relish than others who also held a doctorate in theology, what he was doing was itself in accordance with his "degree and all the honors, rights, privileges and responsibilities thereunto appertaining" (to use the phrasing often uttered at graduation ceremonies even in the present day).

Luther was unquestionably stretching that privilege as far as it could go—and, in the estimation of his opponents, much farther. In doing so, though, he was actually living up to his privileges and responsibilities as a doctor of theology. It is, consequently, difficult to make the charge of subjectivism stick for Luther: his degree and his position (as professor of Bible) authorized a certain degree of independence in his teaching and assertions. Even so, as we will see, he found support in the witness of Christian antiquity—as did the other Reformers.

It is worth noting in this regard that Luther did not extend this privilege of such independent thought to others, though.[8] For Luther, *sola scriptura* did not imply that everyone could thus legitimize his own understanding of Scripture. Any appeal to Scripture required adhering to the proper hermeneutical approach—which Luther had set out. For those who could not or would not abide by these strictures, Luther had little tolerance. *Sola scriptura* did not invite a free-for-all approach to Scripture in which any and all had the right to assert its authority to substantiate whatever insights they claimed to have attained from it.

Religious authority in Luther's thought. It is important, in the face of all this, to ask what *sola scriptura* meant for Luther. Is Scripture a solitary authority, with no other religious authorities even acknowledged? Or is it the only unquestioned authority (thereby allowing that subordinate authorities might exist)? In this regard, it will be helpful to consider how Luther viewed the church fathers, the ancient creeds and the ecumenical councils. It was one thing to turn aside merely human traditions, papal bulls, canon law and the pronouncements of scholastic theology; many others in the sixteenth century—for example, numerous Christian humanists—were ready to go that far. But the church fathers, the ancient creeds and the ecumenical councils were in a different category: hoary antiquity and the reputation of veracity clung closely to them.

The role of the church fathers. Luther appreciated the church fathers; indeed, he quoted them profusely in his works. He summarized his entire program by urging, "Back to the Bible, to Augustine and to the church fathers!" The last two of these may surprise some readers who assume that *sola scriptura* would eliminate them. But Luther's extensive reading of Augustine's works had prepared him to turn to the Scriptures as the ultimate religious authority. He came to see Scripture as superior to patristic writings, to be sure. Even so, Luther repeatedly cited the church fathers—especially Augustine, but also Ambrose, Hilary, Cyprian, John Chrysostom and others—to document his teaching. They spoke with special significance for Luther, as witnesses to the gospel

---

[8]See the treatment of Luther's responses to and relationship with others in the Reformation movement in Mark U. Edwards Jr., *Luther and the False Brethren* (Stanford, Calif.: Stanford University Press, 1975).

and to a purer Christianity than what had developed during the medieval period since their time. Even so, he had learned from Augustine himself not to believe anyone, no matter how allegedly wise or saintly, unless his arguments were founded on Scripture well interpreted.[9]

Luther respected and honored the church fathers, but he did not accept them on par with Scripture: "All the holy fathers, when they speak apart from the Scriptures, are as fallible as anyone else."[10] For Luther, the most reliable and his favorite patristic author was Augustine, but even Augustine sometimes failed to measure up to Luther's exacting standards. For himself, Luther had no desire to differ with the fathers, "but I will take their books and go with them to Christ and his Word as the touchstone and compare the two."[11] Even so, the way Luther expresses this relationship is striking: "we Gentiles must not value the writings of our fathers as highly as Holy Scripture, *but as worth a little less.*"[12]

Luther did not simply disregard the church fathers; he read them with respect and honor. In his estimation, even if they were not infallible, their respect was well deserved. Patristic teaching, if endorsed by Scripture rightly interpreted, should be heeded. They stood as a significant religious authority, subordinate to the overarching and ultimate authority of Scripture. They served to guide in the right understanding of Christian teaching. Patristic works were unquestionably to be preferred to the private judgment of any individual.

This assessment of Luther is corroborated by his Wittenberg colleague, Philip Melanchthon. In response to the Sorbonne theological faculty's 1521 condemnation of Luther's teaching, Melanchthon offered a spirited and insightful defense of Luther. Significantly Melanchthon repeatedly emphasized that Luther stood in critical solidarity and agreement with the church fathers: "he has done nothing else than to

---

[9]A. Skevington Wood, *Captive to the Word—Martin Luther: Doctor of Sacred Scripture* (Grand Rapids: Eerdmans, 1969), pp. 32-33, 125-26.

[10]Cited from the introduction to Luther's 1521 *Avoiding the Doctrines of Men,* in Theodore G. Tappert, ed., *Selected Writings of Martin Luther, 1529-1546* (Philadelphia: Fortress, 1967), p. 204.

[11]This citation (from a work unavailable to me) is found in Wood, *Captive to the Word,* p. 122.

[12]Luther declares this in his *On the Councils and the Church, 1539,* in Tappert, *Selected Writings of Martin Luther,* p. 243 (emphasis added).

call us back to Scripture and also to the fathers who came the closest to the meaning of Scripture"; "in many other places the same things can be shown, that Luther agrees with the ancients"; "for the most part there is general agreement between Luther and the ancient theologians." Melanchthon went on to assert, against the scholastic theology promulgated by the Sorbonne faculty: "It is your theology, my masters, and not Luther's that disagrees with the fathers."[13] To be sure, Melanchthon was no disinterested observer in this regard, but he was himself quite expert in patristic literature. In his estimation, Luther did the better job of standing within the patristic tradition of faithful teaching. This says something significant about the church fathers and religious authority in Luther's teaching.

The role of the ancient creeds. Luther also had great reverence for the ancient creeds; indeed, he often linked Scripture and the creeds as religious authorities. For him, the creeds were rooted in scriptural teaching and embodied the faith held by the whole church since antiquity. They were not equal to or above Scripture; rather, they served to condense basic Christian teaching, especially concerning the person of Christ, the Savior. They responsibly served, then, to limit and guide what could legitimately be claimed as Christian teaching. They were unquestionably superior to the private judgment of any individual. In 1538 Luther wrote *The Three Symbols or Creeds of the Christian Faith*, where he dealt with the Apostles', Nicene and Athanasian creeds, in addition to the fourth-century *Te Deum Laudamus*.[14] This also is an important consideration for assessing Luther's understanding of religious authority.

The role of the ecumenical councils. In the next year, Luther turned to consider the ancient ecumenical councils in *On the Councils and the Church*.[15] This proved to be his most exacting historical treatise. In it he dealt with the first four ecumenical councils—Nicaea (325), Constantinople (381), Ephesus (431) and Chalcedon (451). According to the leading dogma-historian of the twentieth century, Jaroslav Pelikan,

---

[13]Philip Melanchthon, *Luther and the Paris Theologians, 1521* in Hill, *Melanchthon: Selected Writings*, pp. 74-76.

[14]Wood, *Captive to the Word*, pp. 124-25.

[15]Luther's *On the Councils and the Church, 1539* is available in Tappert, *Selected Writings of Martin Luther*, pp. 201-370.

this lengthy work is "the most significant single statement of his critical reverence toward the Catholic substance of tradition."[16]

Luther's careful study of the literature on the councils available to him led him to conclude that councils—no matter how broadly representative of the church, even ecumenical councils—had no authority to promulgate new teachings not based in Scripture. Significantly, he urged that they repudiated any such claim and resolutely focused on preserving the ancient faith passed down from the apostles. The new teachings were propounded by the ancient heresiarchs. These novelties, departures from the faith declared by the apostles, were condemned by the four ancient ecumenical councils.[17] Luther summarizes his treatment in telling fashion:

> These then are the four principal councils and the reasons they were held. The first, in Nicaea, defended the divinity of Christ against Arius; the second, in Constantinople, defended the divinity of the Holy Spirit against Macedonius; the third, in Ephesus, defended the one person of Christ against Nestorius; the fourth, in Chalcedon, defended the two natures in Christ against Eutyches. But no new articles of faith were thereby established.[18]

According to Luther, the councils focused on defending the historic Christian faith presented in Scripture, proclaimed in the gospel and handed down faithfully as the tradition from Christ and the apostles. These councils defended Christian doctrine against novelties introduced by false teachers. The councils thus were bound by the Scripture's teaching, which they sought to protect against perversion. They serve as a religious authority below the ultimate authority of Scripture,[19] to be sure, but they stand superior to any individual.

Summary of Luther on religious authority. Pulling all this together, it is clear that Scripture was the ultimate norm for faithful teaching for

---

[16]Jaroslav Pelikan, *Obedient Rebels: Catholic Substance and Protestant Principle in Luther's Reformation* (New York: Harper & Row, 1964), p. 56.

[17]Luther details these points specifically for the respective councils in *On the Councils:* Nicaea, pp. 246-47, 249-50, 278; Constantinople, pp. 278-29, 283, 284; Ephesus, pp. 285-88, 297; and Chalcedon, pp. 298-99, 310-11.

[18]Luther, *On the Councils*, p. 313.

[19]For a fuller treatment of this issue, see Pelikan, *Obedient Rebels*, pp. 54-76.

Luther. Even so, the church fathers served as a subordinate standard of faithful teaching for him. So did the ancient creeds. The same was true of the ecumenical councils' doctrinal decrees. Luther stood with them, and they stood with him—all under the ultimate authority of Scripture.

A distinction may help clarify this. For Luther, the Scripture was *norma normans*—the norm that norms. In comparison, the church fathers, the ancient creeds and the doctrinal decrees of the ecumenical councils were *normae normatae*—normed norms. As evaluated and approved from Scripture, they were authoritative. *Sola scriptura* thus meant for Luther that Scripture was the *only unquestioned* religious authority. It did not mean that Scripture was the *only* religious authority—as has often been assumed or misunderstood in subsequent Protestantism. As church fathers, ancient creeds and the ecumenical councils' doctrinal decrees passed the test of and thus stood faithfully with Scripture, they were regarded as subordinate religious authorities which must be respected and heeded.

The Other Reformers and *Sola Scriptura*

As we turn to consider the other Protestant Reformers' views on religious authority, it is worth remembering that they were all committed Christian humanists as they came to embrace the Reformation movement. They brought with them their love for ancient literature—Greek, Roman and especially Christian. They were all impressed by and drawn to the wisdom found in antiquity and what it offered to their day. This fed into their understanding of religious authority: like Luther, these Christian humanists turned Protestant Reformers recognized subordinate religious authority inhering in Christian antiquity. For them also, *sola scriptura* did not mean that Scripture was the *only* religious authority, but rather that it was the *only unquestioned* religious authority, beneath which other religious authorities from Christian antiquity were to be recognized.

Philip Melanchthon. The assessment we came to regarding Luther's viewpoint on religious authority is already reflected in Philip Melanchthon's 1519 *Baccalaureate Theses*. He presented these as the last step in receiving the initial degree in theology at the University of Wittenberg.

Luther declared his delight in the theses of his young and gifted colleague. Significantly Melanchthon's sixteenth and seventeenth theses stated: "It is not necessary for a Catholic to believe any other articles of faith than those to which Scripture is a witness. The *authority of councils* is *below* the authority of Scripture."[20] Already in 1519 the young reforming theologian Melanchthon recognized religious authorities subordinate to Scripture. Later in the year, in a letter to his friend Johannes Oecolampadius about the Leipzig Debate, Melanchthon urged, as Luther would twenty years subsequently, "This is clear: A council cannot institute new articles of faith." He went on to state, "He [Luther] maintained nothing with any greater reverence than that councils should possess their own authority."[21]

Even so, the authority of Scripture remained ultimate: "But the authority of councils is so dependent upon Scripture that it is not permissible to decree anything contrary to them." Melanchthon spelled out how these related: "We know that what has been set forth in the Canonical Books is the doctrine of the Holy Spirit. We do not know that what is decided by the councils is the doctrine of the Holy Spirit unless it agrees with Scripture."[22] Councils have genuine religious authority as subordinate to and assessed by the ultimate religious authority, which is Scripture alone.

We have already noted that in Melanchthon's defense of Luther against the Sorbonne theologians, he contended that Luther and the church fathers usually agree. The way Melanchthon wrote indicates his own endorsement of this positive relationship to patristic sources. Clearly expressing his own viewpoint on the question in regard to infant baptism, he noted that the practice "is approved by the ancient authors of the church," and he went on to list some of them—Origen, Augustine, Cyprian and Chrysostom. Then Melanchthon declared, "We must not differ with them without certain and clear testimonies of

---

[20]Philip Melanchthon, *Baccalaureate Theses* (Hill, *Melanchthon: Selected Writings*, p. 18, emphasis added). Melanchthon reaffirms this viewpoint in his 1520 letter to Dr. John Hess of Nuremberg: "A Catholic must believe Scripture alone, and the authority of Scripture is greater than that of the councils" (also in Hill, *Melanchthon: Selected Writings,* p. 49).
[21]Philip Melanchthon, *Letter on the Leipzig Debate* (Hill, *Melanchthon: Selected Writings*, p. 25).
[22]These citations are from Melanchthon's letter to Hess in Hill, pp. 52, 53.

Scripture."[23] This gives a straightforward, striking declaration that the church fathers are religious authorities which, unless they are undermined by Scripture itself, must be heeded and followed. If anything, this is even more forthright than Luther's declarations, though it squares with what we found with him.

In his 1521 *Loci communes*, Melanchthon stressed repeatedly the ultimate authority of Scripture, urging that the main purpose of the work was to promote familiarity with and reliance on Scripture: "There is nothing I should desire more, if possible, than that all Christians be occupied in greatest freedom with the divine Scriptures alone and be thoroughly transformed into their nature." For himself, he intended his work to focus on the Scriptures as the ultimate basis for the Christian faith: "Anyone is mistaken who seeks to ascertain the nature of Christianity from any source except canonical Scripture."[24] He explicitly contrasted that pure source with defiled streams issuing from some patristic authors.[25] Melanchthon subsequently gave evidence that councils can err, which led him to urge that they must be scrutinized and evaluated by Scripture.[26]

In all this, it might seem as if Melanchthon were backtracking from his previous endorsement of an authority inhering in councils and church fathers. But it must be remembered that his concern in the *Loci communes* is to set forth numerous particulars of Christian doctrine. For him, this task belongs to Scripture: "We give the list of only the most common fundamentals so that you may see on what a summary of Christian doctrine depends and why we must refer to Scripture *in preference to everything else*."[27] Whatever authority church fathers, councils and creeds might claim, they were not adequate to establish Christian doctrine: "Articles of faith must be judged simply in accordance with the canon of Holy Scripture. What has been put forth outside Scripture

---

[23]Philip Melanchthon, *Against the Anabaptists, 1528* (Hill, 103-122), p. 110.

[24]Philip Melanchthon, *Loci communes theologici*, in *Melanchthon and Bucer*, ed. Wilhelm Pauck, Library of Christian Classics (Philadelphia: Westminster Press, 1969), p. 19.

[25]The authors he mentions are Origen, Ambrose, Jerome and "with few exceptions the Greeks" (ibid., p. 19).

[26]He asks, "Since it is obvious that councils can err, why are their decrees not scrutinized in the light of Scripture?" (ibid., p. 65); see also his comments at p. 66.

[27]Ibid., p. 49 (emphasis added).

must not be held as an article of faith." Establishing doctrine, Melanchthon declares, belongs to "Scripture alone."[28]

But this did not mean for Melanchthon that one dared dispense with the church fathers, the ancient creeds and the ecumenical councils' doctrinal decrees. He produced the *Loci communes* to help readers become familiar with Scripture: "Surely we have no other aim than to aid in every way possible the studies of those who wish to be versed in the Scriptures,"[29] on which all doctrine must be based. In 1539 he produced another work, *The Church and the Authority of the Word,*[30] to show readers how to deal with and appropriate wisely the witness of the church fathers, the ancient creeds and the doctrinal decrees of the ecumenical councils. This later work is his fullest treatment of the question of religious authority. In it, Scripture remains the unquestioned, ultimate religious authority. This treatise is a masterful little patrology, showing how well the author knew Christian antiquity. Melanchthon offered learned, balanced, critical, but appreciative treatment of a host of church fathers and the first four ecumenical councils' discussions and doctrinal declarations.[31] In this work, Melanchthon continued to insist on the ultimate and unquestioned authority of Scripture, from which all doctrine must emanate and by which all other claimants to religious authority must be evaluated. While it would be impossible to present here a thorough examination of the variegated treatment Melanchthon offered in this treatise, a few points apropos to our considerations should be brought forward.

Melanchthon's stance on *sola scriptura* was well known by this time, and he continued to insist on it unflinchingly in this work. Even so, he

---

[28]Ibid., p. 63; cf. his further statement: "No doctrine and no articles are necessary for salvation except Scripture" (p. 65).

[29]Ibid., p. 20.

[30]Philip Melanchthon, *The Church and the Authority of the Word*, in Hill, *Melanchthon: Selected Writings*, pp. 131-86.

[31]Melanchthon gives particular attention to Irenaeus, Origen, Tertullian, Cyprian, Basil of Caesarea, Epiphanius, Augustine, Pseudo-Dionysius, Chrysostom, Ambrose, Jerome and Gregory I. He refers to but does not specifically discuss the roles also played by Gregory of Neo-Caesarea, Alexander of Alexandria, Cyril of Alexandria, Eustathius of Antioch and Peter of Alexandria. In his examination of the councils, he focuses on Nicaea, Constantinople, Ephesus, and Chalcedon, with further discussion of several regional synods and subsequent councils.

urged that "the authority of the ancients is not to be rashly destroyed,"[32] and since some claimed too much for tradition (intending his Roman opponents) and some far too little (mentioning Servetus as one example), Melanchthon had produced this treatise to show how to appreciate and appropriate that authority: "Therefore it is necessary to warn people in a correct manner about the authority of the church."[33] He offered three main points in this guidance, showing "what the church is, in what respect it must be heard, and how proved testimonies may be used."[34] Each of these points plays a significant role in the argument.

The church, according to Melanchthon, is "the assembly of true believers"[35] and "is to be found among those who retain the true doctrine of the Gospel";[36] it is "bound to the Word of God."[37] This church has stronger and weaker members, so it is not without flaws. These can even somewhat obscure the true doctrine it embraces. Even so, the continued embrace of the Word of God entails the continuity of the church through history. The consensus of the church down through time, submissive to the Word of God, is to be honored. Melanchthon boldly stated: "I always say that that assembly within which the word of God has been honored, and which is called the church, *must be heard*." In this regard, Melanchthon urged, "Let the authority of the Word divinely transmitted be *primary*"—it is noteworthy that he did not say "solitary." This historic attestation of the truth by the church leads us to the Word of God: "Let us, therefore, hear the church when she teaches and admonishes, but not believe merely because of the authority of the church. For the church does not originate articles of faith; she only teaches and admonishes." The two cooperate to teach us: "We see that this teaching has been handed down in the Word of God and the testimonies of the ancient church agree with it."[38]

In this way, Melanchthon insists, Protestants revere the doctrinal

---

[32]Melanchthon, *Church and the Authority of the Word*, p. 131.
[33]Ibid., p. 134.
[34]Ibid., pp. 134-35.
[35]Ibid., p. 135.
[36]Ibid., p. 136.
[37]Ibid., p. 137.
[38]Ibid., pp. 142 (emphases added), 144.

decrees of the ancient ecumenical councils, even though the various synodical statements on numerous moral or practical questions cannot all be endorsed.[39] In a similar fashion, after expanding on strengths and weaknesses to be discerned in numerous church fathers, Melanchthon summed up his approach by noting: "I have not collected these examples of the ancient authors . . . for the purpose of taking away any of *their deserved praise*" as witnesses to the faithful embrace and proclamation of Scripture's teaching. Rather, Melanchthon gloried in them under the overarching approval of Scripture: "It is agreed that we faithfully retain and guard the doctrine of the catholic church of Christ as it has been transmitted in the prophetic and apostolic scriptures and in the confessions—it is clear that we truly hold the same doctrine as the catholic church of Christ." For this, he noted, "I do not appeal to all the authors, but only to the better ones. . . . We follow the clear and sure judgment of divine Scripture. Nor let us forsake the confessions [ancient creeds]. . . . For there is no doubt that the kind of doctrine we profess expresses the very consensus of the catholic church of Christ, as indicated by the confessions, the saner synods, and the more learned fathers."[40] In defending the Protestant Reformation, Melanchthon laid claim to the best and strongest of the church tradition of teaching. For him, *sola scriptura* did not rule out but found itself buttressed by the subordinate religious authority of the church fathers, the ancient creeds and the doctrinal decrees of the ecumenical councils.

Significantly, Melanchthon roundly condemned a misappropriation of the Protestant slogan. He rejected all novel teachings, following the church fathers (and Luther) in this regard. Specifically, Melanchthon repudiated those who claim to follow Scripture but show no interest to stand with the consensus of the faithful through the ages, preferring to posit their new insights instead. He observes, "An example is Servetus when he opposes the church of all ages." This notorious heretic denied both the doctrine of the Trinity and the deity of the Son of God. Melanchthon stressed that Servetus urged that his own understandings

---

[39]Ibid., pp. 146-49.
[40]Ibid., pp. 176-77 (emphasis added); see similar comments at p. 185.

"be preferred to the decrees of the church"[41]—alluding to the Trinitarian and Christological decrees of the ecumenical councils. Melanchthon showed his disdain for this in striking fashion when he commented sarcastically that Servetus thus "proclaims magnificently the authority of the Scriptures."[42] For Melanchthon, a claim to the sole authority of Scripture which disregards the witness of the church through history is a perversion of the authority of Scripture.

For Melanchthon, that is not how *sola scriptura* works. Scripture is the only unquestioned religious authority. The written Word of God assesses all other claimants to religious authority, but once it approves them, they are subordinate religious authorities which must be honored and which guide the church down through time. For Melanchthon "the confessions, the saner synods and the more learned fathers" serve as subordinate religious authorities to guide in understanding the Christian faith and interpreting Scripture—which must always retain the final word as ultimate norm.

Ulrich Zwingli and Johannes Oecolampadius. The contributions of Zwingli and Oecolampadius on this question were cut short by their untimely deaths in 1531. Early in his career in his 1522 sermon, "Of the Clarity and Certainty of the Word of God,"[43] Zwingli held forth vigorously the authority of Scripture, interpreted under the guidance of the Holy Spirit and good reason. Not surprisingly at that point in the development of the Reformation, he did not advert to the question of the possible authority of the church fathers, the ancient creeds or the ecumenical councils.

Zwingli's colleague from Basel, Oecolampadius, also set forth Scripture as the authority for the Reformation's emphases. But he was a formidable patristic scholar who edited and published translations of works by the church fathers John Chrysostom, Gregory Nazianzen, Theodoret and Cyril of Alexandria. At the Colloquy of Marburg in 1529, he boldly claimed overwhelming patristic support for the

---

[41]Ibid., p. 134.
[42]Ibid., p. 142.
[43]Available in G. W. Bromiley, ed., *Zwingli and Bullinger*, Library of Christian Classics (Philadelphia: Westminster Press, 1953), pp. 59-95.

views he held about the Eucharist. Later that year, his friend Philip Melanchthon published a brief treatise attempting to respond, in part, to that claim.[44] Like Melanchthon, Oecolampadius wanted to stand with patristic teaching. The two knew each other well: fellow students earlier at the University of Tübingen, in 1519 Melanchthon had written about the Leipzig Debate to Oecolampadius. In the course of that report, as we have already seen, Melanchthon pointed out with approbation that Luther readily accorded authority to the doctrinal decrees of ecumenical councils. Melanchthon clearly expected that his friend shared that attitude.

In the Baden Disputation of 1526, the formidable debater John Eck exposed the underdeveloped perspectives of Zwingli and Oecolampadius on the authority of the ancient church. Two years later at the Berne Disputation of 1528, they showed that they had refined their views in ways that affirmed the absolute authority of Scripture while simultaneously recognizing and appropriating the authority of Christian antiquity—the church fathers, the ancient creeds and the ecumenical councils' doctrinal decrees—for the Reformation's teaching. In this development, they were assisted by Martin Bucer,[45] their associate from Strasbourg, who had devoted regular attention to this question.

In 1531, the last year of his life, Zwingli published *An Exposition of the Faith*[46] in which he did not deal directly with religious authority in any attempt to pull his perspectives together in a coordinated fashion. Even so, his treatment indicates his emphases. Scripture remained the ultimate religious authority, without any rivals. At the beginning of a section in which he set forth what he believed regarding Christ, Zwingli summarized the definition of faith promulgated at the Council of Chalcedon in 451. He did so without specifically mentioning that fourth ecumenical council by name; in his day, though, the ancient source

---

[44]Philip Melanchthon, *Letter on the Lord's Supper, 1529,* in Hill, *Melanchthon: Selected Writings,* pp. 125-28.

[45]See the painstaking analysis offered by Irena Backus in *The Disputation of Baden, 1526 and Berne, 1528: Neutralizing the Early Church* (see n. 3 above). The title she adopted for this study in its subsequent publication in German makes the relevance of her study evident for our investigations: *Das Prinzip "sola scriptura" und die Kirchenväter in den Disputationen von Baden (1526) und Bern (1528)* (Zürich: Theologischer Verlag, 1997).

[46]Available in Bromiley, *Zwingli and Bullinger,* pp. 245-79.

would have been immediately recognized. As he continued, he pointed out his agreement with what "St. Athanasius taught."[47] Shortly thereafter, he referred with approbation to the teaching of "the holy Fathers" regarding the significance of Christ's resurrection.[48] Throughout this exposition, the Zurich Reformer followed the outlines of the Apostles' Creed, which he clearly accepted as authoritative.[49] He specifically cited "that pillar of theologians, Augustine" for his teaching;[50] subsequently, he referred with approval to what Irenaeus and Gregory Nazianzen had written.[51] It is striking that in defending what he and his colleagues had taught, he affirmed: "We never taught a single word that we have not taken from Holy Scripture or the Fathers."[52] While Scripture was the sole unquestioned religious authority, it was not solitary: the church fathers served as a subsidiary authority. With the way he appropriated the Apostles' Creed and the doctrinal decree of the Council of Chalcedon, it is clear that he also saw them as religious authorities—subordinate to Scripture, indeed, but authorities for all that.

A careful study has shown that Zwingli collected, carefully read and regularly cited several church fathers. These include Irenaeus of Lyons, Origen, Tertullian, Cyprian, Lactantius, Athanasius, Hilary of Poitiers, Basil of Caesarea, Gregory Nazianzen, Ambrose, Cyril of Alexandria, John Chrysostom, Jerome, Augustine, Gregory the Great and John of Damascus.[53] The study concludes strikingly, "There is no doubt that . . . Zwingli read the Bible through the grid of patristic exegesis."[54] This led the Zurich Reformer to a perspective on religious authority in which "a tacit hierarchy of sacred texts is established with the Bible at the top broadening out into a pyramid of patristic evidence, indispensable in its turn for construction of a Biblical theology."[55] For Ulrich

---

[47]Zwingli, *Exposition of the Faith*, p. 251.
[48]Ibid., p. 253.
[49]Ibid., pp. 251-53.
[50]Ibid., p. 255.
[51]Ibid., p. 276.
[52]Ibid., p. 256.
[53]Irena Backus, "Ulrich Zwingli, Martin Bucer and the Church Fathers," in *The Reception of the Church Fathers in the West: From the Carolingians to the Maurists*, ed. Irena Backus, 2 vols. (Leiden: Brill, 2001), 2:627-660; see esp. pp. 630-39.
[54]Ibid., p. 639.
[55]Ibid., p. 644.

Zwingli, *sola scriptura* meant that only Scripture is unquestioned as a religious authority, but beneath it stand the subordinate religious authorities of the church fathers, the ancient creeds and the doctrinal decrees of the ecumenical councils.

Martin Bucer. Before he was even received among the clergy of Strasbourg, Bucer[56] responded to the request of the city council for a defense of the Reformation movement. He began this document of late 1523 with a forthright assertion of the ultimate authority of Scripture as the chief point of the movement. For Bucer, Scripture came from God, with divine authority; all other writings came only from human beings. The chasm between the value of the two was enormous, Bucer affirmed. He argued that this offered no slight to the church fathers, though, since they themselves urged that only what squared with Scripture should be believed. The sole supremacy of Scripture is clearly paramount in Bucer's view. It is worth noting that, even so, the church fathers lined up with what Bucer urged the nascent Reformation movement held.

Over the following years, Bucer continued to insist on *sola scriptura* and to rely on patristic deference to Scripture as witness to that point. Beyond that, he came to emphasize the antiquity shared by Scripture and patristic works. This brought them together much more closely. What had been a chasm in his early argument closed considerably over ensuing years as Bucer thought through the significance of that mutual antiquity. His ongoing study of the church fathers led him to affirm a patristic consensus which closely correlated with the Reformers' emphases.

Bucer proceeded, as a pastor-theologian who stressed the ultimate authority of Scripture, to produce commentaries on Scripture itself. In

---

[56]Helpful works on Bucer's perspectives on religious authority include the item previously noted by Irena Backus, "Ulrich Zwingli, Martin Bucer and the Church Fathers"; also Irena Backus, "Martin Bucer and the Patristic Tradition," in *Martin Bucer and Sixteenth Century Europe: Actes du colloque de Strasbourg (28-31 août 1991)*, ed. Christian Krieger and Marc Lienhard, 2 vols. (Leiden: Brill, 1993), 1:55-69; and David F. Wright, "Martin Bucer 1491-1551: Ecumenical Theologian," in *Common Places of Martin Bucer*, trans. and ed. D. F. Wright, Courtenay Library of Reformation Classics (Appleford, U.K.: Sutton Courtenay, 1972), pp. 17-71. As a trained Bucer scholar, I have also pursued investigations into Bucer and the church fathers, the results of which are not yet published but are drawn on for this treatment.

them, the role played by the church fathers progressively increased. In his 1529 commentary on the Psalms, he regularly cited the church fathers as authorization for Protestant understandings of Scripture and its teachings. In his 1530 commentary on the four Gospels (the second edition of this work), he urged that the church fathers should serve as guides for the exposition and understanding of Scripture. In his 1536 commentary on Romans, he openly acknowledged the authority of the ancient church; it was subordinate to Scripture, indeed, but it was nonetheless authoritative. In the introductory material to the commentary, he indicated that he deferred to patristic views as he expounded Scripture. This was evident in the way he organized his commentary: the exposition was usually divided into four parts, the last of which he entitled *Patres*—church fathers—where he summarized, compared and commented on several church fathers' expositions.

By 1530, when Bucer criticized his Roman opponents, it had become commonplace for him to assert that they did not stand, despite their claims, with the church fathers. Rather, Bucer averred, the church fathers stood with the Protestants. He was so convinced of this that it became a mark of his theological style of argument simply to correlate Scripture and the church fathers as religious authorities. Scripture remained the ultimate norm, but the church fathers showed how it should be interpreted and understood. So Bucer appealed, in various wordings, to "apostolic Scripture *and* the church fathers."[57]

In the midst of all his other endeavors as pastor, theologian and diplomat, Bucer also managed to find time to become conversant with the ecumenical councils and ancient imperial law. In his deference to Christian antiquity he came to embrace them both, as well as the ancient creeds. Thus the whole package of Christian antiquity—as examined and approved by Scripture as the ultimate religious authority—was authoritative for Bucer. In this regard, one can indeed recognize the predilection for antiquity of his humanist background, but he appropriated

---

[57]In a treatment on two other leading Reformers, Wilhelm Pauck observed, "Butzer . . . placed the tradition of antiquity next to the Bible and, in this connection, emphasized . . . the normative character of the doctrines of the Fathers" ("Luther and Melanchthon," in *Luther and Melanchthon,* ed. Vilmos Vajta [Philadelphia: Muhlenberg Press, 1961], p. 20).

this for his service in the Protestant movement to which he devoted his life and service.

In 1548 the victorious Emperor Charles V imposed the Augsburg Interim on the Protestant territories he had so recently defeated in the Smalcald War. The capitulations in doctrine and practice imposed were too much for Bucer, who accepted exile and thus turned away from his nearly quarter-century labors in Strasbourg. Welcomed to England, he gave his last few years to the service of the Reformation movement there. In 1549 he produced *The Restoration of Lawful Ordination for Ministers of the Church* as a contribution to it.[58] In this extended memorandum, he referred to the church fathers (several of them by name, but sometimes generally), the Christian emperors of old and the ancient creeds. In all this, he clearly indicated how important Christian antiquity was for him as a religious authority under Scripture. Bucer urged that, among other questions, a candidate for ordination should be asked "whether he firmly believes all the canonical Scriptures *acknowledged by the early Church* according to the canon of Irenaeus, Origen, Eusebius and Jerome"; "whether he *accepts the three Creeds, Apostles', Nicene and 'Athanasian', as scriptural* and therefore worthy of undoubting faith"; and "whether he holds that any works produced subsequent to the canonical Scriptures, of whatever content or origin, must be tested by the faithful and measured by the Scriptures themselves, and believed and accepted only if shown to be derived from the actual Scriptures: *yet nonetheless that the writings of the early saints and the orthodox Fathers are to be received with respect.*"[59] In these questions, Bucer's insights on religious authority all come to the fore.

John Calvin. As a second-generation Reformer, John Calvin was able to learn from his predecessors in the movement. With them, he held fervently to *sola scriptura*. He also embraced their recognition of a subordinate authority inhering in the ancient creeds, the doctrinal decrees of the ecumenical councils and the church fathers. Indeed Calvin read widely and became thoroughly conversant with the patristic writ-

---

[58]Martin Bucer, *The Restoration of Lawful Ordination for Ministers of the Church*, in Wright, *Common Places of Martin Bucer*, pp. 254-83.
[59]Bucer, *Restoration of Lawful Ordination*, p. 260 (emphases added).

ings, which he cited extensively in his works.

Already in the letter to King Francis which opened the 1536 *Institutes* (and all its subsequent editions), Calvin claimed that patristic teaching supported the Protestant Reformation, rather than the Roman Catholic Church. He appealed to Scripture as the ultimate religious norm, but he pointed out that the church fathers did so as well— thus skillfully claiming both Scripture and patristic witness for the Reformers' teaching. In this letter, Calvin appealed to church fathers some eighteen times; in his 1536 *Institutes*, Calvin offered nearly a hundred patristic citations. In all this, Calvin stood with what his predecessors had urged: Scripture is the sole norm for truth, with the church fathers as subsidiary authorities, subordinate to Scripture but witnessing to the proper understanding of that ultimate norm.[60]

At the Lausanne Disputation, held October 1-8, 1536, Calvin responded to a Roman opponent's challenge that the Reformers disregarded the church fathers. His impromptu response ably countered that charge by contending that the Reformers stood alongside the ancient worthies. In support of his assertion, he impressively offered numerous lengthy quotations of various church fathers apropos to the matters under discussion. Not surprisingly, he urged that the church fathers do not have authority equal to that of the Word of God.[61]

In subsequent editions of his *Institutes*, Calvin lengthened the work and offered more material. This included an increase in the number of patristic citations: in 1539 the number tripled to almost three hundred, and in the final edition of 1559 it increased to approximately eight hundred. Throughout this expansion, Calvin's stance on religious authority remained the same:[62] Scripture is the sole unquestioned authority, but the church fathers serve as a subordinate authority, setting the bounds for a proper understanding of the Word of God. It is interesting that the 1543 edition, strongly influenced by the three years Calvin had spent in Strasbourg in close association with Martin Bucer, is the most

---

[60]Johannes van Oort, "John Calvin and the Church Fathers," in Backus, *The Reception of the Church Fathers in the West*, 2:661-700, esp. pp. 664-71.

[61]See the treatment of the Lausanne Disputation in Anthony N. S. Lane, *John Calvin: Student of the Church Fathers* (Grand Rapids: Baker, 1999), pp. 25-28.

[62]Van Oort, "John Calvin and the Church Fathers," 2:671, 677.

patristic of these editions. Significantly, near the beginning of the work, the way Calvin expresses himself speaks volumes when he observes, "If the authority of the Ancient Church moves us in any way"[63]—clearly assuming that it should do so.

Even so, Calvin's commentaries manifest a different approach than those of his mentor Bucer. Where Bucer wrote for the learned, Calvin wrote for the layperson. Bucer sought to argue for the Reformation through expounding Scripture to theologians; Calvin endeavored to edify the members of the church. This difference resulted in a difference in patristic appeal. Bucer emphasized the fathers greatly in his commentaries; by contrast, Calvin only occasionally referred to them. This betokened no difference in their estimation of the significance of the church fathers; rather, it offered different strategies for reaching different audiences and meeting their needs.

Calvin also clearly embraced the ancient creeds. Indeed, he utilized the Apostles' Creed as the organizational structure for the final edition of his *Institutes*, significantly commenting that he had finally hit on the best way of presenting his material.[64] His approbation of the ecumenical councils was even more forthright: in the 1559 edition he explicitly endorsed the Christological declarations of the first (Nicaea), third and fourth (Ephesus and Chalcedon)[65] ecumenical councils. Turning again to this question later, as he discussed the authority of ecclesiastical councils, Calvin listed the first four ecumenical councils together and declared, "we willingly embrace and reverence as holy the early councils, such as those of Nicaea, Constantinople, Ephesus I, Chalcedon . . . which were concerned with refuting errors—in so far as they relate to the teachings of faith. For they contain nothing but the pure and genuine exposition of Scripture."[66] He leaves no doubt about his view of these ecumenical councils when he affirms, "I venerate them from my heart, and desire that they be honored by all."[67]

---

[63]Ibid., p. 676.
[64]John Calvin, *Institutes of the Christian Religion*, 2 vols., ed. John T. McNeill, trans. Ford Lewis Battles, Library of Christian Classics (Philadelphia: Westminster Press, 1960), 1:3.
[65]Ibid., 1.13.29; 2.14.4.
[66]Ibid., 4.9.8.
[67]Ibid., 4.9.1.

Calvin's understanding of religious authority can be summarized as follows: "*Firstly*, the Scriptures are for Calvin normative and the touchstone by which other writings are to be tested. *Secondly*, the fathers are seen as lesser authorities: they have an authority as those who lived in the 'primitive and purer Church' but their teaching is subject to that of scripture. Calvin treats them as authorities."[68] For Calvin, *sola scriptura* meant that the written Word of God is the ultimate religious authority, the only unquestioned one. The church fathers, the ancient creeds and the doctrinal decrees of the ecumenical councils serve as subsidiary religious authorities. Normed by Scripture, they serve as subordinate norms for right teaching. In Calvin's own words, "Although we hold that the Word of God alone lies beyond the sphere of our judgment, and that Fathers and Councils are of authority only in so far as they agree with the rule of the Word, we still give to Councils and Fathers such rank and honor as it is proper for them to hold, under Christ."[69]

CONCLUSION

Sola scriptura was the formal principle of the Reformation. The Reformers all held to it. But the Reformers did not intend by that phrase to claim that Scripture was the only religious authority; rather, they uniformly held it to be the supreme authority. It stood alone as the only unquestioned authority. The Reformers had tested the other claimants to religious authority and found them all wanting. Some failed miserably—pronouncements of the universities' scholastic theological faculties, papal declarations and canon law—and were discarded. But all the Protestant Reformers looked with respect and admiration on Christian antiquity—specifically on the church fathers, the ancient creeds and the doctrinal decrees of the ecumenical councils—and acknowledged a subordinate religious authority inhering in them.

The Protestant Reformers would not allow that any of these ancient worthies could initiate truth on their own: that was the prerogative of Scripture alone, which was the touchstone of all Christian teaching. If

---

[68]Lane, *John Calvin*, p. 29.
[69]John C. Olin, ed., *A Reformation Debate: Sadoleto's Letter to the Genevans and Calvin's Reply* (Grand Rapids: Baker, 1976), p. 92.

any church father defaulted in humility before a faithful exposition of scriptural truth, that writing or father could be dismissed from consideration. But in the main, the church fathers served as faithful witnesses of Christian teaching. The church fathers, with the ancient creeds which served to encapsulate Scripture's teaching on the one hand, and the ecumenical councils which defended that teaching against heresy and found ways to confess it responsibly on the other, constituted a subordinate religious authority for Christian teaching.

This did not mean that the Reformers expected all believers to be knowledgeable in Christian antiquity and its written monuments. Not surprisingly, the various Reformers differed in how extensively they read in patristic literature and referred to it in their own writings. Even so, they all acknowledged the church fathers, the ancient creeds and the doctrinal decrees of the ecumenical councils as subsidiary religious authorities, beneath and as approved by Scripture.

What this boils down to is that for the Protestant Reformers *sola scriptura* did not mean that the written Word of God is the *only* religious authority; rather, it is the *only unquestioned* religious authority. Scripture stands at the summit of religious authority with no rivals. Any other supposed or alleged religious authority is judged by it; most fail to measure up. The only ones that pass muster in this regard, and so the only ones in which a subordinate religious authority inheres, are the church fathers, the ancient creeds and the doctrinal decrees of the ecumenical councils. They are indeed subordinate to Scripture as religious authorities; but they are nevertheless authoritative. They must not be dispensed with or disregarded.

But what does this mean for contemporary Protestants in the twenty-first century? Does it require members of congregations to be knowledgeable in and able to discourse with insight on these ancient worthies? The Reformers did not expect that of the members of the congregations they served, so they would hardly expect it of others in subsequent centuries. But it does imply that, both in the sixteenth and twenty-first centuries, the faithful must stand with the church fathers, the ancient creeds and the doctrinal decrees of the ecumenical councils.

Must they do so consciously? That would hardly be likely, either then or now. But the Reformers did not envision a situation in which people could claim to be believers and yet stand in opposition to what the church fathers, the ancient creeds and the doctrinal decrees of the ecumenical councils had presented. This perspective of the Reformers implies the necessity of standing with the faithful of all ages—from Christian antiquity, through the Reformation era, to the twenty-first century—in embracing the truth set forth in Scripture. This calls us all to stand in the line of the faithful through the history of the church, whether or not we are aware of that line or of standing in it. In this regard, it would undoubtedly be well for contemporary Protestant churches to offer much more instruction in the history of the church than has been the usual pattern among them. For too long among many descendants of the sixteenth-century Reformers, *sola scriptura* has been misrepresented as obviating concern with anything other than Scripture as a religious authority. This cannot be defended from or charged to the Protestant Reformation.

Sola scriptura has also been misused by some to defend the right of private judgment, as if this assertion of the Reformation legitimized a freedom to come to one's own conclusions on religious matters. Seen in context, such a claim has little to do with the Reformation and far more to do with the freewheeling independence of post-Enlightenment individualism. The subjectivism entailed in such an approach was a reproach thrown in Luther's face. He did not welcome, approve or embrace it; rather, he repudiated it. He found in the clear teaching of Scripture—teaching set forth by the church fathers, the ancient creeds and the doctrinal decrees of the ecumenical councils—the assurance that he was not following his own private opinions. Too often in subsequent centuries, *sola scriptura* has been used as an excuse for a subjectivistic attitude which none of the Reformers allowed as responsible.

There is another common way in which the material principle of the Reformation has been abused in subsequent Protestantism. Whatever might be alleged by some televangelists or other preachers, the "Scripture alone" principle articulated during the Reformation does not legitimize any notion which someone might generate from passages in Scripture. For the Reformers, *sola scriptura* found its boundaries in the faithful teaching of the church fathers, the ancient creeds and the doctrinal decrees of the ecumenical councils. Exposition of Scripture which remained within those limits could be expansive and imaginative. However, to wander outside those limits and produce something "new" was for the Reformers not the mark of someone reading Scripture responsibly and using its authority rightly. How often, though, do Christians in the contemporary world hear about the allegedly scriptural "principle of seed faith" used to invite investment in a ministry? And what about "green prosperity prayer cloths" or the "health and wealth" gospel? None of these (nor similar aberrations) find any support whatsoever from the Protestant Reformation's material principle of *sola scriptura*.

It has been regrettable that the seminary (or Bible college) instruction which has prepared young men and women for ministry in Protestant churches has so often dealt summarily with Christian antiquity. The sixteenth-century Reformers would be astonished and aghast at this neglect. Even so, many of those who end up offering pastoral leadership in congregations and denominations have at best a scanty acquaintance with Christian antiquity. The Reformers might appreciate that we accord the Reformation era in which they labored so mightily such interest and attention, but they would be astonished at how little attention we pay in the contemporary Protestant world to the church fathers, the ancient creeds and the doctrinal decrees of the ecumenical councils.

In this regard, the last fifteen to twenty years have witnessed a notable and encouraging development. For the first time since the days of the Reformers themselves, Christian antiquity has become a "hot" topic. More and more graduates of Protestant seminaries are taking up post-graduate studies in patristics. The first generation of the twenty-first century counts more patristic scholars in the broader evangelical world than in any generation since the time of the Reformers themselves. This puts us in a way possibly to reclaim Christian antiquity— and in a much better space to appreciate what the Reformers intended in their assertion of *sola scriptura*.

- 7 -

How the Anabaptists Fit In

For the last few chapters, we have focused especially on the Protestant Reformation and how it unfolded. Important as those developments were in general (and especially for the Lutheran and Reformed traditions of Protestantism which issued from them), they were not the whole story of the Reformation in the sixteenth century. As earlier chapters indicated, concern for the renewal of society and the reform of Christianity as it was practiced by the beginning of the sixteenth century was widespread. That concern came to vigorous expression in other ways than just the Protestant movement. In this chapter we consider the reform initiatives which came to be known as *Anabaptist*.

In the twenty-first century, the designation *Anabaptist* has taken on a specific meaning: it is used to refer to Mennonites, Hutterites and the Amish—all descendants of their sixteenth-century forebears. Whatever differences these groups manifest from each other in the present, they show a number of similarities as over against contemporary society on the one hand, and Protestant denominations on the other. In the sixteenth century, though, *Anabaptist* was a "catch-all" designation for a much more diverse assortment of religious movements which were neither Roman Catholic nor Protestant. Reformation-era scholarship has expended considerable attention on this phenomenon over the last two or three generations. In addition to scholars from within the Anabaptist tradition itself, numerous others have become specialists in the "Radical Reformation," to use the designation adopted in a magisterial study of what was dubbed *Anabaptist* in the sixteenth century.[1] These investigations have exposed several ways of getting the Reformation wrong in dealing with the Anabaptists.

CONTEMPORARY MISUNDERSTANDINGS

Three of these misunderstandings have arisen from an uncritical embrace of the movement by contemporaries. Two of these approaches have gotten sixteenth-century Anabaptism wrong by assuming a commonality of viewpoint with it. The third builds on a mistaken assumption about the origins of Anabaptism.

Baptistic predecessors. Baptistic and other free church evangelicals who insist that baptism is only for those who can offer a conscious profession of Christian faith have often latched onto the Anabaptists as the presumptive forebears of that perspective. This is significantly mistaken, however. To be sure, Anabaptists practiced baptism of adults, rather than of infants. Indeed, *Anabaptism* means "baptism again"—a rebaptism which repudiated the baptism received as a child. However, while sixteenth-century Anabaptists rejected paedobaptism, they did not practice *believers'* baptism (as it is commonly known today); instead, they practiced *disciples'* baptism. The contemporary option of experiencing a conversion in one church service and being baptized in the next, a practice common in many such church circles, was foreign to sixteenth-century Anabaptists. They reserved baptism for committed disciples who had shown by their steadfast faith, self-discipline and wholehearted following of the ideals of the gathered community that they were genuine disciples.[2] Anabaptism in the sixteenth century prepared the way for further developments which eventually led to the

---

[1] George Huntston Williams, *The Radical Reformation* (Philadelphia: Westminster Press, 1962).

[2] As a further (and not insignificant) difference from contemporary baptistic and other free church emphases, Anabaptists showed little interest in the specific mode of baptism: immersion was certainly not the expectation.

perspectives held by Baptists,[3] but Anabaptism shared only some of those perspectives.

"Genuine" Anabaptism. Another contemporary pattern which gets sixteenth-century Anabaptism wrong has been articulated by some of the movement's descendants. In an understandable desire to trace their movement back to its beginnings, these people have isolated as "genuine" Anabaptism only those groups which manifested the same perspectives as are held in contemporary Anabaptist communities. There is unquestionably a continuity stretching from sixteenth-century Anabaptism to its twenty-first-century manifestation. But this approach overlooks the fact that in the sixteenth century the term *Anabaptist* incorporated a much broader range of emphases than it does in the present day. To be sure, most of these emphases fell away in subsequent generations, and *Anabaptist* received a much more restricted meaning. But during the Reformation era, Anabaptism was not nearly the tidy and well-defined movement which this pattern assumes: it included then far more than what the term includes in the present.

A single source. A third way some contemporaries have gotten the Anabaptists wrong has to do with the movement's beginning. The argument has boiled down to the question of *monogenesis* or *polygenesis*—that is, did Anabaptism begin in one place or many? A significant figure in past generations of Anabaptist scholarship[4] is closely associated with the idea that the movement broke out in Zurich through the endeavors of Conrad Grebel, Felix Manz and others to carry further the appropriate implications of the reformatory insights articulated in the city by Zwingli. According to this perspective, Zwingli balked at these further initiatives, but the others proceeded with them—resulting in the beginnings of Anabaptism. According to this monogenesis perspective, the movement then transplanted itself to the other areas after persecution broke out in Zurich, with these

---

[3]For the beginnings of what could be recognized as contemporary Baptist perspectives, one must wait until the seventeenth century in Britain.

[4]The Mennonite scholar Harold Bender set forth this perspective in several of his works; see especially his "The Anabaptist Vision," *Mennonite Quarterly Review* 31 (1944): 67-88. He also served as editor of this journal, in which this monogenesis perspective found frequent expression.

other areas thus becoming Anabaptist through influence from the original single source in Zurich.

However, numerous studies have shown that what was called Anabaptism in the sixteenth century broke out in several places, roughly contemporaneous with each other and without prior cross-fertilization. These places included not only Switzerland (with what had transpired in Zurich) but also South Germany, Austria, Moravia and the Netherlands.[5] This polygenesis viewpoint recognizes that the spokespersons of the different strains of this general phenomenon initially assumed greater coherence among their respective movements than would later prove to be the case. Indeed some of these would later fail to find their way into what would become the mainstream Anabaptism which issued into its twenty-first-century phenomenon, but as mentioned, in the sixteenth century *Anabaptism* was a generic term which included a considerably wider sweep of viewpoints than it would in subsequent centuries. Our concern is with Anabaptism in the Reformation era.

SIXTEENTH-CENTURY MISUNDERSTANDINGS

Misunderstandings abounded in the sixteenth century as to what this diverse entity which came to be known as Anabaptism was. These misunderstandings arose from the shock occasioned by the implications of their distinguishing mark, their Protestant and Roman Catholic opponents, and the sheer variety of those who claimed to be or were spoken of as Anabaptists.

A radical Reformation. The chaotic situation of the early years of the Reformation had led (among other things) to the Peasants' War of 1524-1525, where people untrained in Scripture or Christian doctrine drew conclusions from what they had heard of Reformation teaching, conclusions which sharply addressed problems those people had wrestled with. This issued in open rebellion, which was ruthlessly put down.

While this revolt cannot unproblematically be styled as an Anabap-

---

[5]A particularly significant treatment of this question is by James M. Stayer, Klaus Deppermann and Werner O. Packull, "From Monogenesis to Polygenesis: The Historical Discussion of Anabaptist Origins," *Mennonite Quarterly Review* 49 (1975): 83-122.

tist movement, it was undeniably a radical event, startling to contemporaries. Significantly it transpired at about the same time as Conrad Grebel and his friends in Zurich were pushing for further modifications in Christian lifestyle and ecclesiastical practice. Zwingli's refusal to take these steps did not keep them from taking them, nor from following that path yet further. This led Grebel and Felix Manz to request and receive baptism as adult disciples in January 1525, a radical act which eventually led to Manz being drowned in the Limmat River on orders of the Zurich city council. He was not the last of the "rebaptized" (i.e., "Anabaptists") to receive capital execution in this manner.

Undeniably this was an extreme response to what they had done.[6] The reaction indicates, though, how radical the step was which these Anabaptists had taken in the estimation of some responsible civic leaders in that day. To be sure, the Zurich council could appeal to provisions of ancient imperial law found in the Justinianic Code, which prohibited rebaptism—a proscription originally enacted against the Donatists in North Africa in the fourth and fifth centuries. But aside from the convenient legal precedent, what was it that led to such a drastic reaction? To a twenty-first-century person, who may well know people who received baptism as adults and profess baptistic beliefs, this reaction is "way over the top." How could such a sentence be passed in the sixteenth century?

It was possible because repudiation of the paedobaptism practiced universally within the church for many centuries with a call for an adult baptism constituted a radical (from *radix*, Latin for "root") attack on society, cutting at its roots as then constituted and accepted. In the expectations that flowed from the Constantinian settlement centuries earlier, membership of state and church corresponded. Baptism—administered to infants in almost all instances—initiated the baptizand not only as a member of the church but also as a citizen of the state. Societal expectations, legal enactments and interpersonal relationships all built on this foundation. So to deny that the paedobaptism of all was legitimate and to insist on a later baptism of only a

---

[6]On June 26, 2004, leaders of the Reformed Church in Zurich asked forgiveness from contemporary Mennonites for what had been done to their sixteenth-century forebears.

few could not be simply a personal decision with the goal of pursuing greater spiritual fidelity. It inevitably also entailed a stinging indictment of the Christian faith of the others and of the legitimacy of the civil state. To seek and receive rebaptism in the sixteenth century could not be just a private spiritual decision: it had momentous consequences, all of which were radical in their societal and ecclesiastical implications. In the instinctive estimation of sixteenth-century leaders, allowing Anabaptism would have been devastating to church, society and government as then constituted.

That the rebaptizing practice soon enough took root elsewhere only stoked fears of a conspiratorial underground network of revolutionaries. In a sixteenth-century perception, the Peasants' War and Anabaptism seemed to be of a piece—as were also the various communitarian, militant, mystical, spiritualist and apocalyptic streams which emerged in relatively short order in discrete areas.[7] These individuals and groups all quickly found themselves opposed by Protestant and Roman Catholic churches alike. Not surprisingly, as these outsiders heard of each other, they found a certain commonality in being the objects of opposition. What transpired among them was similar to what had happened with the early embrace of Luther's teachings, when hearers assumed a shared concern and perspective on what to do with him. These people initially identified with each other, readily adjudging that those with whom they were corresponding or had heard about were of the same ilk as they were. In short order, they were all dubbed *Anabaptist,* even if they had not adopted the expectation of a rebaptism (a requirement some of them never espoused); most of them came to accept the term as a self-designation. Even when some hesitated to identify themselves by it, though, Protestants and Roman Catholics readily discerned a commonality and used the designation for them all. In the sixteenth century, *Anabaptist* came to refer to a wide range of nontraditional approaches to Christian teaching and practice.

Protestant and Roman Catholic opposition. Both Protestant and Ro-

---

[7]See, e.g., the treatment by Werner O. Packull, *Mysticism and the Early South German-Austrian Anabaptist Movement 1525-1531*, Studies in Anabaptist and Mennonite History (Kitchener, Ontario: Herald, 1977).

man Catholic camps viewed these outsiders with considerable suspicion. Not surprisingly, the two camps also interpreted what they found in terms of their own preconceptions and approaches. At the time neither camp could step out of the presuppositions entailed with the Constantinian settlement: both saw the Anabaptists as dangerously subversive in intent and direction, sensing unsettling probable implications of the Anabaptist orientation but unable at the time to think through what those might turn out to be and evaluate them dispassionately.

Further, both camps instinctively interpreted the Anabaptists as if they were bound by the patterns of Protestantism or Roman Catholicism—that is, they viewed the Anabaptists through the lens both camps used, a lens focused on doctrinal articulation and coordinated thought. But such a focus was foreign to the early and diverse Anabaptist movement, which was not concerned with doctrinal patterns the way both Protestantism and Roman Catholicism proved to be. Rather, the various Anabaptist groups sought to step out of all such patterns and try to find a path to a simpler, more basic Christianity. As a recent scholar of Anabaptism has well put the point, Anabaptism was "neither Catholic nor Protestant."[8] It marched to the beat of a different drummer. Both Protestantism and Roman Catholicism misunderstood and misinterpreted Anabaptism.

Diversity among the Anabaptists. The diverse groups within Anabaptism also misunderstood and misinterpreted each other. The natural inclination was to suppose that the concerns which animated one's own group were the same for others in the movement. But as the groups and their leaders interacted with each other, they came to recognize significant differences of emphasis and focus. Reformation-era scholarship has explored what they discovered and has identified several significant groups within what was collectively known in the sixteenth century by the designation Anabaptist.

Swiss Anabaptism. One of these was the group which looked to the

---

[8]Walter Klaassen, *Anabaptism: Neither Catholic nor Protestant* (Waterloo, Ontario: Conrad Press, 1973). Although the author makes this point especially regarding those who would become mainstream Anabaptists, it applies as well to the others in the sixteenth century who also belonged to the amorphous movement.

emphases of Conrad Grebel, Felix Manz and their associates in Zurich and eventually came to be known as Swiss Anabaptism. Its adherents were determined to carry out a more radical reformation of Christian teaching and practice than Zwingli was willing to pursue in Zurich. In due course this led them to acknowledge the necessity of living as a separated body of believers. They sought a repristination of New Testament practice, with special attention to the particulars enjoined in the Sermon on the Mount.

Suspicious of ostensibly Christianized society, this group sought to find their way to a more rigorous, purposeful discipleship than they found possible in either Protestant or Roman Catholic circles. They repudiated oaths and the use of force, distancing themselves from expected societal norms and coming to view magistracy with suspicion—going so far as to declare that no genuine Christian could serve as a magistrate (since he would be expected to avail himself of force). They also embraced pacifism and espoused a basic biblicism—that is, a determination to rely only on the Scriptures, especially the New Testament, without patristic or medieval interpretive glosses. Their hermeneutical approach would become more explicit as they interacted with others who bore the name Anabaptist but whose use of Scripture was jarring to them.

It is intriguing that Swiss Anabaptism vigorously distanced itself not only from the incomplete Reformation (as they saw it) brought by Zwingli, but even more emphatically from their medieval background in the Roman communion. Even so, the orientation of Swiss Anabaptism looked much like the monasticism of medieval religious practice, with the "religious" pledged to a gathered society (a monastery or convent), practicing a rigorous self-discipline to attain greater Christlikeness than could be attained in society generally.[9]

Establishment Anabaptism. An intriguing, albeit short-lived, variety of Anabaptism sought to achieve a small-scale Constantinian settlement on Anabaptist bases. Balthasar Hubmaier led in this effort in

---

[9]For a stimulating treatment of this relationship, see Kenneth Ronald Davis, *Anabaptism and Asceticism: A Study in Intellectual Origins*, Studies in Anabaptist and Mennonite History (Kitchener, Ontario: Herald, 1974).

Waldshut, Germany. Hubmaiaer was the only Anabaptist leader who had received theological training, but it had been thorough: he had earned a doctorate in theology from the University of Ingolstadt under the tutelage of John Eck. He became an adherent of early reform movements and in due course his further reflection led him to a stance similar to that of the Swiss Anabaptists in most regards. A dramatic difference, though, was that he received support from the local rulers in Waldshut, with the result that Anabaptism became the religious commitment of the entire community. This attracted the attention of neighboring powers, however. Hubmaier was eventually captured and taken to Vienna, where he was tried, tortured and executed in 1528. With his arrest and the repression of the movement in the region, this variety of Anabaptism came to a sudden end.

Militant Anabaptism. While Swiss Anabaptism eschewed the use of force, other Anabaptists embraced it.[10] In early 1534, free elections in Münster, in northern Germany, resulted in an Anabaptist majority on the city council. They began to utilize their numbers to bring in legislation and enact policies embodying their religious perspectives. In due course, with the preponderance in the council, the legislation and policies became increasingly radicalized.

This led to the departure of many citizens, including some councilors, to other cities and territories, where they complained to Protestants and Roman Catholics alike about the Anabaptistic excesses toward which Münster increasingly was turning. The hands of the vigorously Anabaptist members of the city council were strengthened when news of these developments attracted more radical Anabaptists to the city, some of whom became leaders in the further developments there. Among them were Jan Matthijs and Jan van Leiden, Dutch Anabaptists who rose to prominence, the first as a new Gideon who would lead the Münsterite forces against their enemies, and the second as the self-proclaimed King David of the "New Jerusalem" (which he had assured the city's inhabitants would descend at Münster). Various bizarre enactments followed, including the acceptance of polygamy (building on

---

[10]The major exposition of this viewpoint is found in James M. Stayer, *Anabaptists and the Sword* (Lawrence, Kans.: Coronado Press, 1972).

Old Testament practices) and permission for public nudity (since sin had ostensibly been outlawed by civil enactments and the return to the Edenic paradise had supposedly already transpired).

Münster was becoming an outlandish oddity—and a perceived danger, which needed to be eliminated. Anabaptist preaching and prophecy there had led to the determination to bring in the coming messianic kingdom with the Münsterite sword. Minor skirmishes with neighboring cities heightened the tensions. Eventually nearby Protestant and Roman Catholic powers put away their mutual suspicion and joined forces against Münster, which was resoundingly defeated. Its leaders were captured and executed.

The Münsterite debacle brought an end to this variety of Anabaptism, but it left a lasting taste in the mouths of European rulers. For them, Anabaptist teachings were the prelude to revolutionary upheaval, and Anabaptists quickly came to experience persecution and heightened opposition. In the wake of Münster, under the leadership of Menno Simons, mainstream Anabaptism would come to follow the Swiss Anabaptist model, eschewing military force and embracing pacifism.

Communitarian Anabaptism. Another interesting variety of Anabaptism practiced community of possessions. This received some impetus during the Peasants' War of 1524-1525, but it remained a pattern followed by scattered groups of Anabaptists subsequently.[11] Basing itself on the practical necessity of providing for themselves as a separated community of committed believers on the one hand, and on the practice of the early church as witnessed in the New Testament (in Acts 2 and 4) on the other, these communitarian Anabaptists developed close-knit and tightly coordinated communities in which each was responsible for all. This variant became less common, however, as the sixteenth century passed. The group known today as the Hutterites is the only descendant of the early Anabaptists to maintain this lifestyle.[12]

Mystical Anabaptism. A further Anabaptist variant in the sixteenth

[11]See James M. Stayer, *The German Peasants' War and Anabaptist Community of Goods* (Montreal: McGill-Queen's University Press, 1991).
[12]For the early history of this group, see Werner O. Packull, *Hutterite Beginnings: Communitarian Experiments During the Reformation* (Baltimore: Johns Hopkins University Press, 1996).

century emphasized mystical connections with God. In such a relationship, the claim went, God communed with the believer who opened up himself or herself to the divine. In this connection, God might vouchsafe to the human being assurances of divine favor or insights into what would shortly transpire on earth. For some, the latter led to quietistic responses, waiting on God to accomplish whatever God had revealed. For others, such as Thomas Müntzer, these alleged revelations led to activism. He openly declared the coming judgment of God in his proclamations. In his notorious "Sermon before the Princes" of 1524, he famously denounced their slackness in following God's will and declaimed God's sure judgment on them.[13] He then threw himself vigorously into the Peasants' War.

This variety of Anabaptism could, at times, dispense with Scripture and sacrament, relying instead on mystical experience and revelations allegedly received from the Holy Spirit. Not surprisingly, this version of Anabaptism remained mostly elitist in nature: leaders received the revelations and hearers humbly listened and followed. Given this, its appeal remained restricted, since few actually experienced these mystical moments or insights.

Spiritualist Anabaptism. A closely related phenomenon was spiritualist Anabaptism. Usually quietistic in orientation, this movement sought and claimed to receive direct interventions from the divine Spirit. Hans Denck and Obbe Philips were notable in this group—which, owing to its emphases, remained largely a collection of isolated individuals, rather than leaders of gathered communities. A somewhat different emphasis was found with David Joris,[14] who nonetheless is to be counted among the spiritualist Anabaptists.

Apocalyptic Anabaptism. This group of Anabaptists included some of the movement's most flamboyant figures. They claimed to have received divine revelation detailing what would shortly happen in preparation for or as concomitant with the second coming of Christ. Such

---

[13]Available in English translation in George H. Williams and Angel M. Mergal, *Spiritual and Anabaptist Writers*, Library of Christian Classics (Philadelphia: Westminster Press, 1957), pp. 49-70.

[14]For a treatment of the life and influence of David Joris, see Gary K. Waite, *David Joris and Dutch Anabaptism 1524-1543* (Waterloo, Ontario: Wilfred Laurier University Press, 1990).

prophecies, of course, generated much fascination and, as prognosticated dates drew near, occasional frenzy. An early figure in this group was Hans Hut, who proclaimed the return of Christ would take place in 1528. Subsequently, Melchior Hofmann predicted that Christ would return at Strasbourg in 1533. True to his vision, he traveled to the city to warn it of its impending judgment. His preaching managed to get him arrested and consigned to the city jail, where he remained until he died, ten years past the date he had declared would be the divine denouement at Strasbourg. This variety of Anabaptism attracted much attention, of course; however, little of it was the sort of attention that would soften the views held about Anabaptists by their Protestant or Roman Catholic opponents.

CONCLUSION

Reformation-era scholarship has teased apart several variations within sixteenth-century Anabaptism. The list above should not be seen as all-inclusive; other varieties may well be identified as investigation into these outsiders proceeds. It should also not be thought that the categories above are hermetically sealed, as if in air-tight containers. Rather, these groups often bled into each other. After all, it took some time for these outsiders' initial assumption of agreement to give way to recognized differences, and various figures moved readily within more than one of these groups as their lives progressed.

But with all this, it is easy to see why the Anabaptists were so often misunderstood and misrepresented in the sixteenth century. They did not fit into the prevailing pattern found in the dominant religious groupings of Roman Catholicism or Protestantism. Further, the various Anabaptist groups only came late to discern the significant differences within the amorphous movement. This contributed to them all being tarred with the same brush, in reaction to the exotic and exaggerated excesses of the extremes. Moreover, the Anabaptists were significantly at odds with accepted societal norms and patterns, which had prevailed for centuries. This was the sort of stuff that fed into a revolutionary mythology about these "radicals" and viewed them as dangerous on numerous levels.

That such perceptions could be widely held of the forebears of today's Mennonites indicates how much has changed about the Anabaptists since the sixteenth century. That such perceptions were commonly
held at the time by otherwise reputable opponents in both the Protestant and the Roman Catholic camps indicates how different the situation was then than it is in the twenty-first century. That these have
taken so long to get sorted out and clarified, even with Reformation-
era scholarship expending so much energy on Anabaptism, indicates
that "getting the Reformation wrong" about the Anabaptists has been
both a historical and a historiographical pattern.

- 8 -

Reformation in Rome

AS THE SIXTEENTH CENTURY DAWNED, the leadership of the
church in Rome showed scant interest in any genuine response to the
longstanding call for *reformatio in capite et membris*. Even a vigorous exhortation to reform offered at the Fifth Lateran Council in 1512 and the
decrees enacted there stimulated no change of heart in this regard.[1]
Throughout the early years of the Reformation movement, papacy and
curia showed minimal interest in the issues raised in Germany and elsewhere, unless they affected the income received for the support of hierarchs, building projects and Renaissance art. Eventually, though, Rome
sensed the seriousness of what had happened and launched what has
come to be known as the Counter Reformation—"counter" because it
rose as a response to and reaction against the Protestant Reformation.

All this is true enough, but it is far from the whole story. It "gets the
Reformation wrong" to limit reform endeavors within the Roman obedience to what issued from the highest levels of the hierarchy, on the
one hand, or to reactions to Protestantism, on the other. This should
hardly be a surprise if we consider the situation. Given a church which

---

[1]See "Egidio da Viterbo's Address to the Fifth Lateran Council, May 3, 1512," in *Catholic Re-
form: From Cardinal Ximenes to the Council of Trent, 1495-1563*, ed. John C. Olin (New York:
Fordham University Press, 1990), pp. 47-60. Olin's work offers an excellent introduction to
Catholic reform and translations of several key works from it.

at the beginning of the sixteenth century encompassed virtually all of Europe outside the Ottoman Empire's holdings, and which had so long yearned for renewal, it should occasion no surprise to discover that movements for reform from within that church had taken root and were bearing substantial fruit, both before and apart from what transpired with the Protestant Reformation. That these initiatives were not sponsored by and did not look to the papacy or curia for encouragement is hardly startling, considering how thoroughly in the two preceding centuries both cardinals and popes had squandered the trust long invested in them by Western Christendom. Nor should it be a shock to discover that these endeavors continued after the Protestant Reformation began, and that they could continue largely unaffected by that significant movement. It should also generate little surprise to learn that the Counter Reformation, for all its obvious and intended reaction to Protestantism, pursued other reform concerns as well.

It has long been recognized that the late Middle Ages witnessed some renewal endeavors within the church. Significant leaders such as Jean Gerson, the chancellor of the University of Paris, and Nicholas of Cusa, a cardinal, had proposed ways and means to deal with the problems. However, these initiatives attracted only a handful of supporters and stimulated no noteworthy changes. A more populist approach appeared with the *devotio moderna* (the "modern devotion"), which sought to inculcate through teaching, writing, preaching and schooling a commitment to faithful Christian discipleship—with the hope that this might catch on broadly and eventually lead to a transformation of the church. Begun by Geert Groote (1340-1384), this movement found an outlet in a society known as "the Brothers of the Common Life," who set up numerous schools in which the ideal was kept alive and the goal was assured by careful rules to guide students in the narrow way of faithful discipleship. In due course, a spiritual classic arose from this movement, Thomas à Kempis's *The Imitation of Christ* (which would go on to become one of the best-selling books of all time). However, by the early sixteenth century, the modern devotion had slipped into stale legalisms which no longer stimulated or challenged faithful Christian life (according to Desiderius Erasmus, who as a youth attended the mother school of the movement in Deventer). Whatever their hopes and intentions, none of these endeavors brought about vital transformation of the church.

In the last two or three generations, Reformation scholarship has moved beyond these to investigate other reform initiatives within the Roman obedience prior to and contemporaneous with the Protestant Reformation. Such scholarship has shown that there was a serious and vibrant Catholic Reform[2] underway in different places, and with different emphases, well before Luther nailed his ninety-five theses to the Wittenberg church door, and that this reform was not absorbed or made irrelevant by what happened among the Protestants. Further, scholarship has more fully brought to light the serious change of heart in curial circles, which indeed led to a determined purpose to react vigorously to the Protestant Reformation, but whose reform initiatives were not limited to responses to Protestantism. Finally, the Roman obedience experienced *reformatio in capite et membris.*

Grasping this significant shift in understanding the reform that transpired within the Roman Catholic Church is essential if we are to avoid "getting the Reformation wrong." What happened in these regards not only shaped the Roman obedience but also transformed the Protestant movements as well (as we shall see in the next chapter). It complicates the story of the Reformation, but it makes that story even more intriguing.

CATHOLIC REFORM

Reformation scholarship has identified four strands of reform initiatives within the Roman obedience which antedated the Protestant Reformation's beginnings. These movements have come to be identified as "the Catholic Reformation" or, more simply, "Catholic Reform." Recent studies have investigated these movements and endeavored to discern their influence on the later reforms enacted at the Council of Trent.

---

[2]In addition to the volume by Olin mentioned above (n. 1), see an earlier version of the work in his *The Catholic Reformation: Savonarola to Ignatius Loyola—Reform in the Church 1495-1540* (New York: Harper & Row, 1969), which includes some documents not included in the later book.

The Northern Christian humanist movement. One of these is already familiar to us. Even so, it is worth noting that northern Christian humanism,[3] in its beginnings and for much of its history, sought reform from within the Roman obedience. While it is true, as we have seen, that large numbers of the younger Christian humanists turned to the Protestant Reformation, that was not the end of the movement. Most of the Christians humanists beyond thirty years of age remained in the Roman church, where they continued to pursue the renewal of piety, society, church life and doctrine. Their efforts bore some fruit in the reinvigoration of learning and doctrine, and continued up to the time of the Council of Trent (1545-1563), contributing to the reformation enacted there.

The Spanish movement. In the late fifteenth century, the kingdoms of Aragon and Castile were united through the marriage of Ferdinand and Isabella. The leading churchman of the realm was Francisco Jiménez de Cisneros, created a cardinal of the Roman church in 1507, who served as Isabella's confessor. The monarchs counted Jiménez a trusted advisor, and Isabella especially lent the increasing power of the state to support the reform endeavors he introduced into the church in Spain. With the explosion of wealth and influence for Spain, in the wake of its colonization of Latin and South America and the enormous amounts of gold and silver which poured into the Spanish coffers, what transpired in Spain caught the attention of much of Europe. In due course, the reform endeavors of Cardinal Jiménez engendered great respect.

Jiménez was convinced that a great deal of the problem with the clergy was that few of its members had received anything beyond a minimal preparation for their duties and that they had not been seriously held to account for their lifestyles. He determined to change this in the church as it existed in Spain. He founded the University of Alcalá chiefly for the training of priests. There they received a rigorous education, which included a strong presentation of scholastic theology, but Jiménez saw to it that the scholasticism inculcated there was pruned of its well-known predilection for delight in distinction and debate. He

---

[3]See the treatment in chapter two.

enhanced this doctrinal training by drawing on the linguistic and patristic endeavors of the Christian humanists. What he thus offered in Spain was the first serious attempt to assure a learned clergy in Western Christendom. This met a main concern which had long been expressed in the call for *reformatio in capite et membris*. The Spanish example would become a main plank in the platform of reform eventually adopted at the Council of Trent.

Beyond this, Jiménez made sure that all priests understood and pledged to live by the demand for celibacy. This emphasis marked the training offered to potential priests in the universities, and the cardinal saw to it through various means that those serving parishes throughout the realm lived by this requirement. With this, Jiménez directly countered one of the core criticisms in the anticlericalism which had arisen and been so vigorously expressed in Western Christendom. This became a basic element in the eventual reforms enacted throughout the whole of the Roman communion.

Furthermore, the cardinal rigorously cracked down on the hierarchy's abuse of finances. His own example in this regard was sterling, as he abided by the provisions of canon law and exercised ascetic discipline on his own use of funds. He insisted that those under his oversight—which included the entirety of the clergy in Spain, from archbishops down to the lowest levels of the ecclesiastical structure—live in ways that openly showed their submission to the provisions of canon law in all these regards. This too became essential to the reforms enacted within the Roman communion.

With the reform Cardinal Jiménez enacted in the church in Spain, he directly met and answered all the chief concerns expressed in the long-heard call for reform of the church from head to toe. In this fashion he breathed new life and vigor into Christian practice in Spain. Moreover, he so well addressed the problems people had long had with the church that when the Protestant Reformation eventually spread to the Iberian Peninsula, it found little welcome. Catholic Reform there had answered the concerns, and the further emphases of the Protestant movement had little appeal. Thus Spain proved to be the Western European country least receptive to Protestant teaching.

The Italian movement. In Italy a reform movement took quite a different direction. Home to over half of the more than seven hundred bishoprics in Western Christendom, Italy boasted numerous cities which were large by late medieval standards. Guilds had arisen in the Italian cities during the Middle Ages as a way of assuring not only quality and price controls for the artisans, but also the honorable burial of members and provision for the needs of their families in case of unexpected demise. This pattern was taken over and modified by the religious "confraternities" (literally, "brotherhoods") established during Renaissance-era Italy: they sought needed reform within Western Christendom by providing social services and promoting personal piety.[4] This all should have been furnished out of the diaconal funds and the efforts of the bishops, as had been the case in Christian antiquity; however, Renaissance-era Italy knew few such bishops. In the Italian movement of Catholic Reform, others stepped purposely into the gap.

The religious confraternities arose among laypeople, often of noble or successful merchant background. Recognizing the privileges they had received, the members of these confraternities sought to provide care for the poor, sick and destitute in their cities. The members of the confraternities met regularly for encouragement and edification; several confraternities became noted for their devotion to prayer. These included groups which came to be known as the Theatines and the Oratory of Divine Love, to mention only two.

Selflessly providing sustenance and care for the needy, these confraternities were soon accorded great respect for their endeavors and purposes. The confraternities' leaders and significant members became known for their piety and philanthropy. Some of them were appointed to high positions in the ecclesiastical hierarchy, so that they could pursue similar endeavors more readily in the name of the church. In due course, as the papacy itself began to turn seriously toward reform, some of the leading figures of the religious confraternities were appointed to

---

[4]See Nicholas Terpstra, *Lay Confraternities in Renaissance Bologna*, Cambridge Studies in Italian History and Culture (New York: Cambridge University Press, 1995); also helpful, although with a broader sweep, is Nicholas Terpstra, ed., *The Politics of Ritual Kinship: Confraternities and Social Order in Early Modern Europe*, Cambridge Studies in Italian History and Culture (New York: Cambridge University Press, 1999).

the cardinalate and played significant roles in the reform endeavors of the 1530s and 1540s.[5]

Apart from the specific concerns for social service and personal piety, one of the chief aims of these leaders was to seek an improvement in the way the more than 350 Italian bishops lived and served. Prior to his elevation to the cardinalate, the layman Gasparo Contarini wrote a thoughtful, respectful, but firm treatise addressing this problem, a work which exhorted them to live up to their calling.[6] In the reforms adopted by the Council of Trent, bishops received strict directives about their lives and the service they were to render, including provision for the needy and destitute. These emphases had arisen in the earlier Catholic Reform movement in Italy associated with the religious confraternities.

The rigorist movement. It should hardly be surprising that a rigorist group also arose seeking reform in the late medieval church. It seems that whenever churches go through a significant transition a group of people will surely arise within them urging a return to "the old-time religion," calling the church back to the "good old days," to the old practices and outlooks from before things got cluttered and off-track. The ostensible result of heeding such a summons would be a renewal of the church by returning to what had seemed to work so well in the past.

Such a group arose in the late fifteenth and early sixteenth centuries. It called Western Christendom back to the glory days of scholastic theology before disputatiousness and logical fractiousness took over, summoned the clergy to live up to its vow of celibacy, and urged the hierarchy to abide by the provisions of canon law and tend to spiritual duties. These rigorists urged a combination of scholastic rigor and punctilious observance of medieval practices as the way to straighten things out in the church. This meant that the rigorist movement had the difficult task of arguing that the medieval church's teachings and practices were really the best way to go—a hard sell, after the debacle of the fourteenth and fifteenth centuries! This was swimming upstream, but several valiant stalwarts for the Roman communion labored for this per-

---

[5]These included Gasparo Contarini, Gian Pietro Caraffa and Giovanni Morone.
[6]Gasparo Contarini, *The Office of a Bishop*, ed. and trans. John Patrick Donnelly (Milwaukee: Marquette University Press, 2002).

spective. Among them were Thomas Murner, Johannes Cochlaeus, Jacobus Latomus and John Eck.

Being the defenders of former practices put these men in the unenviable position of having both to defend Rome and to answer the burgeoning, multifaceted and chaotic early Reformation movement. These scholars thus served as the defenders of and apologists for the Roman church against the criticisms of Luther, Melanchthon, Zwingli, Bucer, Oecolampadius and others. While their task was daunting in both regards, their endeavors helped set the patterns followed later in the Council of Trent's confrontation with and response to Protestantism. In this way, they contributed to reform within the Roman communion, even if that reform did not come packaged in the way they thought it should have been.

COUNTER REFORMATION

The Roman Catholic Church ultimately developed a full-blown response to the long-standing call for *reformatio in capite et membris*. This response drew on the several strands of Catholic Reform we have considered. Beyond this, beginning in the mid-1530s, reform endeavors within the Roman communion received further impetus from three new developments. These were all coordinated into what has been called the Counter Reformation—a vigorous reaction to Protestantism, on the one hand, and a wide-ranging and thorough response to the call for a genuine renewal and transformation of the Roman communion, on the other.

The Society of Jesus. A cannonball shot which shattered the leg of Ignatius Loyola set him on a dramatically different path than he intended for his life.[7] The spiritual transformation which ensued attracted others to him. In due course, they took vows and received papal permission to establish another religious order, which they called "The Society of Jesus." The Jesuits (as they came to be commonly known) became one of the most powerful forces shaping the Counter Reformation.

---

[7]Several biographies and studies of Loyola appeared in or around 1991, the five-hundredth anniversary of his birth. A fine treatment is offered in Philip Caraman, *Ignatius Loyola: A Biography of the Founder of the Jesuits* (San Francisco: Harper & Row, 1990).

A young Spanish noble from an ancient aristocratic family, Loyola (1491-1556) entered into military service as many others from his background did, seeking renown for his exploits and bravery. During the siege of Pamplona in Navarre in May 1521, he received his injury and was taken to the castle of some close friends to recover. Bored and unable to move easily, he finally picked up and began reading some of the devotional literature his kindly and pious hostess had placed in his room. Eventually, he came to a sense of his unworthiness before God and of the greatness of the mercy in Christ which offered grace to sinners. This issued into a determination to become a faithful soldier in the army of Christ.

Loyola lived for a time as a hermit, spending his days in contemplation and prayer. Sensing that he should seek more than his own spiritual well-being, he journeyed to the Holy Land, to offer himself for God's service. The Franciscans there, though, did not welcome the unsolicited assistance of this unknown and untrained enthusiast. Loyola then returned to Spain to receive instruction. Sitting alongside much younger children to establish a better educational basis for himself, he went on to study at the universities of Alcalá, Salamanca and the Collège de Montaigu in Paris. The unmistakable and humble piety he exhibited attracted some younger fellow students to him, and they formed a small group which shared a commitment to devotion and the service of the church. In 1534 they collectively took the typical monastic vows of poverty, chastity and obedience—except that their vows specified absolute obedience to the pope as the leader of the church and Christ's representative on earth. Intending to travel to the Holy Land for mission endeavors, they encountered insurmountable obstacles, so eventually they went to Rome and sought to be received as a new religious order, ready to serve at the pope's behest.

Gasparo Cardinal Contarini became acquainted with them and, impressed, sponsored their application to become a religious order, which was granted by Pope Paul III in 1540. The Society of Jesus would become one of the reformed papacy's most powerful instruments in the Counter Reformation movement and in that regard would go vigorously on the offensive against the Protestants. However, the Jesuits had not been either spawned or developed as a response to Protestantism. This can be recognized from a simple datum: Loyola became the first superior general of the Society of Jesus and in that position engaged in much correspondence, but in all of the almost seven thousand letters included, Luther is mentioned only two or three times. Protestantism played no appreciable role in his understanding of what the Jesuits should be and do, at least not until the last years of his life.[8] While the Jesuits would in due course lead the charge against Protestantism, that was not their original intention. But they had taken a vow of absolute obedience to the pope, and one of the chief tasks the reformed papacy committed to them was to attack Protestantism and win back to the Roman communion as much of the territory which had turned Protestant as possible, and as many people as they could. (Beyond this, the papacy also sent out the members of the Society of Jesus on far-flung mission endeavors, both in the Americas and in the Far East. In this regard, they had huge impact and striking success in establishing Roman Catholicism in these areas.)

For all their dramatic numerical increase and dispersal throughout the known world, the Jesuits were unified by at least the annual practice of "doing" the *Spiritual Exercises*, a rigorous pattern of personal meditation and discipline authored by Ignatius Loyola. Every Jesuit worked through this month-long series of specific devotions every year. The exercises were designed to move the practitioner toward a disciplined activism in the service of Christ and his church and shape him for service. "Doing the exercises" indeed molded the Jesuits into the church's obedient soldiers, but it also promoted their initiative—the challenging and stimulating education insisted on for every Jesuit assured that.

In most of the religious orders established previously within the Roman communion, no particular educational requirements were specified. By stark contrast, the Jesuits insisted on a rigorous education, taking its would-be members through a lengthy "scholasticate" in which they received university education and a thorough training in scholastic theology (as enhanced by the northern Christian humanist emphasis

---

[8]Caraman, *Ignatius Loyola*, pp. 148, 170.

on linguistics and patristics). Those who completed this challenging program could only be accepted as members of the Society of Jesus if they showed during a further year of diligent supervision that they were resolutely committed to serving the church and its leader, the pope, without any mental reservation or hesitation whatsoever. This was unquestionably the most demanding initiation into a religious order the Roman communion had ever witnessed, but—like the old advertisement for the U.S. Marines—the Jesuits were "looking for a few good men." Even so, it became a mark of special distinction to be received into the Society of Jesus, and the Jesuits' numbers increased exponentially in the last half of the sixteenth century.

The Jesuits came along in their strength just as the early generations of Protestant Reformers were dying out: Luther passed on in 1546, Bucer in 1551, Melanchthon in 1560 and Calvin in 1564. The Society of Jesus won renown for the giftedness of its controversialists and for establishing the best schools available anywhere. Through these schools, the Jesuits trained students to become thoroughly committed Roman Catholics, inoculated against Protestant appeals. Invoking a wartime casuistry of "the end justifies the means," the Jesuits readily assured Protestant parents who expressed reservation about sending their children to these excellent educational institutions that the Jesuit instructors would not proselytize their children. From the perspective of the Jesuits, these Protestant parents were on the road to eternal damnation anyway. If lying to them was the only way to win their children back to the Roman Catholic Church, the only path toward salvation (as the Jesuits viewed it), then this was a legitimate deception. In many areas— southern Germany, Hungary and Poland—the deliberate deception was wildly successful: virtually all the Protestant children who entered the institutions had become staunchly committed Roman Catholics by the time they graduated. This was one of the main ways in which the Jesuits won back so many people and so much territory for the Roman Catholic Church from Protestantism.

With all this, plus the extensive missionary enterprises they undertook, the Jesuits proved to be remarkably fruitful in their service to the Roman communion. They were unquestionably a major element in the

Counter Reformation. That movement, though, could not have arisen
without the determined effort of a renewed papacy intent on effecting
drastic reform within the Roman communion.

A renewed papacy. In the first third of the sixteenth century, the
popes continued to walk the notorious paths emblazoned by the Renaissance papacy in prior generations. In 1534, though, Cardinal Ales-
sandro Farnese took office as Pope Paul III (d. 1549), owing to promises
made to German cardinals to call a council to seek the reform of the
church. As a step in that direction, in 1535 he elevated to the cardinalate several men—some laymen, others clergy—who were well known
for their piety and desire to see the church transformed. Among these
were Gasparo Contarini, Gian Pietro Caraffa and Giovanni Morone
(all from Italy); John Fisher and Reginald Pole (from England); and
Jacopo Sadoleto (from France). They served as the nucleus of a curia
which would see a dramatic change in papal policy toward reform.

In 1536 Paul III commissioned several of them, with the assistance
of other hierarchs and monastics[9] respected for their concern for ecclesiastical renewal, to produce an analysis of the state of the church. In
March 1537 the commission presented its report, *Consilium de emen-
danda ecclesia.*[10] The report was a stinging indictment of the malfeasance of preceding popes and the venality of curial practices, and it
called for a stringent refocusing of papal and hierarchical endeavors to
bring about salutary changes in the Roman communion. The report
was ill received by several of the cardinals—especially when it was
somehow leaked to the public, and even more so when it appeared soon
thereafter in published form with Martin Luther's marginal comments!
The pope could do little with the document at that time, but it would
eventually help shape what was decided at the Council of Trent.

Finally, after much delay, Pope Paul III called the long-awaited
council into existence. It began its meetings in December 1545 in the

---

[9]These included Gian Matteo Giberti, bishop of Verona; Gregorio Cortese, abbot of San Giorgio Maggiore monastery in Venice; Federigo Fregoso, bishop of Gubbio; Jerome Aleander,
papal nuncio and archbishop of Brindisi; and Tommaso Badia, a Dominican active in the
pope's service in Rome.

[10]Available in English (with an introduction to the document) in Olin, *Catholic Reformation*, pp.
192-97; and Olin, *Catholic Reform*, pp. 65-79.

northern Italian city of Trent. The Council of Trent met intermittently over the next eighteen years. Pope Paul III presided over its early developments. His successor, the ineffectual Julius III (r. 1549-1555), managed to keep the council going only during some of his pontificate. He was succeeded by a pope who was utterly determined on a drastic reform of Rome and the church headquartered there.

Gian Pietro Caraffa was elected pope and took the name Paul IV (r. 1555-1559). Raised with Contarini to the curial dignity in 1534, he proved quite different from his irenic counterpart. Caraffa had served as papal legate in Spain and had been impressed by the service offered there by the Inquisition. He determined to be as ruthless as necessary in purifying Rome as the Inquisition was in pursuing heretics.

Rome had a notorious reputation as a den of iniquity. What would later become known as "organized crime" flourished there. Brothels were abundant. Large numbers of monks who had been sent on official business to Rome had somehow managed not to find their way to their monastic houses in Rome, but yet managed to find the taverns and brothels—and too many were spotted in the gutters of the streets, sleeping off their intoxication. As a major city, the only international center for all of Western Christendom, Rome faced numerous challenges in all these regards, of course. But even though the papacy was not the ruler of the city, since Rome was the center of Western Christianity, the leaders of the church received scorching denunciation for what Rome had become. Paul IV took drastic measure to address all these problems. Within the short space of his four-year pontificate, he thoroughly transformed the city: the cesspool became virtually spotless.

Dispensing with the finer points of legalities behind which the leaders of organized crime had too long managed to hide, Pope Paul IV dispatched his gendarmes to dispatch the criminals. They were rounded up and disappeared, never to be seen again; the underlings in the criminal organizations soon went missing as well. Papal ruthlessness managed to expunge organized crime from the city.

Brothels had been set up in Rome as a way to protect the women who had become prostitutes against the gang sexual attacks favored by macho youths. With the practice at the time that unmarried daughters were often simply turned out onto the streets by their parents, many young women had virtually no choice except prostitution as a way to provide for themselves. Brothels had been set up as ways to protect these women from such attacks, assure that they were regularly checked for sexually transmitted diseases and place some limitation on prostitution. In due course, clergy of one level or another came to serve as chaplains or administrators at such institutions—resulting in predictable pillorying of the morals of the Roman clergy elsewhere in Western Europe.[11]

Pope Paul IV addressed the issue with a dramatic directive. As of a particular date, all the brothels would become convents. Any woman who decided against becoming a nun would simply be sent back out onto the streets to face whatever future might await her. Even though these women protested that they were not the most likely candidates for such a venture, the pope insisted—and all the brothels in Rome closed.

In regard to the wayward monks, the pope had a notice posted on the city's numerous kiosks (which served to make known public announcements) that all monks must report to their monastic house in the city by a particular date. The day after that date, the pope's gendarmes rounded up some two hundred monks who had not done so. They were faced with the choice between being sent to prison or being consigned to the galleys to row ships. The monks volunteered to go then to their monastic houses, but Paul IV resolutely rejected that idea, and they were all assigned either to prison or the galleys, depending on which they chose.

Pope Paul IV managed thus to purify the city of Rome in dramatic fashion. He intended to renew the Roman communion on his own initiative, since—like most of his predecessors—he feared that a council might get out of hand. So he did not call the Council of Trent back into session during his pontificate. Under his directives, Rome first issued in 1559 the *Index of Prohibited Books*, an official ecclesiastical list of banned books. He took an initial step toward dealing with the longstanding problem of absenteeism by expelling all the non-Italian bishops resident in Rome and sending them back to their dio-

---

[11]On this, see John Bossy, *Christianity in the West, 1400-1700* (New York: Oxford University Press, 1985), pp. 40-41.

ceses to serve there. Furthermore, he sternly reminded bishops of their duty to preach—and regularly did so himself. He enacted also various laws directed toward curbing the misuse of ecclesiastical finances. Further initiatives he may have intended to push the Roman communion toward ecclesiastical renewal were brought to an end by his death in 1559.

His successors turned from his ruthlessness while still vigorously pursuing the reform of the church. To achieve this, they managed to find a way to work through the Council of Trent while still guiding its decisions. With great determination, they directed the Roman Catholic Church toward genuine renewal and reform. Under their guidance, the Council of Trent proclaimed the marching orders of a reinvigorated Roman Catholicism.

The Council of Trent. The Council of Trent played an enormous role in renewing the Roman Catholic Church, establishing what it would be for the next four centuries (until the Second Vatican Council, which began in 1963) and shaping what has come to be known as the Counter Reformation. It may be surprising, then, for readers to learn how much the papacy feared the council. In the preceding century, conciliarism had threatened to transform the government of the church dramatically, putting popes accountable to regularly held church councils. While conciliarism had come to an inglorious end, it nevertheless served as a reminder of what could happen if councils got out of hand. So, while preceding sixteenth-century popes had shrewdly neglected to call a council to deal with the clamor throughout Western Christendom for renewal of the church, even when the renewed papacy developed genuine determination to bring reform to pass the popes were cautious about the Council of Trent. Indeed, for all his resolute determination to straighten out the Roman communion, Pope Paul IV never called the Council of Trent into session throughout the entirety of his pontificate.

The Council of Trent met irregularly from 1545 to 1563. Actually, the council was in session for less than a third of that span of time: it met from 1545-1547, 1551-1552 and 1562-1563. The popes worked diligently behind the scenes to keep a firm hand controlling what took place. Among the ways they did so was by assuring that papal legates presided over all the sessions and by determining the composition of the groups which dealt with various questions. Ultimately one of the reform popes expressed satisfaction with the results of the council and endorsed the canons and decrees of the Council of Trent as binding on the entire Roman Catholic Church. The council dealt both with issues of reform within the Roman communion itself and with the challenge presented by Protestantism.

Reform initiatives encompassed several main concerns, all focused on the bishops and their oversight of the church. One of the strict requirements enacted at Trent was the obligation on bishops, and priests serving under their oversight, to reside in the places where they serve as clergy. The frequent complaint about absenteeism (which was already in violation of canon law) found a hearing and was dealt with summarily in a way that soon resulted in dramatic change in this regard. With this, a strict prohibition of "pluralism"—a practice forbidden in canon law but common in preceding centuries, in which a clergyman might hold more than one ecclesiastical office at the same time—followed apace. Further, Trent insisted that all priests and bishops fulfill all the obligations of their clerical office, including the duty to preach regularly. Bishops were directed to see to it that those under their oversight diligently fulfilled their clerical responsibilities.

To help assure their ability to do so, and to ensure a learned clergy, each bishop was strictly enjoined to establish a clergy-training institution in his diocese, at which candidates would receive a thorough training to prepare them for their priestly duties. This training included not only facility with the various services and rubrics they would be expected to administer, but also thorough training in a rejuvenated scholastic theology (in which Thomas Aquinas was held up as the model to follow). Moreover, the Council of Trent laid the responsibility for careful oversight of all that took place within the diocese squarely on the bishop, who was therefore to be sure to be engaged in those developments and direct them in proper paths.

At the insistence of the popes, the Council of Trent also dealt with doctrine. Whereas the medieval church had allowed a fair degree of latitude in viewpoints, the popes now wanted to nail down what was and was not acceptable teaching within the Roman communion. For this, the council did not enact a general description or package, but produced careful treatments of several doctrinal issues—significantly, each of them as direct responses to what had been taught within Protestantism. In each case, the Protestant teaching was set forth (with varying degrees of thoroughness and accuracy) and condemned;[12] a contrary position was vigorously presented as the doctrine of the Roman Catholic Church. Even so, Trent did not always decide between variations of what had been taught within the Roman communion in preceding generations: some flexibility remained within the overall pattern of Roman Catholic teaching, allowing for some variation within the limits of what was accepted as Roman Catholic doctrine.

The Council of Trent thus declared that the Vulgate (the Latin translation of the Scriptures in use in the Roman Catholic Church) was authoritative. Trent asserted that tradition is a religious authority parallel to Scripture. Against Protestantism, the council pronounced that there are seven sacraments. In that regard, Trent went on to declare that the mass is a true sacrifice. Also against Protestant teaching, the Council of Trent defined that justification is by faith plus good works, that it is a process, and that apart from a special revelation from God no one can know for sure before his demise that he is justified. This package of teaching became the standard for Roman Catholic doctrine.

The Council of Trent closed in 1563. It left to the papacy the task of revising some liturgical materials (the Breviary and the Missal) and of producing an official catechism. In June 1564 Pope Pius IV promulgated the conciliar enactments. The canons and decrees of the Council of Trent demarked Roman Catholicism then and for the next four centuries. Reform had finally come to Rome. Now Rome took the offensive against the Protestants.

---

[12]I read carefully through the canons and decrees of the Council of Trent a few years back and found myself, as a Protestant of Reformed background, consigned to eternal perdition 268 times.

- 9 -

Changing Direction

From the Reformation
to Protestant Scholasticism

JUST AS THE PROTESTANT REFORMATION'S main early leaders were passing from the European scene, Rome's Counter Reformation was gaining its strength. During the 1550s and 1560s, the papacy drew on the vigor of the Jesuits to challenge Protestant teaching with the canons and decrees of the Council of Trent. Rome went on the offensive at a time when Protestantism had lost its outstanding leaders and chief apologists, and the Protestants had diverged into competing Lutheran and Reformed camps. The Jesuits carried the attack to Lutherans and Reformed alike, sending Protestants of both stripes reeling back into defensive postures. Defending Protestantism was rendered more difficult by the conflict within it: the Lutheran and the Reformed camps each drew sharp lines excluding the other, attacked the other and claimed to be the ecclesiastical embodiment of genuine Christian truth.

The Jesuits articulated sophisticated defenses of Roman Catholic doctrine with their masterful use of a rejuvenated scholasticism. Lutheran and Reformed spokesmen needed to respond in kind, both to the Jesuits and to each other. Unlike the early stages of the Reformation, the Protestants were no longer setting the terms for the debate: the Jesuits had seized the initiative and dictated those terms. Lutherans and Reformed both ended up having to appropriate scholastic methodology to defend their perspectives and articulate their teachings. A three-way conflict ensued, fought with weapons of Jesuit choice: scholastic theological methodology and reliance on Aristotelian reason.

During this period the Lutheran and the Reformed streams of the Protestant Reformation sharply diverged from each other. Each fought not only with the resurgent Roman Catholic Church but with the other Protestant body. These intra-Protestant conflicts could be as vicious as anything that transpired between either Lutherans or Reformed and the Jesuits. Each of the three sides laid claim to the fullness of Christian truth for its distinctive perspectives and denied the parallel claims made by the other two. All three fought for supremacy, for victory for their own tradition. This made for a verbally violent epoch.

In Protestant circles, this period came to be known as the age of Protestant scholasticism. It proved to be a significant shift within Protestantism, as the Protestant scholastics sought further to articulate and defend what the Reformers had declared. But did Protestant scholasticism get the Reformation wrong? Opinions have been divided on this question.

ASSESSMENTS OF PROTESTANT SCHOLASTICISM

Conservative Protestants of both Lutheran and Reformed stripes have viewed Protestant scholasticism with great appreciation. For one thing, this period saw the development and articulation of the great systems of Lutheran and Reformed dogmatics—the imposing doctrinal systems presented by Johann Gerhard, Abraham Calovius and Johannes Andreas Quenstedt (among others) for Lutherans, and those by Johannes Wollebius, Gisbertus Voetius and Francis Turretin (also among others) for the Reformed. These magnificently synthesized presentations, with all their careful argument, refined inner connections, abundant appeal to Scripture and compellingly consequential logic, have served ever since as the standards for teaching in the conservative wings of both the major Protestant traditions.

Indeed, for nearly the whole period since the age of Protestant scholasticism itself, whenever an intrachurch renewal movement arose within Lutheran or Reformed circles, it returned to the polished, articulated, carefully constructed systems of its respective Protestant scholastic forebears. In both traditions, Protestant scholasticism served as the reorientation point for correcting the church's doctrine and practice, for a return to the "straight and narrow" of doctrinal faithfulness. In conservative Lutheran and Reformed circles alike, such a move was understood as a return to the faith of the Protestant Reformation— which was apprehended, understood and set forth according to the prototypes of Protestant scholasticism.

Significantly this pattern was interrupted by Protestants deliberately turning back to reconsider the sixteenth-century Reformers. German Protestantism especially engaged in a painful self-assessment in the waning days of World War I. As the four-hundredth anniversary of Luther nailing his theses on the Wittenberg church door drew near, some chastened German Protestant theologians turned a penetrating gaze back beyond Protestant scholasticism to the Protestant Reformers. Karl Barth, Emil Brunner and others sensed how badly German Protestantism had failed in its religious mission and saw hope for renewal, not in the teaching of the Protestant scholastics—as had always been the pattern up to that point—but in that of the Reformers themselves.

Within German Protestantism, liberal scholars had already turned far away from much of historic Christian teaching in general and from Protestant scholasticism in particular. Beyond this, dogma-historical scholars of the late nineteenth and early twentieth centuries, such as Adolf von Harnack and Reinhold Seeberg, had roundly criticized the sophisticated doctrinal systems of Protestant scholasticism as a departure from original Christian teaching. When a war-weary, mortified Protestantism looked for a reorientation point, it fastened on the Reformers instead of the Protestant scholastics. Those yearning thus for a renewal of Protestantism sensed a significant difference between the Reformers and their Protestant scholastic successors and sought to reclaim what the Reformers offered in their teaching.

The relevant point in this regard is not whether Barth and Brunner and their associates "got it right" in their assessment of the Reformers' perspectives. What is noteworthy is that they discerned a departure from the Reformers' teaching in what the Protestant scholastics taught—and vastly preferred the Reformers. The alleged chasm between Reformers and Protestant scholastics stretched through much subsequent twentieth-century scholarship on church history and on the Reformation; indeed it became a virtual default position in most such scholarship.

Not surprisingly, not all agreed. Conservative Protestant scholars have joined in the increased study of the Reformers themselves which has arisen in the aftermath of World War I. These scholars have continued largely to view the Reformers' teaching through the lenses of Protestant scholasticism and its polished, articulated doctrinal systems. In this approach, the Reformers are seen as providing the raw material which their Protestant scholastic successors refined into sophisticated doctrinal systems.

Several scholars in these circles have developed a more articulate response to the denigration of Protestant scholasticism, however. It is common for them to criticize the theoretical perspectives of those who allege the chasm, suggesting that this allegation arises especially from a particular worldview which necessitates the conclusion, rather than letting the data speak to the situation.[1] Beyond this, though, they repudiate some of the specific arguments set forth in criticism of alleged Protestant scholastic departures from the Reformers' teachings, arguing that no real difference arises from these changes. They urge that the Protestant scholastics presented the Reformers' teaching in a different idiom but not with a different sense. Whereas the Reformers spoke primarily to congregations, Protestant scholastics addressed students in classrooms. This entailed a different approach to the material but, ac-

---

[1]For a pointed presentation of such a perspective, see Carl F. Trueman and R. Scott Clark, "Introduction," in *Protestant Scholasticism: Essays in Reassessment*, ed. and trans. Carl R. Trueman and R. Scott Clark, Studies in Christian History and Thought (Waynesboro, Ga.: Paternoster, 1999), pp. xi-xix.

cording to these defenders of Protestant scholasticism, no real change in what was taught.[2]

As someone raised as a Christian believer but outside both the Lutheran and the Reformed traditions, I knew little of either the Reformers or the Protestant scholastics. In graduate studies, I first became acquainted with them both at approximately the same time. Drawn in due course into a conservative Reformed tradition, I imbibed the sense that the Reformers and the Protestant scholastics were "on the same page." Seminary training in such a tradition confirmed me in that assessment, and my initial explorations into the teaching of the Reformers took place within those borders. However, as I embarked on doctoral studies in the Reformers' teachings, I began discerning disconcerting differences between what the Reformers and their Protestant scholastic successors emphasized, did and taught. Further research in and teaching of church history and the history of early modern Europe, the late Middle Ages and eastern Europe have only strengthened this impression.

I am aware of the criticism some defenders of Protestant scholasticism direct against the theological or worldview assumptions of the critics of the movement.[3] I also repudiate those assumptions, but I agree that the critics of Protestant scholasticism are on to something here. I have genuine respect for the careful scholarship which has defended Protestant scholasticism from various unwarranted or ill-advised criticisms and has so ably asserted the value of the Protestant scholastic accomplishment.[4] Even so, I must demur from the consequent endorse-

---

[2]For a condensed assertion of this viewpoint, see ibid., pp. xvii-xviii, which undergirds the argument of another article in that volume: Richard A. Muller, "The Use and Abuse of a Document: Beza's *Tabula praedestinationis*, the Bolsec Controversy, and the Origins of Reformed Orthodoxy," pp. 33-61, esp. pp. 53-55, 60.

[3]For example, in their "Introduction," Trueman and Clark allege that such an assessment is shaped by post-Kantian theological predilections, liberal theology and Neo-Orthodoxy as articulated by Barth and Brunner, as exacerbated by an affirmation of the Enlightenment's turn from Aristotle (pp. xi-xiii).

[4]The preeminent name in this regard is Richard A. Muller. With the numerous books and hundreds of articles he has authored, he has done more than anyone else to rehabilitate Protestant scholasticism; his vigorous scholarship has stimulated and inspired many others to follow in his train. See, among others, Richard A. Muller, *After Calvin: Studies in the Development of a Theological Tradition*, Oxford Studies in Historical Theology (New York: Oxford University Press, 2003); *Christ and the Decree: Christology and Predestination in Reformed Theology from Calvin to*

ment of Protestant scholasticism as the Reformation continued simply on another footing. A methodological shift in "doing" theology un-questionably took place in the transition from the Reformation into the Protestant scholastic period. However, while most defenders of Protestant scholasticism interpret this shift as inconsequential for what was taught, I aver that it constituted such a serious change in direction that it amounted to a change in teaching. From my perspective, Protestant scholasticism was a significant shift from the Protestant Reformation. Indeed, I will boldly assert that Protestant scholasticism long ago and those who defend it today manage in that defense to "get the Reformation wrong." That assertion needs substantiation.

GOING SCHOLASTIC

Protestant scholasticism came along after the Protestant Reformation. Certain historical circumstances contributed to an adjustment of Protestant practice in this direction even during the lifetimes of the Reformers. Three of these circumstances are especially worthy of note, since they played major roles in the transition from one movement to the other.

Historical sequence does not in itself assure historical continuity, though. It is possible to appreciate the challenge each of these circumstances entailed for the Reformation without thereby assuming that any of them individually or that all of them together warrant the transition to scholastic theological methodology and Aristotelian reason as the way to present the Reformers' teaching. The problems with the claim that Protestant scholasticism is the Protestant Reformation presented in another mode cannot be exorcized that simply.

The Reformers' opposition to scholasticism. During the Protestant scholastic period, the defenders of Lutheran and of Reformed teaching adopted scholastic theological methodology to articulate doctrine. This ought to seem utterly anomalous on first examination, since the Reformers themselves had so vigorously excoriated scholastic theology. Both Lu-

---

Perkins (Grand Rapids: Baker, 1988); and *Post-Reformation Reformed Dogmatics*, 4 vols. (Grand Rapids: Baker, 1978-2003). For several others involved in this venture, see the list of contributors and their publications as noted in Trueman and Clark, *Protestant Scholasticism.*

ther and Calvin[5] reserved their hottest denunciations for scholastic theologians, denigrating them regularly and repeatedly as "sophists"—about as disparaging an academic dismissal as was then thinkable. The Reformers did not just reject the results of medieval scholastic teaching in particular doctrines (such as transubstantiation or the treasury of the merits of the saints), they rejected the methodology.

Luther was especially vehement in his disparagement of scholastic theology and its methodology. In 1517 he set forth ninety-seven theses in his *Disputation Against Scholastic Theology*. In this wide-ranging denunciation of scholastic teachings, Luther asserted, "It is an error to say that no man can become a theologian without Aristotle. This in opposition to common opinion. Indeed, no one can become a theologian unless he becomes one without Aristotle. . . . Briefly, the whole of Aristotle is to theology as darkness is to light. This in opposition to the scholastics."[6] In his 1521 response to the Roman theologian Jacobus Latomus, Luther declared, "I think I have sufficiently shown from their own writings that scholastic theology is nothing else than ignorance of the truth and a stumbling block in comparison with Scripture." Shortly afterward he counseled, "My advice has been that a young man avoid scholastic philosophy and theology like the very death of his soul." In assessment of both the great scholastic theologian Thomas Aquinas and the influence of Aristotle, Luther went on to aver, "Thomas wrote a great deal of heresy, and is responsible for the reign of Aristotle, the destroyer of godly doctrine."[7]

To be sure, as we have seen, this did not mean that Luther managed to expel all traces of scholastic approaches from his practice.[8] While he

---

[5]In the treatment in this chapter, I will focus on Luther and Calvin as the progenitors of the Lutheran and the Reformed traditions, respectively. I recognize that Calvin did not play the sort of central role in the latter that Luther did in the former: Heinrich Bullinger and others also influenced the development of the Reformed tradition. However, to be able to keep this treatment within reasonable bounds, I will refer to Calvin as stimulus for the Reformed tradition; however generalizing this may be, it is worth keeping in mind in this regard that the Reformed tradition has often been spoken of as "Calvinist," so there is warrant for the approach adopted here.

[6]Martin Luther, *Disputation Against Scholastic Theology*, in *Selected Writings of Martin Luther: 1517-1520*, ed. Theodore G. Tappert (Philadelphia: Fortress, 1967), p. 38.

[7]Martin Luther, *Against Latomus 1521*, in Tappert, *Selected Writings of Martin Luther: 1517-1520*, pp. 197-98.

[8]While Luther repudiated scholastic theological methodology, he nonetheless continued to

repudiated scholastic theologizing *per se*, he nonetheless manifested the disputatiousness it inculcated and the invective it cherished. As well, the integration of the whole of his teaching on justification *sola fide* followed the scholastic pattern. Nevertheless, he diligently guarded his teaching against scholastic reliance on reason. His assessment of the effects of Aristotelian reason, the foundation of scholastic methodology, on Christian teaching is well known. According to Luther, reason had given Christian teaching "the French pox" (i.e., syphilis) and Aristotle was the pimp who had arranged the tryst. A more pointed declaration of the scurrilous nature of scholastic methodology for teaching Christian doctrine could hardly be imagined. How is it, then, that Luther's would-be faithful followers could so readily turn again to what Luther excoriated as theological fornication?

In similar fashion, if not so earthy in expression, Calvin denounced scholastic theology as contemptible.[9] He resolutely repudiated the methodology of scholastic theology.[10] He disparaged the "babble" the scholastic theologians produced as "slime," "frivolous word battles" and "quibbling."[11] What they presented, Calvin declared, was "mere sophistry, and sophistry so twisted, involved, tortuous, and puzzling, that scholastic theology might well be described as a species of secret magic."[12] Calvin rejected the flights of fancy scholastic theology encouraged and the speculation it spawned. He disparaged its uncritical reliance on bare human reason as a tool to unlock the treasure chest of divine revelation. Even so, as with Luther, the circles that followed in Calvin's line turned to scholastic methodology as the chief way to ex-

---

utilize it himself in certain regards: on this, see D. V. N. Bagchi, "*Sic et Non*: Luther and Scholasticism," in Trueman and Clark, *Protestant Scholasticism*, pp. 3-15.

[9]For an excellent, nuanced summation of Calvin's attitude toward scholastic theological methodology, see David C. Steinmetz, "The Scholastic Calvin," in Trueman and Clark, *Protestant Scholasticism*, pp. 16-30.

[10]William J. Bouwsma expresses Calvin's response to scholastic theology accurately in stating: "[Calvin] despised what passed for systematic theology in his own time" (*John Calvin: A Sixteenth-Century Portrait* [New York: Oxford University Press, 1988], p. 5).

[11]These assessments are found, respectively, in John Calvin, *Institutes of the Christian Religion*, 2 vols., ed. John T. McNeill, trans. Ford Lewis Battles, Library of Christian Classics, vols. 20-21 (Philadelphia: Westminster Press, 1960): 1.17.2; 3.4.1; 3.12.1; 4.18.1 (where Calvin also excoriates their "crabbed subtleties").

[12]John C. Olin, ed., *John Calvin and Jacopo Sadoleto, A Reformation Debate: Sadoleto's Letter to the Genevans and Calvin's Reply* (1966; reprint, Grand Rapids: Baker, 1976), pp. 64-65.

pound Christian teaching. How was this possible?

Challenges facing the successors. For both camps, three consider-ations should be kept in mind. The first is that once the initial enthu-siasm for the Reformation had expended itself and the movement needed to be consolidated, to what pattern could one turn? The bold assertions that had worked with such startling success early in the Reformation movement needed careful articulation in order to be preserved for subsequent generations, to whom the Reformers' asser-tions were already well known. For this, only one system of thought lay at hand—that of Aristotle.

Second, the cautious process of adopting Aristotle had already be-gun during the Reformers' lifetimes; indeed, Philip Melanchthon had led the way in this. His diligent endeavors and marvelous success in rewriting virtually the entire university curriculum to inculcate a Prot-estant approach to learning led to his epithet *Praeceptor Germaniae*— "teacher of Germany." In the early 1520s, Melanchthon was as suspi-cious of Aristotle as Luther, but as the younger colleague set about his curricular revisions, he needed a system to structure and coordinate his productions, and the only available system was the logic of Aristotle. He broached this need with Luther, who allowed his trusted colleague some latitude in this regard. As Melanchthon continued with his en-deavors, he became more and more comfortable with Aristotle and even began utilizing Aristotelian patterns in later editions of his *Loci com-munes theologici*—his presentation of Protestant doctrinal teaching. Melanchthon's students imbibed considerable respect for Aristotelian thought, which prepared many of them—some of them as his defend-ers, some as his opponents—to take up the task of articulating and defending Luther's teaching via the scholastic method.

A similar pattern emerged in Geneva. Calvin finally managed to get the Genevan Academy established in 1559, but several of those he con-tacted were unable to accept an offer to become an instructor there. Theodore Beza had long taught Greek in the academy in Lausanne, but after tensions arose there in 1558, he had come to Geneva. Well known as a capable exegete and a gifted theologian, Beza offered much to the nascent Genevan academy. At Calvin's suggestion, Beza became professor of Greek; he was also appointed rector of the institution.[13] Beza was unusual among Calvin's associates in that he followed Aristotelian patterns of thought as a way of coordinating and articulating his understandings of the Reformation's emphases. While Calvin had no use for scholastic theology, he nonetheless worked closely with Beza over the next handful of years. On his death, Calvin left the academy in Beza's hands. Beza became one of the first Reformed scholastics. He used his expertise in Aristotelian logic to carry on his work as instructor at the Geneva Academy and, as part of that, articulated Reformed doctrine on scholastic bases.[14]

The third consideration to be kept in mind in puzzling out how scholastic methodology so quickly took root in the Protestant movements is what they were facing in the onslaught of the Jesuits, beginning already in the 1560s. Deeply committed to the doctrine articulated at the Council of Trent, the Jesuits were also skilled in scholastic theological methodology. Their schooling had trained them in the strongest traditions of scholasticism, a pattern of thought which had continued and been nurtured within the Roman communion since the thirteenth century. Well-versed in the intricacies of Aristotelian logic, the Jesuits had been trained to utilize it effectively in pressing home the claims of the Roman Catholic Church.

They set their sights on Protestants in both the Lutheran and the Reformed communities. With all the vigor of a young and vibrant movement (much like the situation with Luther and his colleagues in the early Protestant Reformation), the Jesuits went on the offensive and attacked. The Jesuit juggernaut was bearing down on the Lutherans

---

[13]Wulfert de Greef, *The Writings of John Calvin: An Introductory Guide*, expanded ed., trans. Lyle D. Bierma (Louisville: Westminster John Knox Press, 2008), pp. 36-38.

[14]In this regard, an interesting difference in assessment arises in two key defenders of Reformed scholasticism in their respective treatments of Beza's 1555 publication, *Tabula praedestinationis*. In Richard Muller's examination (cf. n. 2 above), he is at pains to dismiss criticisms of Beza's document and its "decree-execution" framework as indications of a turn from Calvin's treatment of the doctrine of predestination; however, Donald Sinnema's "God's Eternal Decree and Its Temporal Execution: The Role of This Distinction in Theodore Beza's Theology" in *Adaptations of Calvinism in Reformation Europe: Essays in Honour of Brian G. Armstrong*, ed. Mack P. Holt (Burlington, Vt.: Ashgate, 2007), pp. 55-78, demonstrated the significance of this distinction in many areas of Beza's writings, even in some not particularly or obviously related to the question, and points out how it departs from Calvin's approaches.

and the Reformed. The controversialists for Roman Catholicism had the momentum and pressed their advantage effectively. The Jesuits forthrightly confronted the Protestant spokesmen with sophisticated and polished scholastic arguments, demanding responses. To counter Roman Catholic claims and to defend their own perspectives (also against each other) the Lutherans and the Reformed alike found it necessary to develop answers and counterclaims which met their opponents squarely. To be able to answer and to argue the case for their own version of Protestant teaching forced both Lutherans and Reformed to become adept in Aristotelian reason and scholastic methodology.

In summary, we note that in both Wittenberg and Geneva the exigencies of carrying further the Reformers' perspectives entailed trusted associates introducing Aristotle as an aid for teaching. Despite the common opposition of Luther and Calvin, Aristotle found support and endorsement in the Reformers' enclaves. This shift also seemed necessary if the successors of the Protestant Reformers were going to respond effectively to the challenges brought by the Counter Reformation and the other Protestant tradition. The die had been cast: Protestantism became scholastic.

OTHER OPTIONS

But putting it this way suggests a certain historical inevitability to this transition. To be sure, it is the way the shift in doctrinal methodology transpired historically. But other options were available to these successors of the Protestant Reformers, options from the Reformers themselves. Two readily come to mind.

In the first place, Luther's way of restructuring doctrinal teaching could have been followed. If nothing else, he had found a way out of the scholastic methodological maze. His vigorous articulation of the perspectives to which he came, with everything related to justification *sola fide*, undeniably offered his successors another path than the scholastic one they chose. As we have seen, he did not thoroughly jettison all the trappings of scholastic theologizing, but he found another way to articulate his insights than that of scholastic *loci* and Aristotelian logic. As much of the abundant scholarship on Luther which poured out

around the five-hundredth anniversary of his birth (in 1983) has shown,
Luther's thought was intricately integrated in this fashion—a fashion
close enough to scholasticism that it might well have been effectively
used to counter the style of argument used by the Roman controversialists. If later scholars can recognize this prized pattern in Luther's
thought, surely his contemporaries—and especially those (who came to
be called *Gnesio-Lutherans*) who assayed to follow him punctiliously in
preference to Melanchthon—might well have perceived in Luther's
corpus another way to articulate their prized legacy than in the approach spawned by the associate of Luther whom they otherwise
spurned. But they did not.

Similarly the heirs of Calvin had in his own approach to doctrine
and Scripture another option than that of scholastic methodology and
Aristotelian reason. While Calvin did not try to be a systematic theologian, he nevertheless showed a way of integrating Christian doctrine
in the structure he adopted for the last edition of his *Institutes of the
Christian Religion* in 1559—and in this regard it is surely worth considering carefully that Calvin expressed satisfaction that he had finally
found the ideal way to present the Christian faith.[15] In following the
general pattern in the Apostles' Creed, Calvin presented Christian
doctrine via the biblical history of redemption: creation, fall, redemption and consummation. A thoughtful follower of Calvin might well
have appropriated this pattern for further setting forth Christian doctrine and articulating responses to Jesuit and Lutheran challenges. But
no one did.[16]

Adopting scholastic methodology was neither historically inevitable
nor necessary for the successors of the Protestant Reformers. Given all
the problems with scholasticism and Aristotelian logic which both Lu-

---

[15]In the prefatory letter, "John Calvin to the Reader," Calvin explicitly noted, "I was never satisfied until the work had been arranged in the order now set forth" (*Institutes*, p. 3); he believed
he had finally found the best way to present Christian doctrine with the structure adopted for
this final edition of the *Institutes*.

[16]It is striking that this pattern was reclaimed later, largely in response to perceived problems
with Reformed scholasticism, by Johannes Cocceius (1603-1669). (Citing Cocceius to this end
does not imply endorsement of all that he set forth as if it were simply Calvin's approach renewed; rather, it indicates that thoughtful successors of the Genevan Reformer could develop
quite a different approach than a scholastic one as a way to present Reformed teaching.)

ther and Calvin so unmistakably and vigorously expressed, it is striking that their successors chose to return to scholastic paths. To discern and articulate the possibilities enshrined in the doctrinal approaches of Luther and Calvin certainly would have entailed some painstaking examination and reflection, and responding to the Jesuits in another format than the scholastic fashion used by these Roman Catholic controversialists would have required sophisticated translation from one idiom of thought to another. But the most obvious approach—and let it be said, the easiest, given the considerations pointed out above—was to reclaim scholastic methodology and Aristotelian reason for the presentation and defense of the Reformers' teaching. But (to co-opt Robert Frost's poem) the path taken has made all the difference—a difference in what was taught and how it was heard.

Changes in Teaching

There is no question that the Protestant scholastics in both the Lutheran and the Reformed camps sought to remain faithful to the Reformers' teaching. These successors adopted scholastic theological methodology and Aristotelian reason as means to preserve and present Reformation doctrine more effectively, both in response to challenges from the Jesuits and the other Protestant camp and as argument for the ultimate validity of the Lutheran or the Reformed scholastic system. Even so, this shift in methodology led demonstrably and incontrovertibly to significant changes in the teaching as offered and received. In this way, Protestant scholasticism, whatever its intentions regarding faithfulness to the Reformers' teachings, "got the Reformation wrong." This can be shown in two related ways.

Fixation on logic. Both the Lutheran and the Reformed scholastics faced the hostile criticism of two opponents: the Jesuits and the other tradition of the Protestant Reformation. All three sides in this intellectual conflict laid out their own teaching and criticized their opponents via the canons of Aristotelian dialectic. The ancient Greek philosopher's passion for reason and logic took hold, not only in the Jesuits, but also in the Protestant scholastics, both Lutheran and Reformed.

The need to defend one's cherished doctrinal perspectives against criticism forced careful logical analysis of opposition arguments and precise answers. The desire to set forth the perspectives held in the Lutheran or Reformed camps called Protestant scholastics to utilize Aristotelian distinctions and terminology to optimal advantage in making the case for their respective systems of thought. This entailed a repackaging of Lutheran and Reformed teaching to comport with these needs. But that repackaging resulted in more than just a different presentation: it changed the content, sometimes in significant ways.

The allegation here is not simply that the Protestant scholastic treatments offered a different presentation of the Lutheran or the Reformed doctrinal perspectives which had been set forth by the Reformers. Clearly that was the case, which in itself need not be problematic—although it might have been, depending on how much ended up being changed and in what direction the change went. Without urging that all such changes were of a momentous nature, and without attempting to deal with the whole of Protestant scholastic teachings—a task beyond the limits of this chapter (and, indeed, of any single monograph)—it can be seen that the fixation on logic that ensued within Protestant scholasticism ended up seriously changing the Reformers' teaching in deleterious ways. One example from each of the Protestant scholastic traditions, taken from a significant theologian of the period and dealing with a major doctrinal issue, should serve to make the general point.

One of the outstanding Lutheran scholastics was Johann Gerhard (1582-1637). In Lutheran circles, it has often been said that Gerhard was the third in the line of great Lutheran theologians in which there is no fourth (with Martin Luther and Martin Chemnitz being the first two in that line). Gerhard unquestionably placed a significant imprint on Lutheran teaching with his labors in articulating and defending a Lutheran systematic doctrinal perspective.[17] Beyond that, he produced some profoundly moving devotional writing: his *Sacred Meditations*[18] is

---

[17]John Gerhard produced a massive treatment of Lutheran systematics in his *Loci theologici*, 9 vols. (1610-1622); indeed, according to Paul Tillich, "Johann Gerhard was the one who developed the classical system in Lutheran theology" (*A History of Christian Thought: From Its Judaic and Hellenistic Origins to Existentialism*, ed. Carl E. Braaten [New York: Simon and Schuster, 1968], p. 279).

[18]Johann Gerhard, *Gerhard's Sacred Meditations*, trans. C. W. Heisler (Philadelphia: Lutheran

a masterful and moving series of fifty-one meditations which manifest profound love for God and humility before him.

Whatever may be the case in that devotional masterpiece, in his systematic theological writing Gerhard operated as a Lutheran with scholastic methodology and utilized Aristotelian reason. In Aristotle's dialectics, terms play key roles. In that regard, the concept of "cause" is especially important, and Aristotle distinguishes a variety of such causes. Gerhard appropriated this Aristotelian pattern to set forth the incarnation of the Son of God. Gerhard taught that with regard to the incarnation, Mary is the *material* cause, the Holy Spirit is the *efficient* cause, human salvation is the *final* cause, and the miraculous conception of Jesus is the *instrumental* cause.[19] In strictly Aristotelian terms, this is all true, but it is a stretch to view this as an exposition of Christian truth. Rather, it is describing how to ratiocinate. The incarnation ends up being overwhelmed by Aristotelian distinctions.

Among the Reformed scholastics, Johannes Wollebius (1586-1629) was respected for his grasp of the whole of Reformed dogmatics and his ability to present it cogently and concisely. In setting forth his presentation of Reformed teaching, he dealt with the doctrine of justification. Calvin had offered a stirring presentation of the doctrine in his *Institutes*, setting forth this fundamental doctrine of the Protestant Reformation in a moving, winsome fashion.[20] Wollebius plunged into his treatment of justification by pointing out that it is God's gracious act to forgive sinners and declare them righteous, heirs of eternal life.[21] Wollebius then expounded the doctrine of justification in a series of propositions as follows:

> III. The *efficient cause* of justification, that is, the agent that does it, is the entire Holy Trinity. . . .
>
> IV. The *internal active cause* is pure grace, or free favor of God. . . .

Publication Society, 1896).

[19]Gerhard, *Loci theologici*, 1:495 (1885 reprint ed.); I am indebted for this reference to Otto W. Heick, *A History of Christian Thought*, 2 vols. (Philadelphia: Fortress, 1965), 1:482.

[20]Calvin dealt with justification at *Institutes* 3.11-14.

[21]Johannes Wollebius, *Compendium Theologiae Christianae*, in John W. Beardslee III, trans. and ed., *Reformed Dogmatics: Seventeenth-Century Reformed Theology through the Writings of Wollebius, Voetius, and Turretin* (Grand Rapids: Baker, 1965), p. 164.

V. The *external active cause* is Christ the God-man. Christ as the Son of God is *efficient cause* of justification together with the Father and the Holy Spirit, but since he is God-man and our mediator, he is the *external active cause* because he secures this gift for us by his merit.

VI. The *instrumental cause* is the word of the gospel. . . .

VII. For justification, *considered in its passive aspect*, with respect to the person who is justified, there is no cause except the *instrumental* one, faith.[22]

After three brief sections (VIII-X) expounding the significance of "faith *alone*," Wollebius returned to his pattern:

XI. The "*matter*" [of justification], *understood actively*, is the entire satisfaction of Christ. . . .

XII. Its "matter," *understood passively*, is man who is wretched in himself, but nevertheless chosen by God, called, and given faith.
. . .

XIII. Its *form, understood actively*, is the imputation of the entire satisfaction of Christ.[23]

It is a challenge to view this as an exposition of what Protestants believe about the doctrine of justification. In this treatment, justification seems little more than window dressing for technical distinctions from the Aristotelian canon about how to think appropriately.

Gerhard and Wollebius were contemporaries. Both stood relatively early in the Protestant scholastic period, which went on through the end of the seventeenth century. This indicates that the problems with the scholastic turn and the deference to Aristotle were not late-blooming weeds: they arose quickly and permeated Protestant scholastic teaching in doctrines which were anything but secondary concerns.

In this regard, it may be helpful to call to mind what a twentieth-century Canadian philosopher, Marshall McLuhan, proclaimed with

---

[22]Ibid., pp. 164-65 (emphases added); it should be noted that the ellipses indicate omissions only of occasional elucidating comments and citation of biblical proof texts.
[23]Ibid., p. 166 (emphases added).

the title of one of his books: *The Medium Is the Message.*[24] We need not explore the philosopher's full teaching on the topic, for the title makes the requisite point adequately for our purposes: the packaging becomes the content, as far as what the recipients hear or learn.[25] This surely seems to describe what we see in Gerhard and Wollebius, for their respective presentations have more to do with Aristotelian thought than they do with the doctrine ostensibly treated.

This can be seen from a different angle in a way that may be helpful. Many of us will have encountered a version of what the author of this book heard from his mother (a loving woman, but no philosopher) when she told her mouthy teenage son, "It's not what you say: it's how you say it." That pearl of wisdom can be applied in many ways, as I have found out through the course of my life. One of the ways is to recognize that even the same words can pass on quite different messages, depending on how the words are said. An "I love you" spoken softly, with a gentle look, communicates an unquestionably different message than when those same words are uttered with an edgy tone as a preface to a sharp criticism. In the latter case, the words may set a context, but they convey little genuine caring. *How* something is said, the *way* doctrine is presented, makes a huge difference in what is heard. Protestant scholasticism managed to communicate Aristotle well; it is questionable how effectively it served to pass on what the Reformers had taught.

Perhaps an analogy will serve well here. The Reformers and the Protestant scholastics offer two contrasting ways of learning Christian doctrine. We can compare this to the ways people can learn about frogs. One way is to watch frogs for hours on end, and the other is to dissect the frogs. The Reformers watched the frogs, and they kept doing so, repeatedly and at great length. The Protestant scholastics dissected the frogs and probably came to quicker conclusions about what could be said about the frogs; the frogs never jumped again, though.

Objectification of doctrine. The Protestant scholastics sought to

---

[24]Marshall McLuhan, *The Medium Is the Message* (New York: Random House, 1967).

[25]It is interesting in this regard that in the media-intense culture of the early twenty-first century, psychologists and educators regularly express concern about how the constant exposure to electronic communication may be changing the way young people process data—that is, how and what they think.

present the case for their particular tradition of doctrine, whether Lutheran or Reformed, in a way that should have been convincing and compelling to any fair-minded and clear-thinking individual. This entailed laying out that doctrine as clearly as possible. Protestant scholasticism in both Lutheran and Reformed camps was thus marked by the endeavor to achieve the objectification of the respective doctrinal viewpoints being presented. This also served to transform the Reformers' teaching.

The perceived need to lay out teaching clearly and effectively entailed objectifying the doctrine as much as possible. That is, the Protestant scholastics had to present their material so that it could be dealt with "out there" and be objectively assessed by those not (as yet, at least) committed to it. This also led to some changes from the emphases and teachings of the Reformers, whose views the Protestant scholastics hoped to present faithfully in a different mode. We can recognize this in the Protestant scholastic presentation of three key doctrines.

With regard to Scripture much can be said, for the Protestant scholastics in both the Lutheran and Reformed traditions developed the doctrine of Scripture to a great degree. However, this entailed a divergence from the Reformers' approach to Scripture. The Reformers had emphasized that Scripture was *revelation*—that God had revealed his mercy in Christ to the unworthy. Revelation is person-to-person: it is communication from one to another. That divine revelation culminates in the *incarnate Word*, in whom is found salvation (this was the heart of the Reformers' message). The *written Word* of revelation communicates God's wrath against sin, his provision for human salvation and the salvation in Christ, and the *proclaimed Word* is God's loving summons to faith in his mercy in Christ.

The Protestant scholastics found it necessary to treat Scripture in a manner that would allow its impact to be set "out there," objectively. In Protestant scholastic hands, the divine *revelation* which the Reformers emphasized came to be treated as divine *inspiration*—as an assurance that what is found in Scripture is objectively *true*, since it comes from God himself. The point of contrast here is not that the Reformers did not believe Scripture was inspired by God, but rather that revelation has to do with communication between persons (God and human beings), while inspiration focuses on the veracity of what is said. These need not be in conflict, but they are not the same. Scripture, for the Protestant scholastics, is "out there," objectively true, guaranteed as veracious because it came from God. They did not repudiate the communication entailed in revelation; it just became a secondary matter for them. In this fashion, Scripture is depersonalized; the personal connection essential to revelation is sidelined. This is certainly a different emphasis and approach than what the Reformers presented.

Similarly, the problem of sin is depersonalized. The Reformers certainly recognized that sin is an infraction of God's law and worthy of divine punishment. However, for the Reformers sin is *unfaithfulness* toward God and *estrangement* from him: indeed, in Scripture, sin is *always* failure to respond appropriately to God. However, the personal component of this makes setting forth objectively what sin is a bit messy, so the Protestant scholastics placed the emphasis elsewhere. For them, sin is a violation of divine law, which renders the offending sinner guilty. These two orientations are, obviously, not opposed to each other; however, they are unquestionably not the same.

The contrast appears also in treating of faith. Under Protestant scholasticism, faith was depersonalized to the acceptance of right doctrine—which could be objectively and convincingly laid out for others to see. For the Reformers, though, faith was first and foremost personal bonding to God—cleaving to him, assured of his loving embrace. Again, these two conceptions of faith need not exclude each other; the important issue is which one receives the chief place. To make the point, we might note that "putTING the emPHAsis on a differENT sylLABle" may well keep the intended message from the hearers. Perhaps the contrast can be better put by noting how the Reformers and the Protestant scholastics might well have sung a hymn popular in evangelical circles. With the hymn-writer, the Reformers would sing, "I know *whom* I have believed," while the Protestant scholastics would rewrite that line to sing, "I know *what* I have believed." And that makes a world of difference.

CONCLUSION

In the presentation in this chapter, I have tried to show that Protestant scholasticism proved to be a change in direction from the paths the Protestant Reformers had taken. The Protestant scholastics intended to be faithful to their forebears; they certainly did not purpose to change what the Reformers had taught. However, good intentions do not necessarily achieve desired goals. What transpired with the adoption of scholastic theological methodology and Aristotelian reason was a significant change in what the Reformers had taught. The Protestant scholastics in that regard "got the Reformation wrong." Those in subsequent centuries, down to the present, who have uncritically looked on the monuments of the Protestant scholastic period as the Reformers' teaching have also thus managed to "get the Reformation wrong."

None of what is presented in this chapter should be taken to imply that the Protestant scholastics taught error. Rather, the point is that despite their intentions they did not present the Reformers' teaching in another mode. The two movements—the Reformation of the Protestant Reformers, on the one hand, and Protestant scholasticism, on the other—faced different contexts, had different foci and brought different emphases. This led to differences in teaching— including what was taught, how it was taught and what was emphasized.

Unquestionably the Protestant scholastics strongly emphasized logic and reason. The Protestant Reformers were neither illogical nor irrational, but—given what they had seen with scholastic theological methodology and Aristotelian reason—they were much more suspicious of logic and reason than their Protestant scholastic successors were. During the period of Protestant scholasticism, logic and reason found increasing emphasis and served to shape what was understood to be true and how that truth was presented. Human reason took center stage, as the successors of the Reformers rushed to adopt scholastic theological methodology and Aristotelian reason. The Protestant scholastic period flourished until near the end of the seventeenth century.

It should not be thought churlish to point out that the intellectual movement which came on the European scene as Protestant scholasticism was fading from it was the Enlightenment. It has been common to

contrast Protestant scholasticism and the Enlightenment as polar op-
posites because of their undeniably antithetical views on the significance of Christian faith. But it is striking that the two otherwise so
opposing viewpoints nonetheless shared a common confidence in human reason. Perhaps, given what we have considered, it would be better
to think of the two movements less as avowed enemies from different
worlds than as estranged siblings.[26]

---

[26]It is evident from the treatment in this chapter that I have serious reservations about Protestant scholasticism's presentation of the Reformers' teachings. But the correlation of Protestant
scholasticism with the rationalism of the Enlightenment here is no unwarranted slap at the
movement. It should be noted that even the most ardent and capable defender of Protestant
scholasticism, Richard A. Muller, acknowledges the link between the later development of the
movement and the coming Enlightenment: see his *After Calvin*, pp. 78-80.

- 10 -

Was the Reformation a Success?

WAS THE REFORMATION A SUCCESS? That may seem like a strange query to some people. How could such a question be answered? What scale or measuring line or standard would one use to come up with a response? As a historical movement, it need not "succeed" (whatever that might mean): it just *was*.

As a historical movement for reform within the church, though, the question at least implies a doctrinal measuring line (or some other Christian standard) which might be employed to assess the Reformation's success (or lack of it). The sixteenth-century movement unquestionably sought to meet the fourteenth- and fifteenth-century clamor in Western Christendom for *reformatio in capite et membris*. How well the Reformation answered that call can be assessed to some degree— even if the particulars expected in such a renovation would not necessarily have been clear to or agreed on by all evaluators.

Within Protestant circles, many would likely respond that the Reformation surely succeeded in pointing anew to apostolic teaching. In that regard, they might well argue, the Reformation succeeded, since it called the church back to the standard it should follow. Beyond that, for many interested folk, the question makes sense since the sixteenth-

century movement led eventually to the establishment of the denomination of which they are now members: if nothing else, the Reformation was successful in that!

In this chapter we want to ask the question, "Was the Reformation a
success?" in ways that allow us to look at the Reformation as a sixteenth-
century phenomenon, not as a harbinger of twenty-first-century concerns and considerations (however important those may be in and of
themselves). We want to ask it in terms of what the Reformers themselves
thought they were doing: did they succeed in what they hoped to accomplish as this unwieldy movement got underway? We will also ask the
question in terms of what happened, not just what twenty-first-century
Protestants think may have happened. For that, we will need to go beyond the boundaries in time and space within which too many treatments and discussions of the Reformation restrict their attention and
look more broadly at what transpired. So we will look at the path the
Reformation took through the whole sixteenth century, not just the first
sixty years or so, and at what happened in eastern Europe. That will put
us in a position to answer this question better. Not doing so will surely
end up with our getting the Reformation wrong.

WHAT THE REFORMERS EXPECTED

If we ask what the various Reformers in the sixteenth century expected,
we come to a medley of answers. These depend, of course, on the situation faced by each Reformer (or group) and what he (or they) thought
should happen—under divine blessing, of course. The answers do not
coincide with each other all that well: indeed, sometimes those answers
are in conflict. Furthermore, the respective answers often do not square
with what subsequent heirs of the Reformation assume their denominational progenitors sought.

The Radical Reformation. Within the several streams of renewal
movements collectively styled the Radical Reformation,[1] various expectations arose as to what should transpire through their endeavors.
Many of them saw their task to be repristinating the experience of the

---

[1]This treatment will deal with the various groups presented in chapter seven; readers are advised
to consult that material as background on the groups discussed below.

church as reflected in the New Testament, complete with the persecution which pursued the infant church then. The various strands of the Radical Reformation might well argue among themselves as to who among them managed this repristination most faithfully. For example, the Hutterites could point to their renewal of the communitarian lifestyles evidenced in the earliest records of church life (Acts 2 and 4), or the Swiss Anabaptists could point to the reclaiming of baptism for faithful disciples as a New Testament practice which they recaptured.

However, establishment Anabaptism turned out to be a resounding failure. Militant Anabaptism also came to bloody defeat at Münster in 1535. Mystical Anabaptism and spiritualist Anabaptism may have found success for some individuals, but they led to no gathered communities which maintained the insights of whoever their founding leaders may have been. Apocalyptic Anabaptists attracted considerable attention and generated plenty of consternation, at least until the dates came and went which the spokesman had identified for the divine intervention that would usher in a new age. But the old age kept on going, so the apocalyptic Anabaptists soon lost all credibility; this was certainly the antithesis of success.

Whatever the particular expectations of each group, all of them could point to the persecution they endured at the hands of Roman Catholics, Lutherans and Reformed for their views. Most of the diverse members of the Radical Reformation expected this, based on the early church's experience. In this regard, the Anabaptists could claim to be "successful"—a dubious and painful success perhaps, but a success nonetheless in attaining their expectations.

Martin Luther. The question would find a very different answer if posed to Martin Luther. The Wittenberg Reformer wanted to proclaim the doctrine of justification by faith alone which had brought him such comfort after the years spent desperately but fruitlessly searching for peace with God. Luther was unquestionably successful in that endeavor: the whole of his teaching, as we have seen, grew out of and was integrated by his insights on justification *sola fide*. Moreover, since the other Protestant Reformers joined with him in proclaiming this foundational doctrinal principle, Luther could look with some satisfaction on the success of this teaching.

But would he have thought of this large movement he launched, the Protestant Reformation, as a success? It may be startling to many readers to discover that Luther had no intention of starting any "reformation." It is striking that he virtually never uses the term itself, and he certainly did not think he was involved in any renewal of the church. In his own understanding, Luther was calling it back to its founding truths, but not as a way of "setting things right again"; rather, he believed that he (and others as associates) had been commissioned to prepare the church for the cataclysm of Christ's impending return. To be sure, Luther was no apocalyptic seer, prognosticating dates for divine interventions to bring history to its end. Even so, he viewed the church and European culture around him as irremediably corrupt, a stench in the divine nostrils that must surely result in the irruption of the endtimes. A reformation would be a work of the future, to be achieved not through human endeavors but by divine power and intervention at the end of history.[2] In the time that still lay at hand, he believed that he and others should proclaim anew what God had revealed through the apostles and so prepare humankind to meet its Maker. For Luther, if this movement in which he was involved took root, that would not be what he expected.

In the meantime, in the brief span before the cataclysm that would bring history to its culmination, Luther hoped to see the proclamation of justification by faith alone which he and others proclaimed bearing fruit. That fruit would include: many embracing God by faith and, like Luther, finding peace with God; lives transformed by the love received from God, a love freely shown by the recipients to others; and the church edified in and committed to the faith so gloriously reclaimed and proclaimed. However, in the last few years of his life, Luther traveled throughout the regions of Germany into which he could safely venture, conducting church visitations. This experience profoundly

---

[2]These emphases recur repeatedly in Heiko A. Oberman, *Luther: Man Between God and the Devil*, trans. Eileen Walliser-Schwarzbart (New Haven, Conn.: Yale University Press, 1989): among others, see the comments at pp. 10, 12, 46-47, 66, 71, 79-80, 177, 264-67, 270 and 302. On Luther's sense of living in the last days, see Mark U. Edwards Jr., *Luther's Last Battles: Politics and Polemics 1531-1546* (Ithaca, N.Y.: Columbia University Press, 1983), pp. 16-18.

dispirited Luther: what he found was so little transformed from what had been common before his labors that he became morose and discouraged. Even the little change he expected to see, a change not leading to a whole-scale reformation of the church but resulting in smaller advances in faithfulness before God, he did not readily find. Furthermore, that his own prince and other German rulers used the movement begun under Luther's efforts to seek their own political ends provoked the Wittenberg Reformer, who viewed this as a perverse misappropriation of his teaching.

Luther found this all profoundly frustrating and irritating. His last years were marked by an edginess with what was taking place in German society and church. At about the same time, he returned to some of his old controversies and renewed them.[3] It seems likely that these two phenomena are linked together. To our question, Luther's perspectives and his response in his later years gives a resounding "No!" as an answer.

Philip Melanchthon. Luther's brilliant young associate might well have looked on what he accomplished with great satisfaction and see it, and the movement in which he was involved so closely with Luther, as resoundingly successful. At a young age, he had been appointed to a professorship at Wittenberg, where he not only could labor with the vibrant Augustinian monk but could also contribute to the movement which had begun. As a gifted young scholar with two books already to his credit, he also penned the Reformation movement's first topical doctrinal treatment, *Loci communes theologici*, in 1521—a volume extolled by Luther. With his remarkable gifts as a young northern Christian humanist, Melanchthon set about revamping the entire university curriculum, an endeavor so widely received and highly praised that he was given the nickname *Praeceptor Germaniae*—"teacher of Germany." But all of this so far speaks to Melanchthon's personal accomplishments, not directly to his expectations of the Reformation itself.

It seems likely that he had a greater sense than his famed older colleague that this movement in which he was involved would indeed be-

---

[3]Mark Edwards has treated these with great insight in *Luther's Last Battles*.

come a Reformation. With his curricular revisions, Melanchthon prepared the materials for future generations of university students to receive a sound Protestant instruction. The various editions of his *Loci*, periodically updated, expanded and improved by the author, also indicate his sense that whatever he and Luther were involved in would last for some time and have ongoing impact on the church. Melanchthon was not as at home as Luther in apocalyptic imminence. He prepared for an unfolding of the future in which the Reformation in which he was involved would take root and bear fruit in coming generations.

But Melanchthon found out that taking a different stance than what Luther's epigones could approve was fraught with danger. While he sometimes experienced working with Luther burdensome, he at least found shelter under his colleague's wings: until his death in 1546, Luther usually deflected the criticisms of Melanchthon proffered by those who wanted to emulate Luther with absolute precision. After his death, though, Melanchthon found himself the target of numerous accusations and rumors that he was undermining Luther's legacy and was unfaithful to the old Wittenberg champion. Hard-line followers of Luther (called "Gnesio-Lutherans") openly resented Melanchthon.

In the aftermath of the Smalcald War (1546-1547), Emperor Charles V imposed a settlement, the Augsburg Interim, on the defeated Protestant territories and cities. While it did not amount to a wholesale reinstitution of the practices and teachings of the Roman communion, it certainly required Protestants to backtrack from much of what they had done. The emperor was unable to enforce the Augsburg Interim in its full demands in some places within Germany; a somewhat scaled-back version came to be known as the "Leipzig Interim." Melanchthon expressed his willingness to live with this. The Gnesio-Lutherans, however, renounced this caviling and withdrew to found the University of Jena—where they did not acquiesce to the Leipzig Interim and the emperor was unable to enforce it on them. From there, Melanchthon's foes continued to heap abuse on him, accusing him of a variety of malfeasances in regard to their champion Luther. This continued to the year of Melanchthon's death in 1560. In his final days, he noted that he welcomed death, for it would free him from the rage of the theologians.

Whatever Philip Melanchthon may have thought in his early days about his own personal successes, he found so much opposition from those who were his colleagues—and almost always his former students—that he took no pleasure in life any longer. He had prepared the Reformation movement to continue, but the way he saw it continuing could bring him no sense of satisfaction. It was certainly not what he had expected. As he went to his grave, Melanchthon could not have viewed the Reformation as a success.

Ulrich Zwingli and Johannes Oecolampadius. It is difficult to assess what Zwingli and Oecolampadius expected and how they might have responded to our question. Unquestionably both men saw significant transformations begun in Zurich and in Basel, respectively. They found their presentations at debates with Roman theologians in the Swiss cantons during the 1520s useful in breaking down obstacles to the Reformation movement and consolidating it. Both Zurich and Basel experienced significant changes in ecclesiastical practice and teaching under their leadership; certain important changes also transpired at their insistence in the way the two cities were governed. In both regards, they might well have seen the endeavors as successful.

But they endured the pain of seeing the nascent Protestant movement rent by tensions over the sacrament of unity, the Eucharist. They put up with the vilification poured out on them by Luther in the Eucharistic controversy, recognizing him as a fellow servant while he excoriated them as minions of Satan. Surely this hostile conflict, which dogged the Reformation movement from 1526-1529 but was not even then resolved, would have raised serious doubts for them about the success of the movement. The fact that both men died in 1531, while their own initiatives for reform were still underway, precludes coming to any sure estimation of how much they might have viewed the Reformation as a success.

Martin Bucer. During the more than quarter-century Martin Bucer labored in Strasbourg (from 1523-1549), he saw the Reformation take deep root. Not long after his arrival, his great gifts led to his being recognized as the leading pastor of the city. His advice was regularly sought and, for the most part, followed by the city councilors—a privilege few of his fellow Reformers enjoyed. He helped initiate significant reform of liturgy, congregational singing and church governance during his tenure in Strasbourg. The city came to be known for its toleration of divergent viewpoints (as long as they did not spin off into open heresy), an openness unusual at the time. Even so, Bucer and his colleagues sought to draw those who benefited from that tolerance into the Reformation movement they led. A noteworthy accomplishment under Bucer's leadership was the establishment of a Protestant version of confirmation, with the youths who had been baptized in infancy giving expression to their personal faith at a designated time after a period of catechetical instruction.

Beyond this, Bucer came to be respected as a gifted biblical scholar. He produced commentaries on various books of the Old and the New Testaments. In the preface to his own commentary on Romans in 1539, John Calvin paid the highest compliments to Bucer's accomplishments as a biblical scholar, specifically praising Bucer's 1536 commentary on the same book but pointing out that it was so detailed and thorough that common readers (for whom Calvin sought to write) could not be expected to try to work their way through that magnificent tome.

Bucer also came to be respected for his unceasing efforts to bring healing to ruptured relationships within the church. His endeavors between 1529 and 1536, as assisted by Philip Melanchthon, led to the Wittenberg Concord of 1536, in which the representatives of the Reformed churches in southern Germany and the Lutherans came to significant enough agreement on the Eucharist that they could both subscribe to the document and share in the sacrament on that momentous occasion. Further, he and Melanchthon set their sites on reunion and reform efforts with theologians whom they trusted within the Roman communion; their collective efforts led to a series of colloquies in which discussion brought a significant measure of agreement. Indeed, at the Colloquy of Regensburg in 1541, agreement was attained on the doctrines of original sin, human will, anthropology and justification. While the colloquy collapsed owing to difficulties on other doctrines which could not be overcome, Bucer undoubtedly looked on this attainment as successful—as was witnessed in 1543, when he worked with the agreements in the city of Cologne at the invitation of the Roman Catholic archbishop there on what proved ultimately to be an abortive effort at reformation.

However, the great accomplishments in which Bucer could rejoice came to a crashing halt in the wake of the Smalcald War. With the Protestants defeated by the imperial forces, the emperor insisted on the imposition of the Augsburg Interim in Strasbourg. While the city fathers yielded to the demand, Bucer preferred exile to what would have amounted in his estimation to a repudiation of much of his work for the preceding twenty-five years. He left Strasbourg for England, where he had been invited by Archbishop Cranmer and the young King Edward VI. In the wake of his departure, and after the emperor's interim measures proved impossible to enforce, the city of Strasbourg turned in a rigidly Lutheran direction, and Bucer's memory was assailed.

In England, Bucer taught as a professor of divinity at Cambridge. In that position he penned *De Regno Christi* at the invitation of the young king, who desired to see further reform achieved throughout his kingdom. Relying on his long experience in Strasbourg and drawing on his wide imagination of how the Reformation could affect both church and society, Bucer sketched out in this volume a suggested strategy which could help spread the Reformation throughout Edward's realm.

Bucer died in 1551 in England; not long afterward, his royal host died as well. Bucer's counsel came to naught: Edward's fervently Roman Catholic half-sister Mary Tudor ascended the throne and sought to reimpose Roman Catholicism throughout England. Bucer's memory was vilified. The great Reformer of Strasbourg had been greatly respected for his own accomplishments, seen much of what he had hoped for come to fruition, helped guide the Reformation there to take what appeared to be deep root, and responded in England to a fascinating invitation from a young king about how to spread the Reformation throughout his domain—but all this came crashing down around Bucer. All he had pursued for more than a quarter-century in Strasbourg and briefly in England collapsed: for Bucer, the Reformation could not be called a success.

John Calvin. Although John Calvin desired a quiet life of scholarship, the imprecations of Guillaume Farel in Geneva in 1536 and Martin Bucer in Strasbourg in 1538 frightened Calvin into pastoral service. While these labors in Strasbourg (1538-1541) were crowned with appreciation and cooperation, those in Geneva, in both installments, proved utterly taxing to Calvin. The first ended with his and Farel's expulsion from the city in 1538. The 1541 invitation to Calvin to return, owing to a supposedly widespread change of heart in the city about his previous labors there, was unwelcome to Calvin. Indeed, he declared that he would rather be crucified 1000 times a day than go back to Geneva! However, Bucer prevailed on him to return again to his first scene of pastoral labors; after consultation with other trusted friends (including Farel), Calvin returned in 1541. He would serve in Geneva until his death in 1564.

It is true that Calvin knew great accomplishment with his publications: his *Institutes of the Christian Religion* received a warm welcome within Protestant circles, in all its editions from 1536 to the final one in 1559; his numerous commentaries on biblical books were honored as paragons of insightful, relevant and accessible exposition; and his many treatises on various topics were read as authoritative treatments of the relevant issues. But in the face of this authorial success, Calvin regularly encountered opposition in Geneva itself. Rather than being the theocratic tyrant of the city (as he has so often been presented), Calvin knew only a handful of years when his supporters held the majority in city council and its various decision-making bodies. Indeed, the opposition grew so intense that in 1553 Calvin preached what he thought would be his farewell sermon in Geneva. He had decided to leave the city, but a surprising result of a city council election brought in a majority of those who followed his advice and looked to him with respect, so he remained in Geneva.

Even so, throughout his second tenure in Geneva, Calvin regularly knew the opposition of a significant portion of the populace. Protests against his preaching found their way frequently to city council, which dealt with the allegations in a languid way that frustrated Calvin, often allowing the allegations to hang in the air for extended periods of time before finally ruling in Calvin's favor. As well, in the sanitary practices of the time, chamber pots were often dumped from upstairs windows onto the streets below, as a way of getting rid of the feces and urine they contained (with the hope that this material would end up washing down the street during rains); it was striking how often these chamber pots "accidentally" were emptied out those upper windows at precisely the moment John Calvin was passing under them. Further, Calvin and his fellow French refugees were disdained by many of the established families of Geneva. This led to serious tensions in hiring, granting citizenship and relationships which were only with difficulty kept in check by a reluctant city council. All in all, Geneva proved to be hostile territory for Calvin for most of his second period of service there.

Only in 1555 did Calvin and the other ministers finally win the right for the church in Geneva to decide on issues of church discipline: although that privilege had been promised to him as part of the arrangement for his 1541 return to Geneva, a difference in wording of that agreement in the copies which Calvin and the city council respectively had in their possession allowed that promise to remain unfulfilled for some fourteen years. Finally—to bring this recounting of frustrations for Calvin to a close, but without exhausting the list of them—it was not until 1559 that Calvin finally saw the Academy of Geneva established. He had asked the city council, as part of the agreement for his return, to support his determination to establish an academy for the purpose of training young people in various fields, but especially in Christian doctrine. He hoped such an institution would produce graduates who could serve Christian society in many fields, but especially as pastors, both in Switzerland and in France. Only eighteen years after his return was Calvin finally able to get this institution established; the city council had simply allowed the proposal to languish in ongoing bureaucratic delays.

In all this time, Calvin knew many hindrances and numerous disappointments. He was eventually able to see much of what had long been promised to him inaugurated in the last nine years of his life. During 1554-1558, when Calvin's supporters held the majority in the city council, John Knox resided in Geneva. He pronounced the city "the most perfect school of Christ on earth since the time of the apostles." Knox's comment responded to the situation he found in the city, in a time when more of what Calvin had hoped to achieve found realization. Even so, some of the further initiatives Calvin desired to see inaugurated remained too often mired in the frequent delays and excuses which civil governments too readily generate. For Calvin, to the end of his days, while he faithfully served the city and the church within it, Geneva remained a vale of frustration.[4]

It is hardly likely that even in the face of his great accomplishments as an author and teacher, Calvin considered the Reformation in Geneva a success. Too much of what he had intended remained undone. He also knew that the gains in Geneva were fragile and needed consolidation in coming years. In that regard, as he faced death in 1564, he recognized that a resurgent Roman Catholicism, invigorated by the Council of Trent and embarking on a spirited and forceful assault against Protestantism, was already having an impact. The Protestant Reformation was not yet secure; as Calvin lay dying, he may well have had questions whether it would be able to resist Rome's assault.

The Jesuits. The Jesuits originally hoped to devote themselves to mission labors in the Holy Land, but that proved to be impossible for them. While the problem of the Protestant Reformation was not even within the purview of the Society of Jesus as it came into existence and received papal approval as a religious order within the Roman communion, the Jesuits soon became the most forceful component of the Counter Reformation's challenge to Protestantism. With their invigorated scholasticism, devotion to Roman Catholicism and educational prowess, the Jesuits became Rome's main assault weapon on territories which had embraced Protestantism. As we will see below, they became wildly successful.

Through mission endeavors in the Far East and in the Americas begun in the sixteenth century, the Jesuits spread Roman Catholicism to non-European areas of the world (well before Protestants began sending

---

[4]For fuller treatment of what Calvin experienced in all this, see Willem van't Spijker, *Calvin: A Brief Guide to His Life and Thought*, trans. Lyle D. Bierma (Louisville: Westminster John Knox Press, 2009), pp. 72-124.

missionaries to such areas). Throughout Europe, the Reformation era also saw the Society of Jesus establishing schools at the secondary and post-secondary levels which were praised as the leading educational institutions of the time. By the Jesuits' indefatigable labors for Rome and against Protestantism, they managed to turn the tide and reclaim vast territories which had embraced Protestantism—an accomplishment not well known among contemporary twenty-first-century Protestants. Of all those involved in the Reformation-era struggles, the Jesuits ended up achieving more of what they expected than anyone else.

Consequently, the Jesuits have the best claim to being successful. What they accomplished needs to be better known. The difference it made for Western Christianity in the sixteenth century and subsequently should be recognized. It will help the twenty-first-century heirs of the Protestant Reformation better understand to what degree that movement was successful and, at the same time, how it also failed.

WHAT TRANSPIRED IN THE LAST HALF OF THE SIXTEENTH CENTURY

Many treatments of the Protestant Reformation end in the late 1550s or early 1560s, around the time the last of the major leaders of the movement passed from the scene. But the Protestant movement continued, of course, and trying to assess whether the Reformation was a success requires considering what transpired in the last decades of the sixteenth century too. For most of this time, frankly, Protestantism was lurching from one crisis to another. During this period, the Counter Reformation was waxing in strength.

Intra-Protestant conflict. In the last years of his life, Luther fanned again into flame the embers of some of his earlier conflicts. His would-be followers picked up that pattern, and strife rent the Lutheran camp in the years after Luther's death in 1546. Melanchthon often served as a lightning rod for these discords: his failure to march in lockstep with his esteemed colleague had earned the suspicion of some Lutherans, but others found Melanchthon's emphases and approach preferable to Luther's. Tensions between the two major segments of Lutheranism led to sharp recriminations and denunciations of one side against the other. Beyond this, additional conflicts arose among the Lutherans, further tearing at the harmony of this segment of Protestantism.[5]

The edginess thus evidenced within Lutheran circles also found outlet in conflict with the Reformed, especially with Calvin in the 1550s, over questions regarding the Eucharist.[6] While Calvin attracted the most attention in this regard, as the preeminent spokesman for the Reformed at the time, the suspicion spread to engulf the entire Reformed camp. The tensions were exacerbated by the uncertain political situation faced by the Protestants.

With the affirmation of Lutheranism's legality, alongside that of Roman Catholicism, within the bounds of the Holy Roman Empire according to the terms of the 1555 Peace of Augsburg, Lutherans had found protection against imperial legislation. The *cuius regio eius religio* ("whose the region, his the religion") perspective set forth in that treaty allowed civil authorities to decide the confessional stance of the region they ruled. No such allowance was accorded to the Reformed, however. Even so, the Reformed tradition soon found welcome from various princes in the empire. The Palatinate serves as one example, where Frederick III adopted the Reformed version of Protestantism, and under his urging, theologians prepared the Heidelberg Catechism in 1563 to set forth what the Reformed church in his domains believed. The Lutherans saw such developments as eating away at their portion of the empire and, potentially, setting the stage for military intervention and the danger that Lutheranism might be stripped of its legitimacy.

Beyond this, the doctrinal conflicts between the two Protestant camps continued unabated. Indeed, with the rise of Protestant scholasticism beginning in the 1560s, those controversies intensified to the degree that each rigidly excluded the other as a viable version of the Christian faith (with both also opposing Roman Catholicism, which returned the favor). This intra-Protestant hostility led to such a pitch that in the 1580s some Reformed adherents were burned at the stake in Saxony as heretics. While the Reformed did not reply in kind in this

---

[5]For a good treatment of these various controversies, see F. Bente, *Historical Introductions to the Book of Concord* (St. Louis: Concordia, 1965).

[6]See the treatment in Wulfert de Greef, *The Writings of John Calvin: An Introductory Guide*, expanded ed., trans. Lyle D. Bierma (Louisville: Westminster John Knox, 2008), pp. 178-81.

regard, they nonetheless manifested hostility toward their Lutheran counterparts.

This all led to some direct confrontation in regions which were in transition between the two camps. In Heidelberg the hostilities reached such a pass that a Reformed preacher and a Lutheran church superintendent traded insults and recriminations from the pulpits in church services in 1559. Princely intervention subsequently banished both of them, but the tensions between the competing viewpoints abated only slightly.[7] This mutual hostility continued throughout the rest of the sixteenth century, and it would find brutal outlet in the Thirty Years' War in the next century. But by the end of the sixteenth century, great damage had already been done to Protestantism. Not only was it divided into warring camps, it had also lost a great deal of ground to a resurgent Roman communion.

The Jesuits and Eastern Europe. Beginning in the 1540s, Protestant teaching made significant headway into eastern Europe—a phenomenon rarely recognized because it is so often not treated in most books on the Reformation.[8] Already in the 1520s, Hungary had opened up to Protestantism, and by 1531 a Protestant seminary had been established in Sárospatak. But as Calvin's writings began entering Hungary in the late 1540s, they quickly attracted large numbers to the Reformed banner. By 1600, almost ninety percent of the population had embraced the Reformed faith. In that year, the Roman Catholic Church had one printing press producing its literature in Hungary, while the Hungarian Reformed Church had twenty-eight of them. Between 1527 and 1600, some 275 religious books were published in Hungary; of those, 244 were by Protestant (mostly Re-

---

[7]See the discussion in Charles D. Gunnoe Jr., "The Reformation of the Palatinate and the Origins of the Heidelberg Catechism, 1500-1562," in Lyle D. Bierma, ed., *An Introduction to the Heidelberg Catechism: Sources, History, and Theology,* Texts and Studies in Reformation and Post-Reformation Thought (Grand Rapids: Baker Academic, 2005), pp. 37-39.

[8]As Andrew Pettegree and Karin Maag comment, "It is a curious fact that one can read most general histories of the Reformation without being strongly aware that there *was* a Reformation in Eastern Europe" ("The Reformation in Eastern and Central Europe," in *The Reformation in Eastern and Central Europe,* ed. Karin Maag [Aldershot: Ashgate, 1997], p. 1); a welcome exception to this observation is Philip Benedict, *Christ's Churches Purely Reformed: A Social History of Calvinism* (New Haven, Conn.: Yale University Press, 2002), which includes a chapter, "Eastern Europe: Local Reformations Under Noble Protection," pp. 255-80.

formed) authors. The Reformed presence in Hungary was so overwhelming that in 1608, the Hapsburg ruler—like his forebears, vigorously committed to Rome—found it politically advisable to legalize
Protestantism in Hungary.[9]

It took a few more years than in Hungary for Protestant teaching to
find a ready audience in Bohemia. The same was true for Poland. The
political situation in both regions helped open the doors.

Bohemia had been swallowed up into Austrian holdings after 1526.
However, resentment at this turn of events helped push Bohemians
toward a religious stance other than that of their Hapsburg rulers, who
were champions of Roman Catholicism. By the 1540s, Bohemians began turning toward Luther's teachings. The Bohemians' Hussite background already predisposed them at the time toward Luther's views,
many of which resonated with Jan Hus's teachings a century earlier.
Before the end of the sixteenth century, most of the noble class had
embraced Protestantism, with the predominance committed to the Reformed tradition—not least because of the greater possibility it offered
for lesser authorities (such as nobles) to resist unjust rulers.

Poland began opening up to Protestantism during the 1540s. While
the Polish kings continued faithful to Rome, they could do little against
the nobles who embraced Protestantism, for the prior development of
Polish royal/noble relationships had kept the king weak vis-à-vis the
nobility and thus unable to enforce a particular religious commitment.
Within Poland the German-speaking territories which became Protestant turned to Lutheranism; among the Slavic nobles, the majority embraced the Reformed tradition.

Both the Lutheran and the Reformed camps grew exponentially,
almost to the end of the sixteenth century. By 1569 half of the *Sejm* (the
Polish parliament), composed of nobles, had become Protestant. By
1580 Poland had approximately one thousand Protestant congregations, divided about equally between the Lutheran and Reformed
camps. By 1591 one in every six parishes throughout Poland was Prot-

---

[9]See Ferenc Szakály, "The Early Ottoman Period, Including Royal Hungary, 1526-1606," in *A
History of Hungary*, ed. Peter F. Sugar, Péter Hanák and Tibor Frank (Bloomington: Indiana
University Press, 1994), pp. 93-94.

estant.[10] To be sure, Protestantism remained confined largely to the noble classes; it had not spread much among the common people. But it had managed astonishing headway among the nobility, who held the real power in Poland.

By shortly after 1600, though, the remarkable Protestant advance had almost entirely been rolled back. Much of this was due to the initiatives of the Jesuits. As we have already seen,[11] they established the best schooling system available, managed to get Protestant nobility to send their children also to these schools, and drew those children back into the Roman Catholic Church. But their extraordinary success in this regard was aided and abetted by intra-Protestant rivalries.

As elsewhere, so too in Poland, Protestant scholasticism became the mode of teaching and interaction between the Lutherans and the Reformed in the later sixteenth century. The mutual hostility it engendered served to divide the potentially powerful Protestant influence within Poland, as both Lutherans and Reformed as vigorously excoriated the other as they did the Roman Catholics—who, under the Jesuits, were educating their children! The warring Protestant camps could not see their way through to work with each other. This had an enormous influence on the fate of Protestantism in Poland. By 1625 the Protestant movement in Poland had been decimated,[12] never to return to the public prominence and political potential it had known in the last forty years of the sixteenth century.[13]

Jesuit endeavors, encouraged by Roman Catholic monarchs, also led to the recapture of much of Hungary and Bohemia for Roman Catholicism. By shortly after 1600, Rome had reclaimed a significant por-

---

[10]For these details, I rely on the information in Janusz Małłek, "The Reformation in Poland and Prussia in the sixteenth century: similarities and differences," in *The Reformation in Eastern and Central Europe*, ed. Karin Maag (Aldershot: Ashgate, 1997), pp. 182-91; and Michael G. Müller, "Late Reformation and Protestant confessionalization in the major towns of Royal Prussia," in ibid., pp. 192-210.

[11]See the treatment in chapter eight.

[12]On the above, see any good history of Poland, such as Adam Zamoyski, *The Polish Way: A Thousand-Year History of the Poles and their Culture* (New York: Hippocrene Books, 1987), or O. Halecki, *A History of Poland*, new ed. (New York: Barnes & Noble, 1993).

[13]In 1999 I met a representative of the Polish Reformed Church at a small international ecumenical conference in New York City; in conversation, he noted that his denomination had a total of ten churches, all of which traced themselves back to the sixteenth century.

tion of the Hungarian populace: about two-thirds had returned to the Roman communion, with the other third remaining Protestant (mostly Reformed). The Jesuits knew somewhat more limited success in Bohemia in the period to the end of the sixteenth century. The Protestant (primarily Reformed) presence was definitively brought to an end with the defeat of the Bohemian forces early in the Thirty Years' War at the Battle of White Mountain ("Bila Hora") in 1620. The entire Bohemian noble class was destroyed. Many nobles died in the battle, many others were subsequently captured and beheaded, and the rest fled the country. Some two thousand noble families—the vast majority of the Protestant movement in Bohemia—suffered this fate.[14] Bohemia returned, reluctantly, to the Roman communion.

The embarrassment of Antitrinitarianism. In any assessment of whether the Protestant Reformation was a success, it is necessary to take into consideration a strange phenomenon which is often overlooked— the development of antitrinitarianism.[15] For a movement which intended to reclaim apostolic teaching and remain faithful to historic Christianity, it was more than slightly embarrassing for the Protestant Reformation to have to count such spawn among its progeny.

Among those in Italy who embraced Reformation emphases, some moved beyond criticism of medieval teachings to challenge ancient Christian doctrine, rejecting the deity of Jesus Christ and, correlatively, the doctrine of the Trinity. They included Lelio Sozzini and his nephew Fausto, Matteo Gribaldi, Giovanni Valentino Gentile, Gian Paolo Alciati and Giorgio Biandrata. In due course many of them ended up leaving Italy and traveling through or settling in Geneva in the 1550s and 1560s.

Like some other immigrant groups, the Italians had their own con-

---

[14]On this, see any good history of the Czechs, such as Hugh LeCaine Agnew, *The Czechs and the Lands of the Bohemian Crown*, Studies of Nationalities (Stanford, Calif.: Hoover Institution Press, 2004), or Derek Sayer, *The Coasts of Bohemia: A Czech History* (Princeton, N.J.: Princeton University Press, 1998).

[15]The most complete presentation of this is found in Stanislas Lubieniecki, *History of the Polish Reformation and Nine Related Documents*, trans. George Huntston Williams, Harvard Theological Studies (Minneapolis: Fortress, 1995), pp. 211-313, 336-41; see also the brief overview in Williston Walker et al., *A History of the Christian Church*, 4th ed. (New York: Charles Scribner's Sons, 1985), pp. 535-38.

gregation in the city. When Calvin learned that a few in that community were expressing antitrinitarian perspectives, he arranged that the Italian congregation adopt a statement of faith which forthrightly confessed trinitarianism. While most of the congregation readily subscribed to the statement, some refused to do so, while yet others did so only reluctantly (and subsequently returned to antitrinitarianism after departing from Geneva).[16] Those who could not sign the statement left for other venues; most ended up settling in Poland.

As already noted, in Poland a wide-ranging religious toleration reigned during the sixteenth century. Soon enough the immigrants who had turned toward antitrinitarianism affiliated themselves again with Reformed congregations in the country. Rejecting the terms and teaching adopted in historic trinitarianism, these teachers urged that Jesus Christ was only a man, but that he lived so faithfully before God that God rewarded him (after raising him from the dead, following his unjust execution) by elevating him to a sort of "associate divine" status. Thus they held to an exalted view of Jesus Christ as far as his humanity was concerned; in conflict with historic Christian teaching, though, they rejected his deity. With this, the doctrine of the Trinity collapsed for them as well, and they urged a unitarian view of God. Some of them accepted, but others denied, that the exalted Jesus Christ could be worshiped.[17]

As this viewpoint became known within the Reformed churches in Poland, many were aghast that such views had surfaced among them; however, others were drawn to the unitarian viewpoint. At the Diet of Piotrków in 1565, this led to such conflict that the Reformed Church in Poland split: the Major Reformed Church remained trinitarian, while the Minor Reformed Church embraced antitrinitarianism. These two groups found it impossible to work together. So, in addition to the hostile tensions between Lutherans and Reformed which had arisen in

---

[16]Van't Spijker, *Calvin*, p. 115.

[17]These views, with further elaborations, came to expression in the Racovian Catechism of 1605, the doctrinal standard accepted by the Polish Brethren (the self-designation eventually accepted by the antitrinitarians in Poland); for a summary of the antitrinitarian views, see Jaroslav Pelikan, *Reformation of Church and Dogma (1300-1700)*, The Christian Tradition: A History of the Development of Doctrine (Chicago: University of Chicago Press, 1984), 4:322-31.

the Protestant Reformation's homelands and been aped in Poland as
the Protestant scholastic period was beginning, now the Reformed
found themselves also in conflict with a group that claimed relationship to them but rejected historic trinitarianism.

Not surprisingly, the Jesuits threw this development in the face of
the Protestants in Poland, urging that such heretical notions must arise
from the Protestant assertion of *sola scriptura*, which they alleged
opened the floodgates for all to decide for themselves what they thought
the Scriptures taught. For themselves, Lutherans did not hesitate to
point out that this aberration had not arisen within their midst, and
they gladly pointed the finger accusingly at the Reformed. The Reformed protested that the unitarian viewpoint was a misappropriation
of what they believed, and the Reformed stood as far aloof as they could
from the antitrinitarian Minor Reformed Church.

Eventually this antitrinitarian group came to be known as the Polish
Brethren. Their influence spawned a similar group in Transylvania,
which had been wrenched out of Hungary's control by the Ottoman
conquests earlier in the sixteenth century. The uncertain political situation of the inhabitants, who still had a Hungarian ruler but feared the
overwhelming Ottoman threat, forced them all to work together as
much as possible. This led to an open tolerance (similar to Poland) in
which antitrinitarianism could be taught without fear of reprisal. As in
Poland, so too in Transylvania, a Unitarian church took root. In 1571 it
obtained legal standing by decree of John Sigismund, ruler of Transylvania and son of John Zápolya, King of Hungary. The chief architect
of this community was Giorgio Biandrata, ably assisted by Francis
Dávid.[18] But the tables turned in Poland: Jesuit opposition eventually
resulted in the banishment of the Polish Brethren in 1658.

CONCLUSION

As we wrap up our considerations in this chapter, we come again to
the question with which we began: "Was the Reformation a success?"

---

[18]Francis Dávid was an extraordinary character: he served as superintendent of three church
bodies in Transylvania: first as a Lutheran, then as Reformed and finally as a Unitarian
(Walker, *History of the Christian Church*, p. 535).

Answering that question is neither easy nor simple. Doing justice to it has required us to go considerably beyond what many people instinctively bring to the fore as they think about what the Reformation accomplished.

Undeniably the Reformation sought to return to apostolic teaching, specifically to the understanding of finding peace with God through faith in his incarnate Son, the Savior, Jesus Christ. Over against the confused messages imparted by the church as it stumbled from the late medieval period into the Reformation era, the message proclaimed by the Protestant Reformers unquestionably showed how to hear again the good news in Jesus Christ as proclaimed by the apostles and the early church.

As we turned to consider the Reformers themselves, remembering the wide group which would be included in that designation in sixteenth-century estimation, we came to a mixed assessment. Some of the Anabaptists proved successful in emulating the practice of the earliest church, as recorded in the New Testament; others saw their particular emphases founder on the shoals of what transpired during their own time. But all experienced some measure of persecution—thus proving successful in repristinating the earliest church's experience in that regard.

As to the Protestant Reformers, each of them found considerable success, even eminence, in the teaching and writing tasks to which they turned. They found a ready audience for their teaching and a wide readership which appreciated their efforts. However, all the Protestant Reformers also encountered serious, dispiriting obstacles in their paths. As each came to the end of his life, none could be sanguine about what he had accomplished or certain that it would survive. The struggles all of them faced in achieving the changes which they hoped to see effected in church and society remained unresolved at their deaths.

Furthermore, a resurgent Roman communion was hammering at what the Protestant Reformers had accomplished, seeking to roll back the advances Protestantism had made. In this regard, the Jesuits managed to reclaim some regions which had embraced Protestant teaching—especially in eastern Europe. Indeed, as the sixteenth century came to an end, the Jesuits were unquestionably the most successful of all the Reformers in achieving their objectives.

Much of the Jesuit success can be credited to the hostile intra-Protestant conflicts that stained the last half of the sixteenth century and continued under Protestant scholastic auspices. Had the Lutherans and the Reformed found a way to collaborate in the face of the Jesuit onslaught in the Holy Roman Empire and eastern Europe, the story of the sixteenth century might have turned out very differently. However, their constant attacks on each other divided the Protestant movement irremediably against itself during the last half of the sixteenth century (and on through the seventeenth). Each camp prided itself on holding the pristine truth of Christianity, but neither managed to hold the hearts and commitment of multitudes who found the Jesuit ministrations more inviting.

The rise of antitrinitarianism shocked all of Western Christendom. Since it arose in Protestant circles, appealing to the Reformers' slogans, Roman Catholic controversialists cogently argued that Protestant teaching exposed itself to such rabid results: that is, the appeal to *sola scriptura* opened the door to a subjectivism which could dispense with the consensus teaching of historic Christianity. Lutherans were only too happy to point out that such unitarian teaching was not endemically Protestant: it had not arisen within their circles, but only among the Reformed. Lutherans could boast that their approach to the Scripture principle led to no such dogma-historical malfeasance. The Reformed rejected the notion that their appropriation of *sola scriptura* could be twisted in an antitrinitarian direction, legitimating that claim by appealing to the example of Geneva in Calvin's time, where the intimations of such teaching led to a confessional stance that excluded such doctrinal aberrations, and to the division that arose in Poland in which the Major Reformed Church and the Minor Reformed Church split and the trinitarian body refused to have anything positive to do with its unitarian counterpart.

Even so, the Reformed could not deny that it was in their circles alone that the unitarian teaching emerged. This was not the last time this would happen: in the seventeenth century the pattern recurred in England, among some Presbyterians and Baptists—who claimed Reformed doctrinal heritage.[19] However carefully the Protestant Reformers, and the Reformed camp among them, had couched *sola scriptura* within boundaries to keep it from wandering into subjectivism, some followers within the larger Reformed world transgressed the boundaries—if not with impunity, then at least with audacity. Evidently, something in the way the Reformed taught, communicated, embodied or dealt with *sola scriptura* left the door open to the possibility of dismissing historic Christianity.[20]

Given all this, the question "Was the Reformation a success?" requires a carefully nuanced answer. While the Protestant Reformation unquestionably transformed Western Christendom, the fuller story of the Reformation—one that includes all of Europe and the entire sixteenth century—manifests many problems, failures, frustrations and difficulties. It proved to be a significant but flawed product, often victor over opposition but also victim of its own weaknesses.

In this regard, the Protestant Reformation of the sixteenth century was much like any other movement or century in recorded history. Without doubt, what transpired in the sixteenth century was momentous. The claim, though, that it was a success—however vigorously asserted and desperately held by subsequent Protestants—is hard to sustain, if the whole story of the Reformation is kept in mind.

---

[19]For a brief treatment of this, see Walker, *History of the Christian Church*, pp. 585-86.

[20]I am not aware of any careful scholarly analysis of how and why antitrinitarianism could have arisen in Reformed circles in the sixteenth and the seventeenth centuries. It seems worthy to note, though, that in succeeding generations Lutherans have encouraged patristic scholarship (and thus awareness of the church fathers' contributions to historic Christianity) more than the Reformed tradition has, at least until the last few years. Such emphasis may well serve to encourage greater appreciation of the ancient church and, correlatively, deeper respect for its contribution to the articulation of Christian teaching.

- 11 -

Is the Reformation a Norm?

IN THIS CHAPTER WE MOVE FROM our historical examination of the Protestant Reformation itself to reflect on one of the ways the heirs of the movement often view it. Those not affiliated with a Protestant denomination are welcome to follow along, but the issues we consider here may seem a bit distant from their concerns or interests. To Protestants of many backgrounds, though, what we are looking at is significant, for we are going to reflect on whether we grateful heirs of the sixteenth-century Reformation should view it as a "golden age" which can point the way for Protestant churches today. Is the Reformation a norm for Protestantism in subsequent generations including our own?

It is hardly surprising that Protestants look back on the Protestant Reformation of the sixteenth century with great appreciation—and, perhaps, even a bit of envy. It may almost appear, whatever flaws the Reformation had, to have been a golden age. For a Protestant committed to the doctrine of justification *sola fide* as basic to understanding the good news of the apostolic message and embracing *sola scriptura* (with its appropriate qualifications and nuances) as guideline for what we believe, the sixteenth-century Reformation resonates with doctrinal and historical significance, and we are strongly drawn to it.

In this movement we discern divine blessing that lashed the church again to its apostolic moorings. Given the struggles the church in general, and the numerous varieties of Protestantism in particular, have faced in subsequent centuries, the era of the Protestant Reformers seems to shine with a special luminosity that contrasts sharply with the shadows too often encountered later. In the face of a widespread cultural indifference to Christianity in the contemporary Western world, the sixteenth century's concentrated focus on the issues presented by the Protestant Reformers easily engenders a certain wistfulness for the Reformation era.

But is the Reformation a norm for later Protestantism? Should the heirs of the Reformation look on the sixteenth-century phenomenon as somehow setting a pattern which we ought to emulate in our day? Is it appropriate for subsequent Protestants to view the Reformation as a golden age?[1] To be sure, these questions may not be consciously asked by Protestants in the present day. Even so, they underlie attitudes expressed in numerous sermons, conversations and articles in denominational magazines. We will deal with that substratum in this chapter.

As we do, we need to limit our focus. It is necessary to recognize that the "should-ness" of the question implies obligation or ethical propriety. That is an interesting perspective, but not one that historical study can particularly address. So, however interesting it would be to examine such a perspective, it will not be our focus here. We will approach the issue historically.

We will deal with the question, first, by looking closely at what the Reformers themselves said about their churches in their day. Then we will consider the recommendation the Reformers themselves offered

---

[1]Carl R. Trueman and R. Scott Clark criticize the idea of a "golden age" to be found in any era of church history in their "Introduction," in *Protestant Scholasticism: Essays in Reassessment*, ed. Carl R. Trueman and R. Scott Clark, Studies in Christian History and Thought (Waynesboro, Ga.: Paternoster, 1999), p. xvi. Their basic point—that no such past age was perfect—is both obvious and unremarkable. But it is surely possible to think of an age as "golden" or as a norm without endowing it with perfection, i.e., to differentiate among various eras in church history and find one more helpful in offering guidance or a pattern to emulate in contemporary church life and practice. The question then becomes, which of the preferable eras is the most desirable one? This is a question that need not imply that it was or needs to be perfect to be so chosen. The question in this chapter asks whether the Protestant Reformation can and should be viewed in this way.

about a historical pattern to be followed. This will give us a significant and directly relevant historical vantage point and perspective from which to consider the question, "Is the Reformation a norm?" If we are not going to get the Reformation wrong, it is important to get this question right.

THE REFORMATION A GOLDEN AGE?

The notion of a golden age sometime in the past has been common in human history. Looking back at some presumably better era as preferable to one's own is no new phenomenon: one encounters it already in the ancient world.[2] It marks the Middle Ages: after the chaos brought on in the wake of the Germanic invasions, when civilization again took root and led to the establishment of schools, those who wanted to teach the young looked to whatever material they had from the ancient world as the best resources available for instructing students. Similarly, with the coming of the Renaissance, yearning for the ancient past took on special poignancy, as Renaissance figures looked backward, beyond the medieval period and the scholasticism that had taken over in education, to the ancient worthies of Greece and Rome. For Renaissance humanism, the cry *ad fontes* intended both return to and preference for the unadulterated, unexpurgated, unabridged and unexcerpted writings of antiquity as the embodiment of wisdom. With virtually all the Protestant Reformers having been steeped in and committed to northern Christian humanism, it is hardly surprising to find them looking back to antiquity for guidance—specifically, to Scripture and the church fathers.

The various Reformers were unquestionably aware of the idea of a golden age in the past that would serve as a standard which could critique what they found in their own day. That notion was at the heart of both Renaissance and northern Christian humanism. With numerous others in the sixteenth century, they viewed the contemporary church, its teaching and its ministrations with considerable disdain: the long-heard cry for *reformatio in capite et membris*, after all, had some serious

---

[2]E.g., in *The Third Satire*, written early in the second century A.D. by the Roman poet and satirist Juvenal, the author yearned for Rome as it had been in bygone generations before the influx of so many non-Romans led to changes in society, culture and mores in the city.

and unmistakable points of reference. The Renaissance and its northern Christian humanist counterpart certainly summoned Western Christendom back to antiquity as a golden age, which the humanists desired to see reborn in their day.

With the rebirth of ancient learning in both Renaissance Italy and sixteenth-century northern Europe, and with the welcome accorded to northern Christian humanism's directives for promoting piety and more cogently presenting Christian teaching, it is hardly surprising that some enthusiasts for the movement—including those who ultimately embraced the Protestant Reformation—sensed that they were witnessing the birth of a new golden age. They recognized that momentous changes were afoot in the movements in which they were engaged, changes they interpreted as divine blessing as they and others sought to return to apostolic teaching, scriptural practice and patristic patterns. Many of them could nod affirmatively to Desiderius Erasmus's assessment: in April 1517—the year in which Martin Luther would nail his ninety-five theses to the church door in Wittenberg— Erasmus wrote to Pope Leo X, optimistically opining that they were living at the dawn of a golden age.[3] Those of Erasmus's devotees who subsequently embraced the Protestant Reformation similarly shared fond expectations of what would transpire in their day.

This is why it is striking to hear the assessments of those Protestant Reformers as they later commented on the state of their churches. After all the hope and expectation for dramatic reformation and renewal through their endeavors to proclaim anew the doctrine of justification *sola fide* and to urge *sola scriptura*, what the Reformers saw as actually arising from their endeavors disabused them of any notion that a golden age was dawning. Although we have evidence for this view earlier, by the 1530s at the latest the Reformers had come to a much more sober assessment of what was transpiring through the Protestant movement.

---

[3]In the letter, Erasmus expressed his confident hope that with the recovery of the teaching and practice of Christian antiquity, learning, piety and righteousness would flourish anew: see R. A. B. Mynors and D. F. S. Thomson, trans., *The Collected Works of Erasmus* (Toronto: University of Toronto Press, 1977), 4:566, ll. 38-45; earlier in the same year, in a letter of February 26, 1517 to Wolfgang Capito, Erasmus had also written that they lived at the beginning of a golden age (4:541, ll. 12-13).

They rejoiced that the apostolic message of good news was again being proclaimed with clarity, and that it was taking root in their communities, but they were under no illusions about the evidence for much actual renewal in their congregations or personal transformation in their congregants.

In his 1521 defense of Luther against the allegations of the Sorbonne theologians, Philip Melanchthon commended patristic teaching and practice as "the purer Christianity before today." He went on to assess Christian antiquity and his own times: "Perchance that was the noonday of the Gospel, but now it is the evening."[4] Melanchthon certainly criticized the Roman communion with this contrast, but he could not do so without also pointing the finger at the movement in which he and Luther were so deeply involved. He undoubtedly hoped to see bright sunlight again in this nascent Reformation movement, but he did not claim that it had managed to gather much luminescence yet.

In 1533 Martin Bucer published a lengthy dialogue[5] which he intended to serve as preparation for a proposed ecclesiastical and civil council which would deal with the division between the Protestants and the Roman communion. The council was not summoned, but his comments about the Protestant churches are telling. In the introduction to the dialogue, Bucer pointed out that Rome had often charged that the Protestants were unfaithful to the pattern of Christian antiquity, but he urged this was a false calumny, for the Protestants agreed with the ancient churches and holy fathers.[6] Even so, he later lamented that Protestant practice did not measure up to the standards of the ancient church: "we are still so far from the earnestness and zeal for genuine, true faith in Christ, as it was found among the ancients."[7] He ada-

---

[4]Philip Melanchthon, *Luther and the Paris Theologians 1521*, in *Melanchthon: Selected Writings*, ed. Elmer Ellsworth Flack and Lowell J. Satre, trans. Charles Leander Hill (Minneapolis: Augsburg Publishing House, 1962), pp. 75-76.

[5]The document was entitled, *Furbereytung zum Concilio wie alle recht Gotßfortigen von beden yetz fürnemmen theylen so man alt- und newgleubige, Bapsttische und Lutherische nennet, Zu einigkeit Christlicher kirchen kommen und sich darin unbewegt halten mogen.* Not yet available in English translation, it has been critically edited and published in a multi-volume series: Robert Stupperich, ed., *Martin Bucers Deutsche Schriften* [hereafter MBDS] (Gütersloh: Verlagshaus Gerd Mohn, 1960-), 5:270-360.

[6]Ibid., pp. 274-75.

[7]Ibid., p. 309.

mantly asserted that the practice of the faith was purer among the Protestants than it was within the Roman communion; even so, Protestant practice fell far short—not only of what it should be ideally, but of what it had been in antiquity.

This was no passing notion on Bucer's part. In 1539 he published another dialogue,[8] again intended to prepare for a council to deal with the ecclesiastical division (a council also never summoned). In commenting on the diversity of ceremonies found in antiquity (but opposed by his Roman Catholic interlocutor), Bucer noted that the ancient churches had known, even with this diversity, a higher degree of true piety than had since been known.[9] The criticism of Roman expectations in this comment entailed no less a criticism of what could be found within Protestantism in his day.

John Calvin declared himself in similar fashion. In all the editions of his *Institutes of the Christian Religion*, from 1536 to 1559, the prefatory letter he wrote to King Francis I appeared. In this letter he referred to "the ancient fathers," whom he went on to describe as "the ancient writers *of a better age of the church*."[10] The clearly intended criticism of the Roman church was unmistakable; even so, for all his defense of the Protestants in this apologetic to the French king, he never implied that the Protestant churches escape this criticism. This was corroborated in 1539 in his address to Emperor Charles V, where Calvin appealed to "the primitive *and purer* Church"[11]—which again criticized both the Roman and the Protestant churches of his day.

It would not be warranted to dismiss these comments simply as the sort of apposite humility one would expect in godly servants. To be

---

[8]The document was entitled, *Etliche gesprech aus götlichen und geschribnen Rechten vom Nürnbergischen fridestand.* Also unavailable in English translation, a critical edition can be found in MBDS 7:402-502.

[9]Ibid., p. 439.

[10]John Calvin, *Institutes of the Christian Religion: 1536 edition,* trans. and ed. Ford Lewis Battles, rev. ed. (Grand Rapids: Collins/Eerdmans, 1986), p. 6 (emphasis added); for the 1559 edition, see John Calvin, *Institutes of the Christian Religion,* 2 vols., ed. John T. McNeill, trans. Ford Lewis Battles, Library of Christian Classics (Philadelphia: Westminster Press, 1960), 1.18 (emphasis added).

[11]John Calvin, *The Necessity of Reforming the Church,* in *Calvin: Theological Treatises,* trans. J. K. S. Reid, Library of Christian Classics (Philadelphia: Westminster Press, 1954), p. 215 (emphasis added).

sure, Renaissance communication practiced an effusive humility and self-derogation that sometimes drifted into insincere ostentation, so we might assume that these Christian humanists-turned-Reformers had adopted this tactic in describing the churches in which they had labored for some time. Against that, we need to recall Martin Luther's assessment of the Protestant congregations as he encountered them in his church visitations during the last years of his life. When we remember that Luther had scant exposure to northern Christian humanism, and that even when he did under his colleague Philip Melanchthon he nevertheless maintained so much of his scholastic orientation in dealing with others, we should hardly expect a deferential or exaggerated Renaissance humility to bubble to his surface. When we recall how profoundly these visitations dispirited Luther and that he did not think reformation or renewal would ensue from what he and his colleagues were doing, we are in a better place to accept the assessment of his fellow Reformers.

Beyond these indications, we have the comments of Desiderius Erasmus in correspondence exchanged with Martin Bucer in late 1527. Bucer had urged Erasmus to recognize that his northern Christian humanist emphases and inclinations fit more appropriately within the Protestant movement than they did in the Roman communion (in which Erasmus had remained). In his response, Erasmus acknowledged that the Roman church was badly flawed, but he declared that he saw no particular or noteworthy improvement in life, godliness or piety in the Protestant ones; until he did, he advised Bucer, he would stay with the church in which he had been raised.[12] A later interchange between Melanchthon and Erasmus had the same focus and response. Significantly neither Bucer nor Melanchthon disputed Erasmus's assessment of the Protestant churches. Given how dearly they hoped that the great Christian humanist leader would embrace Protestantism, it is unques-

---

[12]Erasmus's letter is dated November 11, 1527; it is conveniently available in Johan Huizinga, *Erasmus and the Age of Reformation* (New York: Harper Torchbooks, 1957), pp. 243-46; beyond this letter, see also the extract of another (unidentified by date or recipient) in which Erasmus scathingly assessed what he saw as the failure of the Protestant Reformers' message to summon the members of their churches to greater godliness or humility (also in Huizinga, *Erasmus and the Age of Reformation*, p. 177).

tionably telling that they did not challenge Erasmus on his assessment or pursue the matter further with him.

The Protestant Reformers, then, bar the way to subsequent Protestants viewing the Reformation as a golden age. They viewed their churches as still "on the way" to what they should become, but far from what they should have been by that time. If someone wants to treat the Reformation as a norm, then, which should be emulated in subsequent generations, that person must either remain ignorant of or disregard the Reformers' assessment of their movement. Neither path is open to those who take the Protestant Reformers seriously: the first would be a strange way to adhere to the supposed norm, and the second would necessitate a violation of it.

THE REFORMERS' RECOMMENDATION

However, while the Protestant Reformers would prohibit subsequent generations from looking wistfully at the sixteenth-century Protestant Reformation as a norm to be followed, they point out where we can find a gold standard for church life. Whenever the idea of an ideal pattern—not perfect, to be sure, but superior to whatever could be found in any other historical era—is broached, they point uniformly to the ancient church. In this they indeed follow northern Christian humanist emphases, which is not surprising, since the Protestant Reformers (except Luther) had all been steeped in those emphases. Even so, these humanists-turned-Reformers all offered nuance and qualification to this appeal beyond what fit straightforwardly with their northern Christian humanist attitudes.

The Reformers prized the ancient church, not just because of its antiquity, but because of the faithfulness they perceived in the way it lived out of and honored Scripture and apostolic teaching. Martin Bucer looked to the ancient church as a model of purity;[13] indeed, as the leading Protestant pastor in Strasbourg, he saw to it that the clergy there studied the history of the early church in order to learn how to lead a

---

[13]Irena Backus, "Ulrich Zwingli, Martin Bucer and the Church Fathers," in *The Reception of the Church Fathers in the West: From the Carolingians to the Maurists*, ed. Irena Backus, 2 vols. (Leiden: Brill Academic Publishers, 2001), 2:650.

parish.[14] Bucer pushed for this because he was firmly convinced that the ancient church had lived according to scriptural teaching. The fact that, as he saw it, the teaching and practice of that early church squared with what Strasbourg and other Protestant urban churches offered served to confirm Protestants in their teaching and practice.[15] With this conviction Bucer defended Protestantism from his Roman opponents' charge that it presented novelties: he declared that the Reformers' teaching was a republication of the teaching of Christian antiquity. This was no idle boast or mere bold claim useful for argument, for Bucer was a prodigious patristics scholar by sixteenth-century standards.[16]

While John Calvin was not as learned in patristics as Bucer, Calvin nevertheless knew the church fathers and Christian antiquity well. Like other northern Christian humanists and Reformers, including Bucer, Calvin thought of the ancient church "as a golden classical period."[17] While he recognized it was certainly not perfect or an absolute model, Calvin nevertheless believed that the ancient church had remained faithful to Scripture's message.[18] With Bucer (and the other Reformers), Calvin saw what the Reformers were teaching and practicing as faithful to ancient ecclesiastical teaching and practice. In the prefatory letter to every edition of his *Institutes*, Calvin boldly asserted, "If the contest were to be determined by patristic authority, the tide of victory—to put it very modestly—would turn to our side. . . . I could with no trouble at all prove that the greater part of what we are saying today meets their [the church fathers'] approval."[19]

However, the Reformers did not view Christian antiquity as flawless. In Melanchthon's little patrology of 1539, in which he sought to show readers how to acknowledge and utilize the authority of the church

---

[14]The Strasbourg church ordinances of 1534 laid the necessary groundwork for this by specifying certain patristic works which had to be available in each parish library (ibid., p. 655).

[15]Irena Backus, "Martin Bucer and the Patristic Tradition," in *Martin Bucer and Sixteenth Century Europe: Actes du colloque de Strasbourg (28-31 août 1991)*, ed. Christian Krieger and Marc Lienhard, 2 vols. (Leiden: Brill, 1993), p. 58.

[16]Ibid., p. 68.

[17]Anthony N. S. Lane, *John Calvin: Student of the Church Fathers* (Grand Rapids: Baker Books, 1999), p. 40.

[18]Johannes van Oort, "John Calvin and the Church Fathers," in Backus, *The Reception of the Church Fathers in the West*, p. 697.

[19]Calvin *Institutes* 1.18.

rightly, he urged that Christian antiquity was not without its problems, that Augustine in the fifth century found some things in church practice displeasing, and that church fathers had sometimes erred and failed to follow Scripture. Even so, Melanchthon acknowledged a general consensus of faithful teaching that pervaded the patristic era, a consensus faithfully set forth in his day within Protestantism.[20]

For his part, Calvin also recognized a pattern of faithful teaching in Christian antiquity that persisted beyond Augustine's time.[21] His Strasbourg mentor, Martin Bucer, pointed out that the church subsequently fell into corruption, but that the church fathers had lived and flourished before that transpired.[22] The corruption worked its way gradually into the church, such that it was impossible to accept the total teaching and practice of any period of the ancient church as absolute and normative.[23] Even so, although the ancient church had some few flaws, there was a patristic consensus through Augustine's time which included an acceptance of what the Protestants came to designate as *sola scriptura* and justification *sola fide*.[24] With this confidence, Bucer urged vigorously that the Protestants had not turned from the ancient church and had rejected neither holy antiquity nor the consensus of the

---

[20]Philip Melanchthon, *The Church and the Authority of the Word, 1529*, in Charles Leander Hill, trans., and Elmer Ellsworth Flack and Lowell J. Satre, ed., *Melanchthon: Selected Writings* (Minneapolis: Augsburg, 1962), pp. 149, 167, 171, 185.

[21]"If the authority of the ancient church moves us in any way, we will recall that for about five hundred years . . . religion was still flourishing, and a purer doctrine thriving" (Calvin *Institutes* 1.11.13).

[22]David F. Wright, "Martin Bucer 1491-1551: Ecumenical Theologian," in *Common Places of Martin Bucer*, ed. and trans. D. F. Wright, Courtenay Library of Reformation Classics (Appleford, U.K.: Sutton Courtenay, 1972), p. 41.

[23]In the 1539 Colloquy of Leipzig, Bucer and Melanchthlon were faced with the invitation to reunite with reform-minded Roman Catholics and seek the renewal of the church on the basis of Scripture and the ancient church up to A.D. 600; when the two Protestant Reformers pointed out that the church already had flaws in teaching and practice by that time, the *terminus ad quem* was reduced to A.D. 500. However, they said that the same criticism would have to be made even about that time period (although the problems were not as great as they were a century later). For a discussion of this colloquy, see C. Augustijn, *De Godsdienstgesprekken tussen Rooms-Katholieken en Protestanten van 1538 tot 1541*, Verhandelingen rakende den Natuurlijken en Geopenbaarden Godsdienst, uitgeven door Teylers Godgeleerd Genootschap, new series, vol. 30 (Haarlem: De Erven F. Bohn N.V., 1967), pp. 16-24.

[24]Martin Bucer, "The Church," in *Common Places of Martin Bucer*, ed. and trans. D. F. Wright, Courtenay Library of Reformation Classics (Appleford, U.K.: Sutton Courtenay, 1972), pp. 222-23.

church fathers. For Bucer, the ancient church had an authority which must be recognized, and according to him, the Protestants recognized it faithfully.[25]

Clearly the Protestant Reformers recognized a kinship between their teaching and practice and that of Christian antiquity. For the Reformers, the ancient church had managed to stay, for the largest part, in concert with apostolic teaching. Furthermore, again for the most part, Christian antiquity had manifested a consensus on Christian faith and practice. This consensus, according to the Protestant Reformers, set the historical pattern for subsequent faithfulness within the church.

CONCLUSION

The Protestant Reformers lamented that their own churches did not yet live up to the ancient standard. They would thus prohibit their successors from thinking of the Protestant Reformation as a golden age to be emulated—however readily some of those successors might be enthusiastically inclined to do so. But the Reformers did not then leave subsequent Protestantism with no suggestion in this regard. The Reformers invited clergy and laypeople in their day, and their successors in subsequent generations, to look to the ancient church as a golden age, as a norm to strive to emulate.

This norm was itself subject to Scripture, of course. It was a subordinate norm, itself normed by Scripture. The Reformers' idea of a golden age of the church thus meshed with their understanding of religious authority—which ought not to be surprising, since we are talking about norms after all. As we have seen, for the Protestant Reformers *sola scriptura* entailed according Scripture the ultimate status, as the only unquestioned religious authority. But in total congruity with their deference to the ancient church as a subordinate religious authority normed by Scripture, they pointed Protestants in their day and subsequently to Christian antiquity as a pattern to be followed.

Significantly, though, the study of Christian antiquity fell off in the generations after the Reformers. While the reading and study of the

---

[25]Wright, "Martin Bucer 1491-1551: Ecumenical Theologian," pp. 39, 40.

church fathers continued within the Roman Catholic Church and, to a lesser extent, within Lutheranism, in the larger Reformed tradition and in the evangelicalism which subsequently arose within Protestant circles, Christian antiquity became a neglected field in church history. It remained so until the late 1980s—over four hundred years since the last of the major Protestant Reformers died. But over the last twenty years or so, the study of patristics has caught on within evangelical and Reformed circles. To meet a growing demand for patristic materials and scholarship, Christian publishing houses serving these constituencies have recently spawned book series offering studies of Christian antiquity in general and the church fathers more particularly.[26]

It is worth noting that this is an unprecedented phenomenon: never before have significant numbers in evangelical and Reformed circles shown anything beyond a faint interest in Christian antiquity or patristic materials. In the early twenty-first century, though, these circles can boast several accomplished patristic scholars and numerous significant volumes on the ancient church. Thus only now, more than four centuries later, are Protestant churches really in a position to hear, appreciate and respond to the Protestant Reformers' recommendation of the golden age which should serve as a norm for Protestant churches.

---

[26]In the late twentieth century, both InterVarsity Press and Wm. B. Eerdmans Publishing Company launched book series to provide primary and secondary sources of patristic writings and scholarship.

- 12 -

The Reformation as Triumph and Tragedy

As we bring our considerations of the sixteenth-century Reformation to a close, we come to the question of how to evaluate it. Was the Reformation a triumph? Or was it a tragedy? This concern takes us in a somewhat different direction than the earlier chapter in which we considered whether or not the Reformation was a success. We were able to consider that question on relatively straightforward historical bases, asking whether what the various Reformers sought with their efforts came to fruition.

But the questions we consider in this chapter demand something beyond merely historical assessment. They entail value judgments rooted in scriptural and doctrinal concerns at the heart of the Christian faith. In this regard, we must recognize that the sixteenth-century Reformation sought to recover and reclaim the message of salvation in Christ preached by the apostles and propounded by the church fathers. The Protestant Reformers endeavored to uncover and proclaim the Christian gospel by returning anew to Scripture, recognizing its focus, embracing its comfort and proclaiming its promises.

Because of this, it is both warranted and appropriate to evaluate the sixteenth-century Reformation accordingly. It was, after all, not just another historical phenomenon. The Reformation was an attempt to right the wrongs in the church, wrongs against which Western Christendom had long cried out. The Reformation sought to do so by trying to find again and bring explicitly to the fore the gospel of free grace in Christ in which all Scripture found its center and fulfillment. The Scriptures offer grounds for assessing the Reformation and evaluating it in this regard, and in this chapter we will give explicit consideration to relevant scriptural passages for that purpose. In the conservative Christian circles for which this book is primarily intended, this should be a welcome approach, one in keeping with those circles' own basic instincts. So, then, from a scriptural perspective was the sixteenth-century Reformation a triumph or a tragedy?

This pushes us far beyond the simplistic observation some might instinctively offer, adjudging the Reformation a triumph since it led, eventually, to the founding of their particular denomination. The assessment needs to probe deeper: it must look beyond discrete results to consider more fundamental issues. It has to examine the Reformation as to its impact on the Christian gospel itself. Put that way, some Protestants might well assume the answer should be clear. However, we should not prejudge the question: answering it too quickly may result in getting the Reformation wrong. The answer to the question posed is more complicated than we might immediately think.

THE TRIUMPH OF THE REFORMATION

The longstanding clamor for *reformatio in capite et membris* leaves no room to question whether the late medieval church had defaulted on its responsibilities. The universal assessment of Western Christendom was that the church desperately needed serious renewal. Our previous investigations have given us abundant opportunity to recognize that.

During the fourteenth and fifteenth centuries, the financial chicanery and sexual profligacy in the hierarchy, the dereliction of clerical duty in the depths of the Black Death, the ineptitude of local priests, the exotic manifestations of scholastic intellectual tomfoolery, and the scandal of papal malfeasance (from the Avignon Papacy to the Great Schism to the Renaissance Papacy) were all bad enough to warrant the anticlericalism that marked the period. But beyond all these problems lay a more momentous one—the undeniable loss of clarity as to what the Christian faith was all about. The apostolic tidings of free grace in Christ was notable in the late Middle Ages mostly by its absence. Apart from that message, the church has no reason to exist.

That message had not ceased, to be sure: it was still to be found in the Scriptures and the writings of the church fathers. Indeed both these ancient sources continued to be copied and read in the medieval church. But they had been overlaid with the clutter of ecclesiastical paraphernalia and precedent, which mounted up higher and higher as generations passed, increasingly obscuring the foundation of the Christian faith until that foundation could hardly even be discerned. By the early sixteenth century, Western Christendom had long since lost touch with it. To be sure, no one had maliciously sought to render the apostolic message obscure, but as other important pastoral or ecclesiastical issues demanded and received attention, the basic Christian message was taken for granted, underemphasized and—unintentionally but nonetheless unmistakably—neglected. These other issues had been so pressing along the church's way through the medieval period that it was understandable that they had become the focus of attention. By the time of Luther, though, even a serious, studious, committed monk— one of "the religious," and thus supposedly more in tune with and open to the ways of God—could not figure out what the "good news" was in the Christian gospel.

The struggles of Luther to discover a way to peace with God eventually led him to affirm justification *sola fide*. His rediscovery of a gracious God who pardons sinners and accepts them in Christ was embraced by the other Protestant Reformers, who proclaimed it in concert with him. This was no new teaching, they averred; rather, it was a renewed declaration of the apostolic message in which the church discovered its foundation, the scriptural *fundamentum* on which the church fathers had faithfully built.

Through the efforts of the Protestant Reformers to expound and defend this reading of the message of Scripture, they sought to reacquaint the church with its deepest treasures—the assurance that

"God so *loved* the world that he *gave his only Son*, so that everyone who *believes in him* may not perish but may have eternal life"; that "since we are *justified by faith*, we have *peace with God* through our Lord Jesus Christ"; and that "there is therefore now *no condemnation* for those who are in Christ Jesus" (Jn 3:16; Rom 5:1; 8:1; emphases added). The Protestant Reformers sought to wake the church out of its spiritual torpor by making clear again what Christianity was all about—the unmerited favor of God in Christ graciously bestowed on the undeserving, the assurance of divine love to sinful humanity. What had been lost to sight in the medieval centuries the Protestant Reformers uncovered again. They roughly pushed aside the accumulated clutter that had overlain it and called Western Christendom to see again what it had long yearned for—a clear, ringing affirmation of what God expects of humankind in response to what he has done out of love for us.[1]

We who stand in the train of the Protestant Reformers, in whichever tradition we find ourselves, gladly remember and celebrate the sixteenth-century Reformation as the period in which our brave forebears managed to call the church back to its roots. The Protestant Reformers enabled their own generation to recognize again the main point of the Christian faith and hear the gospel anew. Shaped by their legacy and indebted to them for their insights, their followers in intervening centu-

---

[1]The assessment above focuses on the Protestant Reformers' teaching as a way to deal with contemporary Protestant assessments of the Reformation. But while it is outside the specific purview of this chapter, it is important to note that what the Protestant Reformers urged so vigorously also spurred the radical Reformers to discern anew the church's calling to be a pilgrim community, traveling toward the celestial city and distinct from the surrounding culture, whether or not that culture called itself Christian. That ended up turning a bright light again on a fundamental characteristic of Christianity—that it was not and must "not be conformed to this world" (Rom 12:2), but should be a gathered community devoted to disciplined, faithful living before a merciful God.

Moreover, it is important not to overlook the startling renovation within the Roman communion. After so many generations' frustrated yearning for "reformation from head to toe," the first half of the sixteenth century so shocked the Roman leadership that it finally got serious about straightening out its own household of faith. Picking up elements of earlier reform movements within its own communion, Rome found a new vigor with which it galvanized its considerable resources and incorporated new movements to transform itself. By the mid-sixteenth century, the Roman Catholic Church had engaged in a stinging self-criticism leading to internal renewal and had generated a new strength with which it would go on the offensive against its Protestant and radical detractors. The see of St. Peter sought to reassert itself again as the body intended by Christ when he promised, "on this rock I will build my church, and the gates of Hades will not prevail against it" (Mt 16:18).

ries have revered the Protestant Reformers as new heralds of the ancient message, heralds who made the gospel clear again in their day, whose teaching reverberates down through intervening times to our own.

Rather than fear and uncertainty because of real and imagined failures before an implacable, omniscient and omnipotent Judge, the Protestant Reformers urged faith and assurance. They inculcated a humble confidence because of Jesus Christ in which believers dare approach God as loving Father. According to the sixteenth-century Reformers, the Christian gospel calls people to rely on Christ alone for their righteousness, not on their own feeble and flawed attainments. This free gift of salvation entailed an assurance of God's love in Christ that issued into determined discipleship, offered freely and joyfully in gratitude for divine grace—a grace that continued to extend pardon for the faults and failures against which believers continued to struggle. The Protestant Reformers thus again made divine grace central, rather than focusing on human accomplishment. In so doing, they both rediscovered and powerfully proclaimed the original apostolic message. Centuries later, their grateful heirs recognize and celebrate what they achieved—namely, the recovery of the Christian gospel.

In all this, the Protestant Reformers returned to the deepest wellsprings of the Christian faith. The Reformation movement found itself confronted by the challenge to explore, set forth and defend its understanding of dominical and apostolic teaching. From the perspective of its grateful heirs, it did so faithfully and with integrity. In returning thus to the apostolic message, the sixteenth-century Reformation proved to be a great triumph for the Christian gospel.

It might appear that our investigations are complete. But we have not yet considered all the relevant data. There is more to this story.

THE TRAGEDY OF THE REFORMATION

While the Protestant Reformers managed to remove the clutter that had obscured the apostolic message by their day and to set forth the gospel again with boldness and vigor, the story of the Reformation is not just one of triumph. In the hands of its descendants, the Reformation has proved also to be a great tragedy for the Christian gospel. Indeed, as we have seen, that process began already in the heady days of the sixteenth-century Reformation itself, among the Protestant Reformers themselves. But down through the intervening centuries, their followers have built on this unfortunate strand of the Reformation's legacy and made it much worse.

To appreciate this fully, we must give careful attention to the way Jesus Christ spoke in the prayer he uttered the night before he was betrayed. In this prayer he interceded for his disciples, through whom his message would be proclaimed to the world. Then he continued, "I ask not only on behalf of these, but also on behalf of *those who will believe in me through their word*, that they *may all* be *one*. As you, Father, are in me and I am in you, may they also be *one* in us, *so that the world may believe* that you have sent me."[2]

If as Christians (of whatever denominational stripe) we believe that Jesus Christ had some insight into what would affect the reception of the gospel as proclaimed by his apostles, then we cannot bypass the correlation he explicitly declares here. According to Jesus Christ himself, for those who would come to faith in him through the apostolic message to be *one* would constitute a compelling argument to the rest of *the world* that God the Father had, indeed, *sent his Son* into world. Conversely, for such believers *not* to be *one* would offer *the world* at least an excuse *not to believe* the gospel. It will not do to try to escape the unmistakable implication of what Christ specifically prayed in this regard. However uncomfortable it may leave us, however much we might wish this dominical dictum were not there, it will not go away; neither will it let us be comfortable in our post-Reformation situation.

The Protestant Reformers did not set about to establish other churches. They did not unfurl banners and march victoriously out of the Roman communion; they were expelled from it by a corrupt leadership. United in the message of the gospel, they nonetheless quickly stumbled into heated quarrels over other issues (such as—of all things!—the Eucharist, the sacrament of unity). As we have seen, this degenerated into vilification and hostile defamation. It served to divide the

---

[2]Jn 17:20-21 (emphasis added); see also the continuation and elaboration of this correlation in Jn 17:22-23.

incipient Protestant Reformation into competing groups of Lutheran and Reformed.

Soon enough, even these groups found their own internal conflicts. Within Lutheranism, the Gnesio-Lutherans denounced Melanchthon and his associates as allegedly unfaithful to the Wittenberg hero; within the Reformed tradition, conflict arose between Zwingli's vigorous followers and those who inclined toward Bucer's emphases.[3] The coming of Protestant scholasticism served to exacerbate the situation with its eagerness for sharp distinctions and readiness to denounce all deviance. Both the Lutheran and the Reformed camps scathingly critiqued each other, claiming the truth exclusively for their side. In due course within each camp this claim became ever more exclusive, resulting in further fissures within both Protestant traditions. Protestantism in general picked up this virus, and the various free churches established from the seventeenth century onward in England, North America and elsewhere separated from allegedly unfaithful church organizations, stepping out on their own, each claiming (humbly, of course) before the divine Judge to speak "the truth, the whole truth and nothing but the truth." But has this allegedly faithful witness been heard in the court of the world?

This unedifying spectacle has continued to the present day. Protestant and other free churches have continued to split time and again, with competing ecclesiastical organizations bearing the same general denominational designation (Lutheran, Reformed, Presbyterian, Congregationalist, Methodist, Baptist, Pentecostal, etc.) numbering into the hundreds, even thousands. By the present day, we heirs of the Protestant Reformation have made this situation exponentially worse than it was in the Reformation era and the heyday of Protestant scholasticism. An organization based in California that keeps track of such dreary statistics noted that, as of the beginning of the third mil-

---

[3]We have not given special attention to this rift in our treatment; even so, it became a significant problem which Calvin had to deal with carefully: see Willem van't Spijker, *Calvin: A Brief Guide to his Life and Thought*, trans. Lyle D. Bierma (Louisville: Westminster John Knox Press, 2009), pp. 118-21; see also Wulfert de Greef, *The Writings of John Calvin: An Introductory Guide*, expanded ed., trans. Lyle D. Bierma (Louisville: Westminster John Knox Press, 2008), p. 176.

lennium, there were more than twenty-six thousand Protestant de-nominations.[4] If we consider this and reflect on what Christ prayed for, and if we look at contemporary culture, should we really be sur-prised that the Christian message we proclaim seems to have little impact on the world around us? Undeniably, that situation cannot be reduced to merely one issue, as if the unwieldy multiplicity of Protes-tant denominations has all by itself led to this situation. Even so, no one who listens carefully to what Christ prayed ought really to be confounded by this result.

The excuses fly aplenty, of course. "We have to stand for truth!" Indeed—but what truth is it that we end up dividing the church over? Protestant and free churches have argued and ended up splitting into rival denominations over issues of baptism (who should receive it? in what mode?), the Lord's Supper, predestination versus free will, escha-tology, church governance, charismatic gifts, creation versus evolution, the ordination of women to ecclesiastical offices—to name only a few. However heatedly some might insist on the importance of these issues and urge the necessity for faithful believers to stand firm on them no matter the cost, it is important to count the cost of such an approach for the gospel itself. Christ's accounting, in this regard, is unmistakable, and it clearly differs considerably from the bookkeeping practiced in Protestant circles for far too long.

In this circumstance, we would do well to heed the wise words of-fered by the apostolic father Clement of Rome (d. c. A.D. 95),[5] who urged, "Be contentious and zealous, *but only about the things that relate to salvation.*"[6] For him, as for the rest of the church fathers, contention must be reserved for the defense of the gospel. This was the pattern found in Christian antiquity, as it moved through the trinitarian and christological controversies which issued into the decisions and doctri-nal declarations of the ancient ecumenical councils. For the church fa-

---

[4]An even more dismal accounting was published by the *International Bulletin of Missionary Re-search* in early 2009: by their reckoning, there are now more than thirty-four thousand Chris-tian denominations.

[5]According to the ancient church, Clement was the companion of Paul referred to in Philip-pians 4:3.

[6]Clement of Rome *Letter of the Romans to the Corinthians* 45:1 (emphasis added).

thers, focusing on anything else would only serve to divide what must not be divided, the church. Irenaeus of Lyons addressed this concern straightforwardly and in a way that must raise serious questions about much of what we heirs of the Protestant Reformation have done, when he stated:

> He [God] will also judge those who cause schisms, who have no love for God and instead desire their own way more than the unity of the church, who for trifling reasons (or some other reason important to them) cut in pieces and divide the great and glorious body of Christ and (as far as they can) destroy it—those who speak about peace while causing war, who strain out a gnat but swallow a camel [Matt. 23:24]. They can effect no reformation great enough to compensate for the harm their schism causes.[7]

Similarly Cyprian of Carthage averred, "Can anyone be so lawless and faithless, so insane in his zeal for quarrelling, as to believe it possible that *the oneness* of God, the garment of the Lord, *the church of Christ* should be torn apart, *or dare to divide it himself?*"[8]

The longstanding failure in Protestantism to become conversant with the church fathers' teachings until the last generation has probably insured that most of those who have encouraged or led or participated in such divisions have not been aware of the patristic assessment of such attitudes and actions. Both the practice and the forthright teaching of the church fathers oppose the pattern which has become all too common in our Protestant and free church circles. Whether we knew of it or not, though, the patristic evaluation stands firm.

But what excuse can we offer for not heeding the explicit teaching of the apostles on such matters? If *sola scriptura* means anything significant, it surely entails the responsibility for those who profess it to keep scriptural teaching as the ultimate and only unquestioned norm for teaching and practice. How, then, is it that we have so cavalierly disregarded the explicit condemnation of divisiveness, of a "party spirit," within the church? St. Paul did not leave that as an option

---

[7]Irenaeus of Lyons *Against Heresies* 4:33.7.
[8]Cyprian *Unity of the Catholic Church* 8 (emphasis added).

when he urged the Corinthian church in his day, "I appeal to you, brothers and sisters, by the name of our Lord Jesus Christ, that all of you be in agreement and *that there be no divisions among you*" (1 Cor 1:10). He made the problem unmistakable and resolutely repudiated it when he went on forthrightly to challenge them, "Each of you says, 'I belong to Paul,' or 'I belong to Apollos,' or 'I belong to Cephas,' or 'I belong to Christ'" (1 Cor 1:12). Even so, among the heirs of the Protestant Reformation, we "belong" to a rarified, distinct, separated version of one or another of the ecclesiastical traditions generated during the sixteenth-century Reformation or the denominations that arose subsequently in their wake.

To return to the imagery used earlier in this chapter, we heirs of the Protestant Reformation have dropped layer of denominational clutter over layer of doctrinal distinctiveness in so many strata on the apostolic foundation that the gospel itself has been covered over. No one did this maliciously or with the intent to obscure the basic Christian message, to be sure. Even so, these "upper layers" have attracted so much of our attention and emphasis that the fundamentum has been obscured. Our penchant for division stands in stark contrast to Christ's concern in his prayer for our unity.

Some may think this assessment too strong. If so, it is worth noting that, beginning in the nineteenth century, it was none other than Christian missionaries on far-flung fields who began to lament the divisions within the church as obstacles to their proclamation of the Christian gospel. The competing allegiances of missionaries from several denominations, with their general lack of acquaintance with the emphases and approaches of other Christian missionaries, generated confusion among the people to whom the various missionaries sought to bring the gospel. Already in 1806 William Carey (a Baptist missionary) wrote back to his supporters in England about this problem. He urged that various denominations "back home" should try to get to know each other and find ways to work together, for this would be beneficial there and would have ripple effects among their respective missionaries serving in distant lands. Some kind of mutual respect and cooperation, he urged, was necessary for the sake of the gospel. Without at least such minimal endeavors toward oneness, the missionary efforts would continue to be undermined.

Carey's plea did not lead to any such changes early in the century. But the problem did not evaporate on the mission fields. In due course, through the nineteenth and into the early twentieth centuries, more and more missionaries recognized and declaimed against the anomaly of competing missions assaying to proclaim the Christian gospel. Missionaries continued to raise this issue; it eventually resulted in the establishment of the International Missionary Council (IMC) in 1921. The IMC called for cooperation among churches and missionaries, for mutual respect and collaboration, under its motto, "The whole church taking the whole gospel into the whole world."

Why had the IMC been organized? The purpose of the IMC was to coordinate efforts and avoid rivalry, to help missionaries understand and work with each other (in their different traditions and denominations), rather than as rivals or competitors. What had been the stimulus for this unusual development? It was concern for the gospel—specifically, how the proclamation of that gospel was undercut by the lack of unity in the church.

So whether we consider the question from the perspective of actual endeavors in mission fields, or from that of what Christ prayed for, the plethora of divisions among Protestants indicates clearly that the Reformation—initially already in the hands of the Protestant Reformers but much more in those of their heirs down through the intervening centuries—has been a tragedy for the Christian gospel.

CONCLUSION

Our examination leads to the conclusion that the Reformation was, on the one hand, a triumph: it rediscovered and boldly proclaimed the apostolic message, the Christian gospel. Our considerations also lead, on the other hand, to the conclusion that the Reformation was a tragedy for the Christian gospel: divisions began among the Protestant Reformers and have mushroomed among their descendants in contravention of the explicit words of Jesus Christ himself. It is at least a horrendous anomaly that the sixteenth-century Reformation got rid of the clutter that obscured the foundation of the Christian faith, only to have Protestants cover that foundation again with the clutter of our manifold divisions.

We must qualify this conclusion somewhat. Because of the Protestant Reformers' efforts and clear teaching, the Christian gospel was recovered and proclaimed. The heirs of the Protestant Reformation have not forgotten how to proclaim that fundamental Christian message: it continues to echo in the multitude of denominations which have issued from our Protestant penchant for divisiveness. So the gospel itself has not disappeared from view in the way that it had by the end of the fifteenth century.

Even so, the multitudes of church splits which have ensued in Protestant ranks—beginning already in the sixteenth century, increasing in frequency subsequently and achieving breakneck pace by the early twenty-first century—have unquestionably managed to undermine the integrity of that gospel. The converse of what Jesus Christ prayed for has come to pass: our lack of unity has rendered the gospel less credible in the eyes of the world. In this regard, we have sown the wind and have reaped the whirlwind.

What can be done, though, in this day to address this situation? Without getting into a rehearsal of the development of ecumenical initiatives and assessing their respective merits, we can nonetheless recognize that those initiatives have arisen out of a desire to overcome our divisions, our rampant denominationalism, in favor of a greater manifestation before the eyes of the world of that unity which we ultimately have in Jesus Christ. It would be fatuous and grotesquely naïve to think that through our endeavors, no matter how well intentioned or humbly pursued, the organizational divisions could be overcome in favor of a fully coordinated church encompassing all Christians. Anyone with any experience of organizations and institutions recognizes that is way beyond anything we could hope to see achieved in the foreseeable future.

It would also be simplistic to expect that the heirs of the Protestant Reformation, with all their denominational differences and the various ways they have learned to view other church groups, would find their way readily into only one ecumenical organization. At present, and for some time into the future, we can only expect that the various ecumenical initiatives with their respective inclinations and emphases will continue to gather certain groups of churches, but will be looked on with some hesitation by yet others.

Even so, we should welcome these endeavors, recognizing in them the desire to overcome the divisions which have too long demarked Protestantism. The more we can give evidence by our respectful collaboration and cooperation with others who bear different denominational names but who embrace the Christian gospel that we are one in that regard, the better it will be—for each of our denominations, for that ecumenical organization, for the gospel itself and for the world into which that gospel is proclaimed. If we do, then like the Protestant Reformers whose heirs we claim to be, we will sweep away some of the clutter we have piled up which has obscured the Christian gospel.

We might find some significant help in this regard by listening to the Protestant Reformers' recommendation that we look to the ancient church as a pattern to follow. While the Reformers held patristic teaching and practice in high regard in a host of ways, one of the undeniable strengths of Christian antiquity was the unity it manifested. Across the wide expanse of the then-known world, in its various cultures and several languages, the ancient church managed to remain one. This unity was not a bland sameness: it allowed room for differences of emphasis, even for strong differences of opinion. But these were "family squabbles" between brothers and sisters in Christ, not occasions for leaving the household and starting another. Learning from our patristic forebears would be a good way of listening to our Protestant ones. The fact that the evangelical and Reformed segments of Protestantism are currently witnessing a surge of interest in Christian antiquity and the works of the church fathers suggests that we may find more help from ancient sources in this regard than ever before.

So, was the Reformation a triumph? Yes. Was it a tragedy? Yes. The question now, though, for us who follow in the train of the sixteenth-century Reformation is, which trajectory will we follow? It is not hard to figure out what "getting the Reformation wrong" would entail and what genuinely "getting the Reformation *right*" would mean. Put that way, it should be clear how we can best honor our forebears, the Protestant Reformers of the sixteenth-century Reformation.

Name Index

Adrian VI, Pope, 31 n. 6
Albert the Great, 44
Alciati, Gian Paolo, 228
Aleander, papal nuncio, 82, 83
Alexander V, Pope (1409–1410), 35
Alexander VI, Pope (1492–1503), 41-42
Aquinas, Thomas, 44, 45-46, 93, 196
archbishop of Bari as Pope Urban VI (1378), 33
archbishop of Trier, Luther and, 136
Aristotle, 62, 110, 194 n. 3
    Albert the Great on, 44
    Beza on, 199
    Luther on, 196, 197
    Melanchthon on, 198
    Thomas Aquinas on, 44
Barth, Karl, 192, 194 n. 3
Basil of Caesarea, 67
Bender, Harold, 162 n. 4
Bernardino of Siena, 50
Beza, Theodore, 198-99
Biandrata, Giorgio, 228, 230
Birgitta, St., of Sweden, 33
Boccaccio, Giovanni, 56
Borgia, Lucrezia, 41
Brunner, Emil, 192, 194 n. 3
Bucer, Martin, 88, 92, 97-98, 149, 154-55
    on the ancient church, 241-44
    on ancient creeds, 152
    as biblical scholar, 218
    Calvin, friendship with, 107
    Calvin on, 218
    as Christian humanist, 115
    on church fathers, 151, 152, 243-44
    city leaders and, 106-7
    at Colloquy of Leipzig, 243 n. 23
    on correlation between faith and good works, 125-26
    denounced by Luther, 113
    on diversity of ceremonies in antiquity, 239
    on ecumenical councils, 152
    Erasmus and, 70, 240, 240 n. 12
    exiled to England, 153, 219
    on justification by faith alone, 120-21
    on Lord's Supper, 112
    Luther and, 99-101, 109
    Melanchthon and, 218
    parish life, reforms of, 101
    as pastor, Strasbourg church, 241-42
    on Protestant churches, 238-39
    on Scripture as divine authority, 151-53
    on *sola fide*, 108-9
    on *sola scriptura*, 151-53
    on "two-kingdom" approach, 104
Bugenhagen, Johannes, 88
Burckhardt, Jacob, 58-63, 59 n. 5
Calovius, Abraham, 191
Calvin, John, 107
    Academy of Geneva and, 221
    on the ancient church, 242, 243
    on ancient creeds, 143, 155, 156
    on antitrinitarianism, 229
    Apostles' Creed and, 201
    on Bucer, 218
    Bucer, friendship with, 107
    Charles V, Emperor, address to, 239
    on church fathers, 153-55, 242
    on ecumenical councils, 153, 155-56
    on Eucharist, 224
    Francis I, King, and, 154, 239
    in Geneva, 220-22
    Genevan Academy, established by, 198-99
    on justifying faith, 126-27
    Lausanne Disputation, response at, 154
    Reformed movement and, 196 n. 5
    on scholastic methodology, 197-200
    on scholastic theology, 196, 197-98
    on *sola fide*, 121
    on *sola scriptura*, 153-56
Capistrano, John, 50
Caraffa, Gian Pietro (Cardinal), 184
    as Pope Paul IV (1555–1559), 185-87
Carey, William, 255-56
Catherine, St., of Siena, 33
Charles V, Emperor
    Augsburg Interim imposed on Protestant territories, 153, 219
    Calvin, address to, on Catholic and Protestant churches, 239
    Luther and, 83
    Smalcald War and, 153, 216
Chemnitz, Martin, 203
Clement of Rome, 253
Clement V, Pope, 31
Clement VII, Pope, 33
Cochlaeus, Johannes, 180
Contarini, Gasparo (Cardinal), 178, 181, 184
Cranmer, Thomas, Archbishop, 219

Subject Index

Academy of Geneva, 221. *See also* Genevan
 Academy
ad fontes, 57, 100, 236
Amish, 160
Anabaptism, 161-63, 167-71
 apocalyptic, 170-71
 central Europe and, 163
 communitarian, 169
 defined, 161
 establishment, 167-68
 "genuine," 162
 militant, 168-69
 mystical, 169-70
 polygamy and, 168
 public nudity and, 168
 spiritualist, 170
 Swiss, 166-67
 Zwingli and, 162
Anabaptists, 160-72, 213, 231
 Baptistic predecessors of, 161-62
 capital execution of, 164, 164 n. 6
 diversity among, 166-71
 free elections in Münster and, 168-69
 misunderstandings, contemporary,
 161-63
 misunderstandings, sixteenth-century,
 163-71
 opposition to by Protestants and Roman
 Catholics, 165-66
 paedobaptism, rejection by, 161, 164-65
 Peasants' War and, 85-86, 163-64, 169,
 170
 as "Radical Reformation," 161
 source of, 162-63
 of Zurich, 162-63
anachronism, 56-57
ancient church
 Bucer on, 241-44
 Calvin on, 242, 243
 Reformers on, 241-44
ancient creeds, 153-59
 Bucer on, 152
 Calvin on, 153, 155, 156
 Luther on, 138, 140, 142
 Melanchthon on, 145
 Oecolampadius on, 144
 Scotus on, 46
 Scripture and, 132
 Zwingli on, 148, 149, 151
anticlericalism, 41-43, 247-48

Alexander VI and, 42
 Bamberg, diocese of, 42
 Black Death and, 41-42
 celibacy, violations of, 42
 Constance, diocese of, 42
 Jiménez on, 177
antitrinitarianism, 228-230, 232, 233 n. 20
 Diet of Piotrkow (1565) and, 229-30
Apology for the Augsburg Confession
 (Melanchthon), 125
Apostles' Creed, 201
Aristotelian logic, 45, 67, 111, 195, 202
 Gerhard on, 204
 Jesuits and, 191, 199
 Protestants and, 198, 200-205, 209
 Wollebius on, 205-6
Augsburg Interim, 13, 153, 216, 219
Avignon Papacy (1309–1378)
 church leadership and, 31-33
 deposition of, 35-36
 moral depravity of, 32-33
 simony and, 31-32, 31 n. 8
Baccalaureate Theses (Melanchthon), 142-43
Baden Disputation of 1526, Eck on Zwingli
 and Oecolampadius, 149
Bamberg, diocese of, 42
baptism, 161 n. 2
Baptistic predecessors of Anabaptists,
 161-62
Baptists, 162 n. 3
Battle of White Mountain, 228
believers' baptism, 161
Berne Disputation of 1528, Zwingli and
 Oecolampadius on Scriptural authority,
 149
bishop of Rome
 evangelization of Western Europe and,
 29
 nationalities of, 31, 31 n. 6, 33
 See also popes
bishops
 Council of Trent directives to, 179
 Council of Trent on clerical duties of,
 188
Black Death, 26-28, 41-42
Bohemia, Protestantism in, 226
brothels converted to convents, 186
"the Brothers of the Common Life," 174
Bubonic Plague. *See* Black Death
Bucer, Martin. *See* name index